The Welsh Gold King

The Welsh Gold King

The Life of William Pritchard Morgan, MP

Norena Shopland

First published in Great Britain in 2021 by
Pen & Sword History
An imprint of
Pen & Sword Books Ltd
Yorkshire – Philadelphia

Copyright © Norena Shopland 2021

ISBN 978 1 39909 060 5

The right of Norena Shopland to be identified as Author of this work has been asserted by her in accordance with the Copyright, Designs and Patents Act 1988.

A CIP catalogue record for this book is
available from the British Library.

All rights reserved. No part of this book may be reproduced or transmitted in any form or by any means, electronic or mechanical including photocopying, recording or by any information storage and retrieval system, without permission from the Publisher in writing.

Typeset by Mac Style
Printed and bound in the UK by CPI Group (UK) Ltd,
Croydon, CR0 4YY.

Pen & Sword Books Limited incorporates the imprints of Atlas, Archaeology, Aviation, Discovery, Family History, Fiction, History, Maritime, Military, Military Classics, Politics, Select, Transport, True Crime, Air World, Frontline Publishing, Leo Cooper, Remember When, Seaforth Publishing, The Praetorian Press, Wharncliffe Local History, Wharncliffe Transport, Wharncliffe True Crime and White Owl.

For a complete list of Pen & Sword titles please contact

PEN & SWORD BOOKS LIMITED
47 Church Street, Barnsley, South Yorkshire, S70 2AS, England
E-mail: enquiries@pen-and-sword.co.uk
Website: www.pen-and-sword.co.uk

Or

PEN AND SWORD BOOKS
1950 Lawrence Rd, Havertown, PA 19083, USA
E-mail: Uspen-and-sword@casematepublishers.com
Website: www.penandswordbooks.com

Contents

Acknowledgements vi
Introduction vii

Chapter 1   Becoming Rich   1
Chapter 2   The Turbulent Goldfield   16
Chapter 3   Finding Welsh Gold   30
Chapter 4   Entitled to a Seat in Parliament   46
Chapter 5   The Classes and the Masses   60
Chapter 6   Merthyr Decides   75
Chapter 7   After the Election   90
Chapter 8   The Dead Hand of Antiquity   104
Chapter 9   The Bryntirion Injustice   119
Chapter 10   A Man with a Grievance   135
Chapter 11   Persistent Endeavours   151
Chapter 12   The Red Dragon and the Red Flag   168
Chapter 13   Standing Alone in a Strange Land   183
Chapter 14   Welsh Gold after Morgan   199

Notes   210
Bibliography   226
Index   228

Acknowledgements

To my wife, Julie Carpenter, for help with the editing and always useful comments, and my father, Robert Shopland, for his support; to Glamorgan Archives; Charters Towers Archives Group and Charters Towers Regional Council; and Monmouthshire County Council/Cyngor Sir Fynwy Register Office.

Introduction

When Prime Minister Margaret Thatcher welcomed Chun Doo Huan, the Korean President, to No. 10 Downing Street in 1986, the first visit to Britain by a Korean head of state, she mentioned in her speech 'Mr Pritchard Morgan, one of the Welsh mining experts who helped you to mine gold and was once your Consul-General in London.'[1]

It is unlikely that anyone in the audience had a clue who she was speaking about. Like many individuals from the past whose fame once stretched across the world, William Pritchard Morgan, the 'Welsh Gold King', is now largely forgotten.

Morgan was a fascinating figure with fingers in many pies and those fingerprints remain on many aspects of UK life. In his article, *To Silence a Jackdaw: Gagging the Northern Miner* (1994), Donald Hector Johnson wrote that Morgan, 'not the last diminutive Welshman to trouble the antipodes', was 'another of those goldfield characters in whose career it is difficult to separate fact from fiction.'[2]

In 1891, Theodore Dodd (probably a pseudonym for the journalist Llewelyn Williams (1867–1922)) wrote a series of satirical articles called *Open Letters to Leaders of Welsh Opinion*, including Morgan. He wrote that if Morgan's biography ever came to be written 'without eliminations or embellishments, it will be the funniest record ever traced for the delectation of a wondering world.'[3] Dodd put his finger on the many conflicting characters of his subject: Morgan considered himself a Welshman, yet spent his first forty years in Australia and was reluctant to relinquish his identity as a Queenslander; his burning desire was to be a politician but he treated the offices he won with negligence; he fought to change the laws of the UK to suit his own interests but because they were the interests of other mine owners, they saw him as a national hero; and he became a thorn in the government's side when he gained power to speak on behalf of China and Korea. He was a Marmite character, loved or loathed – there seemed to be no middle ground.

I had long wanted to write a book on gold-mining in Wales but publishers were unconvinced the dry subject of mining would make a popular book. Besides, Pritchard Morgan was a much more colourful subject. But trying to write a biography during a pandemic lockdown was not going to be easy, as direct access to primary sources in archives was largely impossible. Having said that, primary sources for Morgan's life are, for the most part, limited in any case. No personal archives have been located and apart from odd letters and documents in archives, nothing substantial remains for a man who was such a huge public figure. Due to his popularity and controversy, he was rarely out of the newspapers and so this life has been constructed mainly from that source, and that of Hansard, the official report of all Parliamentary debates.

Morgan was a man of boundless energy, throwing himself into project after project and often bumping heads with people as he steamrolled his way through life. Indeed, so myriad were his activities that a full biography would consist of several volumes, his life in Australia filling at least one, so this book must stand as an introduction to his life rather than a definitive account of it all.

Chapter 1

Becoming Rich

As author Donald Hector Johnson pointed out, Morgan's career can be difficult to separate fact from fiction, and none more so than his origins. Little is known, although several stories are told, of the early days of the man who was to become known across the globe as the Welsh Gold King.

His father, William Morgan, was born in 1816 in the small town of Pillgwenlly, in Newport, the eponymous home of a cruel pirate-turned-saint, as well as that of the tramp poet W. H. Davies. Only a few details are known about Morgan senior's life; but years later, when his son was being interviewed, he described his father as a clergyman who 'took a very active part in the reformation of the construction of the Wesleyan body.' Between 1849 and 1850, Morgan senior worked hard in the cause advocated by Dr James Everett (1784–1872), an English Methodist and writer who had, along with others, been expelled by the Wesleyan Methodists for disagreeing with some of the church's principles, so they created the Wesleyan Reform Movement in 1859. Morgan senior joined this movement and was, continued his son, 'a preacher of considerable influence in Monmouthshire.'[1]

Methodism was characterised by an emphasis on charity and support for the sick and poor; and it crossed class boundaries with preachers making a point of seeking out those not usually embraced by orthodox religions. One of the tenets of the Wesleyan reformers and a principal point of difference with the Methodist Church was that churches should be self-governing. For a young Morgan growing up in a liberal household that also rejected orthodox authority, the bedrock of his beliefs was firmly established. Throughout his life, such beliefs dominated Morgan's work and politics and his refusal to blindly accept authority would regularly resurface.

Morgan's mother Catherine (née Pritchard) was born in 1819 at Hay, Breconshire. When her son made his great discovery of gold in 1887, *The Weekly Mail* reported:

By the mother's side he is a descendant of the very ancient family of Pritchard, of Glamorganshire, a family, according to Mr Clarke, Talygarn, which is directly descended from Eynon and Nest, of Miskin Nest being the only daughter of Iescyn ap Gwrgan, the last native King of Glamorgan and Morganwg. Eynon was a prince of Ceredigion. As I, with that information in mind, watched the quick movements of Mr P. Morgan, I could not help fancying he was a fit representative of the energetic, if somewhat impulsive Eynon. We will forgive Eynon from bringing the Normans into Morganwg now that one of his descendants has, as it appears by his discovery, made Wales one of the richest corners of the earth![2]

Morgan also told the newspaper *Y Celt* that his mother was the descendant of a famous seventeenth-century vicar of Llandovery, the Reverend Prichard, author of *Canwyll y Cymry* (The Welshman's Candle), then the most popular book in the Welsh language.[3] This may give some insight into why Morgan turned one of his first names, Pritchard, into a surname – Pritchard Morgan – to reflect his mother's ancestry.

As with many working-class families, very little is known about the Morgans' lives. According to Morgan's later interviews, they moved shortly after his birth on 2 July 1844 from Old Market Street, Usk to Newport. There they appear in the census of 1851: William and Catherine with five children, William Pritchard, Sarah Anne, Edward, Joshua and Augusta.

As well as being a lay preacher, Morgan senior ran a private school but in January 1852, he, 'in crossing the Usk at Newport after preaching in one of the villages caught a chill and, in a few days, expired' on the 26th.[4] His will shows the family were living at 127 Commercial Street, Newport; although he is referred to as 'Reverend' in some of Morgan's biographies, he appears as 'Mr' in probate and his profession is recorded as schoolmaster. Morgan's birth certificate, however, identifies his father as being a carpenter. Morgan, his mother and his siblings were still living in Newport in 1861.

The family was not rich. The assessor valued Morgan senior's possessions at just £84 (roughly £12,000 today) when the average yearly wage for a teacher in the 1850s was around £81. There certainly was nothing valuable in the will, which lists old carpets and pans, an aged piano; about twenty books and a German clock, but nothing of silver or gold and no money. The accommodation described was not large, consisting of a back parlour, kitchen and pantry, and three bedrooms in which five people lived.

Despite being extensively interviewed in later life, Morgan gave very few details about those early days. He 'received a good, but by no means exceptional, commercial education'[5] but whether that included his father, he does not say. Following his father's death, Morgan was sent to J.C. Roberts' school at Newport and from there, he was 'articled' to work for Robert James Cathcart, an 'advocate of prominence in Newport'[6] in Dock Street, although Morgan did not stay to complete his articles. According to a *Tatler* biographical sketch, he and Cathcart had a 'lively quarrel' in 1864 when Morgan took exception to something his superior had said and 'without further ado young Morgan put on his hat and took himself off.' In *Y Celt* he said it was because 'the salary paid did not correspond to the demand.'[7] Without consulting anyone, he joined a Newport ship heading for the Mediterranean on which he served for six months but disliked the work – although this story appears nowhere else.

Not caring to return home to his mother after the step he had taken, Morgan made up his mind to run away, so he sold his watch and law books and travelled to Liverpool, where he took a ship to Australia, arriving penniless and friendless sometime in the mid-1860s.

The British had been in Australia since 1770 and had since expanded their control to cover the whole land, witnessing a small but steady population growth – until gold was found in the early 1850s and new migrants swarmed in.

This type of gold rush was not new, for just a few years before Morgan's birth, the world had been hit by the Californian rush. People had been prospecting and mining for hundreds of years but this was the first time an ordinary citizen could stake a claim. The 1848–1855 California gold rush became one of the biggest mass migrations in human history. Some went to get rich, others to flee from harsh conditions at home but whatever their reason, they went by their thousands.

By the 1850s, emigration to America and Australia reached its peak and the media was reporting regularly on life in the goldfields, publishing letters that had been sent home, advertisements and guidance for emigration. Books on how to find gold were published in enormous numbers.

The Welsh joined the rush and emigrated in their thousands. Between 1815 and 1850, some three-quarters of Welsh emigrants came from the south-west counties of Carmarthenshire and Cardiganshire and the central upland counties of Montgomeryshire and Merionethshire.[8]

By the mid-1850s, those travelling to California were struggling to find gold as most alluvial deposits had been exhausted and the remaining deeper claims were already taken, leaving little for newcomers. When gold was discovered in Australia in 1851, those who had missed out in California headed south – and the Welsh went with them. The heart of gold country was Victoria and the town of Ballarat had a huge Welsh presence. Between 1851 and the late 1860s, the Australian population nearly tripled; in 1851, the Welsh in Australia numbered 1,800, rising to 9,500 in just ten years. By 1900, some 13,000 Welsh-born people were living in Australia.[9]

However, in 1861, only 155 Welsh-born people lived in Queensland, so why did Morgan head there and not elsewhere? One possible answer, that appears in Donald Hector Johnson's 1994 article *To Silence a Jackdaw*, is that when the penniless 20-year-old Morgan landed at Sydney, he was desperate for any employment so he took work as a common labourer. Morgan later told *Y Celt* that he laid pebbles on new roads for just 6 shillings a day in wages. However, with so many people hunting gold, other jobs became difficult to fill, especially in agriculture where many farmers offered shares in farms or livestock in lieu of wages. Morgan switched to farm labour and, always a hard worker, began to build up his own holdings and start his own farm, becoming prosperous within just a few years.

Now, with money behind him, he decided to return to his legal studies and having qualified, abandoned farming to set himself up as a solicitor in Brisbane.[10] Within two years, he had a lucrative practice and was gaining fame through high-profile cases.

An alternative version of Morgan's emigration is given in an anonymous article entitled *A Reminiscence*, which states that he had not run away but had been sent to Queensland to stay with the Cribb family and money was sent over 'pending good behaviour'. Sadly, young Morgan was a spendthrift (and would be for most of his life) so Cribb cut off his money to try and curb his spending habits. Undaunted, Morgan bought a shoe-cleaning kit and set up business on the doorstep of Cribb's store – three days later, Morgan's money was restored.[11] A variation of this story appears in Johnson's article but Cribb is not mentioned, only that Morgan cleaned shoes because he found himself 'pecuniary stranded'.

If this story is true, then it may be more likely that it was Cribb's partner, John Clarke Foote, that Morgan stayed with. Cribb and Foote's general store was in Ipswich, a suburb of Brisbane, set up in 1849 by Benjamin Cribb who later took on his manager Foote as a partner. It is difficult to find a link between Cribb, who came from Poole in Dorset, and Morgan's family but Foote came from Frampton Cotterell in South Gloucestershire about 30 miles from Newport. Foote was also heavily involved in the Wesleyan Church which may suggest a possible association between Morgan senior and the Foote family. It is also known that Morgan began his legal career in Ipswich where Cribb and Foote's store was located, so there may be some credence to the story.

The only other reference to why Morgan went to Australia is an 1888 *Western Mail* article where he states that he went to seek his fortune, boasting 'of having worked his own way and made a fortune for himself in the world, and is not ashamed of having worked as a labourer for his livelihood.'[12]

Another early record of Morgan in Australia, written from his home at Bellevue Cottage, Brisbane, is an 1866 statement in the *Brisbane Courier*. In 'To the Ratepayers of the East Ward', he turned down an offer to represent them on the town council. Throughout his life, Morgan chased a political career, however, after some 'serious consideration', he decided

> in consequence of the poverty of the City, I am under the necessity of declining, what they may have considered an honor, so graciously accorded me; and, furthermore, that I now consider the conduct of the Brisbanites such an indignity to myself that it must of necessity result in the termination of our acquaintance.[13]

Why he had such an animosity towards the Brisbanites is not known.

In April 1867, having passed his preliminary legal exams, Morgan became clerk to C.H. Stedman in Brisbane[14] and from this point on, he is rarely out of the press. Morgan seemed unable to stay out of trouble and once faced with a difficulty, he would do whatever was necessary to secure a positive outcome for himself. The press contains numerous stories of his clashes with various people and institutions, both personal and professional.

Two years later, he was in trouble again, but this time it could affect his whole life. In May 1872, in the Supreme Court at the Admission of Attorneys, a Mr Lilley appealed on behalf of Morgan, as his certificate of competency to practise law had been refused on the grounds he had not passed a satisfactory examination – but the reason why he had not passed had not been explained by the examiners.[15] In the following court cases, a muddled story appeared concerning one examiner who refused a pass because he had been informed by 'some person' that Morgan had books in the exam room.[16] Any sustained accusation of cheating would effectively ruin Morgan's legal career.

However, it later appeared that it was the examiners who had breached protocol because each had signed the certificate outside an official meeting. As all the examiners were at the court case, the judge suggested they should retire and remedy the situation, adding that it was unfair for Morgan to suffer from the irregularities of the Board. Instead, another meeting was called but two members were unable to attend so someone was sent out for their signatures, effectively returning them back to square one. In the end, a resolution was passed rescinding all previous resolutions and Morgan got his certificate.[17]

What is interesting about this case is that Morgan already seems to be alienating people – one accused him of cheating – and for members of the profession and the Board of Examiners to align against him for an 'irregularity' seems curious. Added to his comments, when refusing to stand for the town council, and his 'termination of his acquaintance with the Brisbanites', it does seem that Morgan was already a controversial figure.

Once free to practise, Morgan wasted no time in setting himself up as a solicitor and, by October 1872, advertisements for his practice at Mount Perry, about 370 kilometres north of Brisbane, were appearing – and he very quickly secured a high reputation. He also got married. On 9 December 1872, he and Harriet Attwood, of Beauaraba (now Pittsworth), Maryborough were wed at Saint Paul's Church.

Harriet was born in Birmingham, England, in 1851, so she was seven years younger than her husband but it is not known why she emigrated to Australia. Indeed, very little is known about her and she was to remain firmly in the background throughout his high-profile life. A son, named Herbert Pritchard Morgan, was born in 1868, four years before their marriage, but it is not known what the circumstances surrounding this are. It would have been shameful for Harriet to have a child out of wedlock so possibly she had been married before and Morgan took on the child as his own. A daughter, Catherine Augusta (possibly named after his mother), was born in 1874.

A year after his marriage, Morgan decided to stand again for local office, the only other candidate being Walter Scott for the Squatter-Conservative Party. Morgan was not identified with any party so he probably stood as an Independent. His political beliefs were equally vague, a criticism that was to follow him for his whole political life, but from the little that was published, Morgan appeared to have liberal leanings and advocated support for working-class people. In the end, the more popular Scott won with 92 votes to 63.[18] In response, Morgan published a letter full of bravado and positive spin:

> Taking into consideration the fact of my coming into the field so late, I cannot but feel proud that I should have polled an equal number of votes with Mr Scott at Mount Perry, a large majority of the votes at Maryborough, and three-fourths of the votes at Musket Flat.
>
> I am pleased to find that my political principles were approved of by so many of the intelligent portion of the community; and notwithstanding the combined efforts of those opposed to progression and the rights of the people, I should not hesitate in again seeking the suffrages of this, one of the most important electorates of the colony.[19]

Morgan was not to stand for political office again for two years. In the meantime, he moved his business from Mount Perry to Maryborough[20] and over the following years, a stream of Morgan's cases appeared in the newspapers, most containing little detail. He split with his business partner, for reasons unknown, and moved again, this time confident enough to set up on his own.

His move to Cooktown in Queensland made sense because it was a rapidly growing town. In 1872, gold had been discovered in the Palmer

8   The Welsh Gold King

River and in the following years, vast amounts of gold flowed through the town. A well-known journalist, Julian Thomas, writing for several papers as 'The Vagabond', drew a graphic picture of the primitive condition of Cooktown and the independent character of the inhabitants:

> There was nothing surreptitious in the drinking in Cooktown. They all did it. Magistrates and miner alike drank, and occasionally got drunk at the same place. The wandering digger, who had made a lucky stroke on the Palmer, played billiards in the same room as the Superintendent of the Police, the swell banker, Dr Ahearn, and Pritchard Morgan, whilst grave Carl Feilberg, then editor of one of the local papers, looked on. There was a camaraderie and freedom between the different classes such as I have never seen anywhere else in Australia. Money was plentiful, and it was spent as it was earned. And in the midst of all the fun and excitement Morgan, lawyer and advocate, was to front, often earning £100 a week in the profession, but losing £75 of this in mining speculations. He was the best amateur billiard player in the North, a daring rider, a fighting man if necessary, and with a power of speech and sweetness of voice heritage of his Welsh race. I have seen him sit down at a piano in a mean public house and play plaintiff airs, and sing still more plaintive verse, till the tears stood in the eyes of the rough diggers who formed his audience, but if any one of these were insolent, Morgan's coat, if he was wearing one, was off. Yet in a drawing room no man was a greater success or a greater favourite. Morgan was emphatically the man for Galway, that is Cooktown. He knew his world. He talked to miners in their own language, and often with an imagery of vituperation which none other could rival. [21]

As the writer Vagabond noted, Morgan was a 'fighting man', particularly if he felt his reputation was being impugned and he was never shy in resorting to the courts, often finding obscure legal arguments to support his actions.

In January 1874, the *Mount Perry Mail*, which was often at loggerheads with Morgan, published an article that he felt damaged his reputation. Many derogatory articles at this time did not name individuals but texts were designed to implicate an individual, often making it difficult to sue for libel. Morgan took a different route and reported the *Mount Perry Mail* to the police for not having a licence to print, so they immediately shut down the publication to the horror of many other publishers. The *Mount Perry Mail* did reappear, complete with a new licence, but it was a salient lesson for those taking on Morgan – he did not play by the rules.[22]

Most described Morgan as a small man with big, black flashing eyes, always amusing his friends with a song or a story, and a brilliant billiard player. Years later, a friend recalled him using his musical talents to get his own way when his Cooktown house was opposite a church where the 'hideous…jangling of the bell' greatly annoyed him. He told the parson,

> if your congregation, rev. sir, really desire to worship God, they'll do it without the intermediary of a cow-bell. I like to take my breakfast in bed on Sunday morning and then go to sleep, and you apparently are determined that I shall not sleep. Very well. My house has been here much longer than your church and much longer than your ghastly…bell.

The following Sunday during the sermon, Morgan flung open the drawing room window, put his foot on the bass pedal of the grand piano, sang at the top of his voice for two solid hours, and 'That parson soon came to terms.'[23]

In the meantime, his reputation as a lawyer was growing dramatically. An early murder case brought him fame when 'there was a long and tedious argument upon a matter of law, but Mr Morgan secured every point, proved himself more than a match for the judge and opposition counsel combined, and, by a powerful and stirring speech, obtained a verdict of "Not Guilty" to the utter amazement of all present.'[24]

This was from an 1888 article when Morgan was at the height of his fame and eager to prove how resourceful he was. According to the same piece, Morgan became so popular among criminals that the local authorities tried to derail this by retaining him for the prosecution. In this capacity, he was even more popular as he liked to master every detail, arguing the smallest point of law – boasting that 'he never prosecuted a murderer without getting him hanged, or defended one without getting him acquitted.'

Morgan gained and nurtured a reputation for never losing, which was not true. One of his most famous losses was the murder of 'Frank the Austrian' in 1877. Frank, a packer, had been murdered by James Cunningham despite, as the judge told Cunningham, Morgan doing 'everything in his power to obtain your acquittal.'[25] On another occasion, he was defending a man and a woman charged with the murder of the woman's husband. A friend asked, 'Do you think you'll get him off?' to which Morgan replied, with tremendous emphasis, 'If I do, I'll shoot him,' but a verdict of guilty was found, and the man was hanged.[26]

In January 1876, Morgan once again stood for political office, the *Brisbane Courier* describing him as 'the leading local solicitor' who had 'got the public by the ear'. However, the *Capricornian* noted he 'does not receive much encouragement.'[27] Other contenders included a barrister, a solicitor, a tailor, a tinsmith and a tentmaker but W.E. Murphy, a solicitor in Brisbane, was the favourite.[28] Morgan played on the fact that he was the only local Cooktown candidate,[29] the *Capricornian* noting 'Mr Morgan is so well known to our readers that we need not remark on his candidature at present'. However, when Morgan issued his address, the *Brisbane Courier* pointed out that it 'expresses no politics whatever', merely his established repute and fitness for public life.[30]

Any gold rush area will attract a diverse array of immigrants and some were treated better than others. Non-whites often received unfair treatment, including Cooktown's large population of Chinese. Recently, there had been a move to increase 'alien' miners' fees from 10 shillings to £3, and from £4 to £10 for businesses. In reality, most of the miners were 'aliens' and this proposal was little more than a discriminatory attempt to regulate Chinese immigration.

About 400 people, principally working class, gathered at a meeting to argue that this would be detrimental to local business and when Morgan spoke, he was loudly cheered. His argument was that enforcing the fees would cost more than it would gain and he proceeded to read a long list of charges incurred to chase those who had failed to pay, including the cost of arrest, imprisonment and taking them to court. His calculation showed that if seven out of eight Chinamen paid the £3 fee, it would take all their money to punish the one who had not paid.[31] This, however, did not address the fact that essentially the Chinese were not wanted amid concerns that if they did pay the £3, they would then demand the same rights as white miners. Some believed it was better to let them keep the 10-shilling fee and have no rights.

The writer Vagabond in his 1888 description of Morgan wrote, 'The Orangemen and the Romans would have often come to hand blows but they became united in front of a common enemy – the heathen Chinese. Mr Morgan and myself had many long discussions on this Chinese question. I do not know the position he would have taken on this subject if he had ever entered the Queensland Parliament. Lucky for him that he did not.'[32]

It seems Morgan's sympathies for the Chinese were ambivalent, as he wrote in the *Cooktown Courier* 'some Chinese had been speared by the savages, and a few of them had died, but this was not near so bad as Borghero losing several horses by the same agency.'[33] Louis Borghero was a mailman who had six horses speared by aborigines.

Perhaps to avail himself of a better press, Morgan, along with Francis Charles Hodel, bought the newspaper the *Cooktown Courier*, but this did not stop criticism. One electioneering article in the *Cooktown Herald* drove Morgan to physical violence when he attacked its proprietor, William Henry Leighton Bailey, a sailor-turned-journalist, with a horsewhip in the middle of the main street. Morgan was on horseback and Bailey returned the assault, quickly unseating him and a fight between the two men ensued with Morgan coming off the worse. He had to return to his hotel to get his head dressed.

Trouble between the two men intensified when, shortly after this incident, Morgan was accused of being behind a 'disgusting assault'. A well-known thug, known as the 'Sogar', threw the contents of a bucket of night-soil over Bailey on Cooktown Wharf in the presence of a large number of spectators especially invited to witness the event at, it was claimed, the instigation of Morgan. Sogar received 18 months' imprisonment with hard labour and 'it is a great pity,' added the *South Australian Register* that 'his principal cannot be convicted, and receive a similar punishment.'[34]

Morgan once again lost the election and so returned to his life as a solicitor. On 27 May 1876, at Cooktown, his second daughter Gwendoline Pritchard was born, her father endowing her with the same middle name as his. A third daughter was born in December 1879 but was stillborn.

In 1879, Morgan renewed his efforts to get into political office, standing for one of the two seats at Cooktown. This election was noted for the fact that the previous six parliaments had been dominated by the Conservatives and this time, there was a demand for a more liberal representation. Cooktown was in its prime, the gold of the Palmer was at its peak, and it had become an important seat.

Five men stood: John Walsh (1842–1893), an Irish storekeeper and mayor; a tailor; Fred W. Eicke, an old one-eyed, rough and ready carrier but he was too poor to be taken seriously; Fred Cooper, a solicitor; and Morgan. Morgan had already bumped heads with Cooper four years earlier when he tried to prevent him appearing in court because he was a solicitor, not a barrister, and the rules forbade members of one branch of the profession practising in another. The judge declined to get involved.[35]

This time, Morgan's chances looked promising, the *Brisbane Courier* noting 'his chance of being returned is good, provided he is not opposed by some other local man. Rumour has it that there is a "dark horse" in the background whose winning is certain.'[36]

Decades later, a 'Cooktown resident', identified only as C.J.J., recalled Morgan's campaign:

> a splendid fellow, liked by the miners because of his Bohemianism and free and easy style. He was an amusing talker with heaps of wit, and could tell funny stories and sing, accompanying himself on the banjo. Between sections in his address, he would lighten proceedings with a song or story. Morgan would visit miners' camps and sing his favourite songs, a parody of 'Just Before the Battle Mother' and 'A Split in the Opposite Party', which he would accompany himself on the banjo.[37]

The journalist and newspaper editor, Spencer Browne (1856–1943) also described Morgan as 'a wonderful natural musician'[38] and a 'Brisbane writer' described him as 'a very bright musician, with the Welsh temperament. He sang delightfully to his own accompaniments on piano or banjo, and on one occasion very nearly sang himself into Parliament for Cook.'[39]

In the election, Morgan had declared himself an Independent and, as C.J.J. recalled, 'as the time grew closer towards polling day his popularity was evident. Many who formerly supported the Government openly stated they were going for Morgan.'[40]

However, to complicate matters, John Murtagh Macrossan (1833–1891), an Irishman and Minister for Works and Mines came to support Cooper. Macrossan was highly popular and very active in fighting for miners' rights but having lost his seat in Kennedy was standing for Townsville, and his 'fiery eloquence and steam-hammered propaganda'[41] were expected to tip the scales in his favour.

On 4 October 1878 at a large meeting at the Masonic Hall, described as crowded, noisy and frequently interrupted,[42] Macrossan was enthusiastically received. He spoke at length, stating that it was important to return members of Parliament who would work with him and the six other northern representatives in order for them to get a share of public money for the North. H. Menzies, a local JP, put forward a pledge for the meeting to support only those men who would join Macrossan, but Morgan moved an amendment to the effect that while approving of the political career of Macrossan, the meeting should not pledge itself to any man or any party but 'through groans and yells they refused to hear him.'[43]

As polling day approached, Morgan was in high spirits – he was extremely popular with the miners and spent a great deal of time riding around the camps and his expectations were high.

Voting in Australia at this time was not always easy because electors were scattered across the vast area and getting to polling booths could be a struggle. The *Brisbane Courier*, never a friend to Morgan, rarely missed an opportunity to ridicule him:

> Alarming sacrifice! Mr Morgan Pritchard Morgan, of Cooktown, solicitor, stated in his speech at the nomination for Cook electorate, that he had ridden seventy miles the previous day with only one drink of water to quench his thirst in order to be present. There was patriotism, if you like. Let Mr Groom after that cease to immortalise the two gentlemen who walked twenty miles to vote for him.[44]

The *Morning Bulleting* also criticised Morgan simply for standing, as they believed that because of Macrossan's backing, Cooper should be unopposed.

Worried about Morgan's popularity, a few dirty tricks were played against him and unsurprisingly, Walsh and Cooper won. But the results were so close that several recounts took place until on 11 January, the final figures were published:

Walsh   579
Cooper   477
Morgan   473
Palmer   201
Eicke   125

Morgan later claimed that the dodge by Walsh and Cooper had cost him around 100 votes and, in anger, he attempted to have the election of Cooper declared invalid[45] to no avail.

The matter did not end there. Macrossan had failed to win Townsville and the seat had been taken by John Deane (1842–1913) who promptly resigned after only two months in office. Morgan quickly threw his hat into that by-election. The *Brisbane Courier* claimed 'his address consisted chiefly in abusing the Government.'[46]

Morgan claimed that Deane had no intention of retaining his seat, which Deane denied, however, it is now accepted that he did sacrifice his seat for Macrossan.

Morgan was determined to derail this undemocratic personal agreement and was highly critical of Deane, as was the *Northern Standard* who accused Deane of abandoning his constituency. On the other hand, the *Townsville Herald* defended the patriotic course arguing that Deane had won his seat supporting the policies of Macrossan and that he showed greater care for the future of the constituency than for his own career as a politician.[47] They damned Morgan as:

> a contradiction of fact; for this gentleman has throughout admitted the intellectual superiority of Mr Macrossan, and has always allowed that he would be the best representative we could have if the seat was not coveted by Morgan for himself. That the Electorate should have been put to the trouble and expense of a contested poll is due altogether to the inexcusable vanity and ambition of Mr Morgan, who as we all know, has not stopped at trifles to damage his opponent by slander and misrepresentation.[48]

Macrossan was tipped to win by a huge margin and he did, polling 670 against Morgan's 222. Morgan had never denied Macrossan was a good politician, it was the manner of this election he objected to, yet years later Morgan was to use this same dodge himself.

All of these failed attempts to gain political office helped to form Morgan's future campaign strategy. While he would have willingly stood for a political party, none accepted him because he would not follow a party line, particularly if it was corrupt or unfair, so he became a maverick. He, and others like him, were contending with politics which were beginning to change; no longer could the Conservatives, the rulers of the empire, be confident of holding power as democracy was growing and others wanted a place.

Morgan, Macrossan, Walsh and Cooper were typical of this new breed, coming from modest backgrounds with high ambitions, but Morgan was hot-headed, lacked diplomacy and was too willing to criticise others, particularly if he saw a wrong being perpetrated. In his political views, he would always be accused of the same things: no clear political manifesto and a lack of understanding of political issues. Nonetheless, he later stated that from these early days, he wanted to be a politician.

Chapter 2

The Turbulent Goldfield

In 1880, Morgan moved his family down the south coast to Charters Towers, in Northern Queensland, and in July, he suffered a severe fall from his horse while out 'kangarooing' (hunting kangaroos). The horse he rode was 'very fresh' and crashed into another whose stirrup iron broke Morgan's leg, leaving him laid up for at least a fortnight.[1]

As soon as he had recovered, he decided to stand for political office again, this time against the Liberal Leader and judge, Sir Samuel Griffith (1845–1920). A fellow Welshman (he was born at Merthyr Tydfil), Griffith had been in Australia from the age of eight and was the current Premier of Queensland. Despite this position, Griffith had continued to sit as a judge and Morgan was often 'pitted in deadly combat in the courts of Queensland' against him.[2]

At a rowdy meeting in February 1880, organised to oppose Griffith's re-election, the audience shouted down various candidates. Morgan tried to take the stage and was eventually allowed to speak but he accused Thadeus O'Kane (1820–1890), editor of the *Northern Miner*, as being the cause of all the disunion with the articles he was printing in his newspaper. In reply, O'Kane leapt onto the stage in an effort to throw Morgan off. A scuffle ensued, with the audience cheering them on, until the chairman finally managed to break them apart and restored some order. After another, verbal, fight with a William Doonan, Morgan left the hall in a 'high state of indignation.'[3]

His fight for the seat was also unsuccessful, claiming, 'I was beaten by one vote, because my opponent shot the man who was bringing in a ballot box from a district known to be in my favour and threw the voting papers into the river.'[4]

The *West Coast Times* claimed Morgan was always defeated by the efforts of the Irish 'Catholic party' against whom he often stood and 'between whom and Mr Morgan existed a bitter vendetta. His remarks upon Messrs Macrossan and Perkins,[5] and their criticisms upon him, cannot be repeated. Mr Pritchard Morgan was, by a certain class, better hated than any man in Queensland.'[6]

Morgan's move to Charters Towers in 1880 was welcomed by many, including O'Kane (who has since been lauded as one of the most influential figures in Australian journalism), due to the few lawyers in the town at that time.

Morgan's reason for moving to Charters Towers is unknown but the area was rapidly expanding. Spencer Browne described it as a 'stirring town, the field was rich, money was abundant, the consumption of strong beverages was enormous (partly a climatic and partly a social phenomenon) and the miner was the king pin.'[7]

Morgan may have wanted to get away from his political rivals and start anew. His friend, the Vagabond, wrote

> He made many bitter enemies during the elections which he contested. He had cause to be bitter ... Morgan had a majority in the Kennedy district, but the ballot-boxes at the Burdekin Bridge were broken open by a band of ex-Fenians. At this time in the North nearly every policeman and every public officer was an Irish Roman Catholic, and justice was very hard to obtain in political cases. Free speech almost was stopped. No gentleman was anxious to ask a question at any political meeting.[8]

Irishman Thadeus O'Kane hated Morgan more than any other. O'Kane was a colourful and dominant character who fought against corruption during Queensland's population growth to become the second largest state in Australia. His newspaper, the *Northern Miner*, became highly influential and, as editor, O'Kane refused to simply echo the words of the government, as many other publications did, but produced independent articles and editorials that annoyed many.

Charters Towers was the second largest town in Queensland after Brisbane and was riven by small corruptions which O'Kane was determined to highlight. He would not stand for the underhand deals and activities, so spoke openly about them and was frequently sued. Those he offended, including the town council, refused to advertise in his paper but the miners stood by him, as did the public.

When Morgan first arrived, O'Kane described him as 'the smartest solicitor in the north,' adding, 'There has been a sad lack of legal brains here, and it will be quite refreshing to see a man start who knows the law and is able to plead.'[9] A few days after Morgan's arrival, O'Kane contested a by-election at Bowen for the Liberal Party and Morgan accompanied him on the boat down. The opposition candidates, however, combed through back issues of the *Northern Miner* for anything derogatory O'Kane had said about Bowen and, as a result, he was defeated.

In the beginning the *Northern Miner* gave Morgan a reasonable press and O'Kane employed him in 1880 in a series of cases against an alcoholic and slightly deranged former employee.

Constantly being sued for libel, Morgan defended O'Kane in two actions. One, in April 1881, concerned an American gold-digger, Marcus Flanagan McNamara, O'Kane's friend of about seven years, who had contributed articles to the *Northern Miner* until, he claimed, he discovered O'Kane had been taking credit for his work. McNamara wrote an open letter of complaint in the *Charters Towers Herald* and O'Kane responded in the same paper. The judge, in his summing up, pointed out that both had libelled each other which seemed to confuse the jury because when they found for the defendant, they then corrected themselves and said they would found for the plaintiff and awarded McNamara £20 plus costs (about £2,000 today).[10] As soon as that case came to an end, a counter action began with O'Kane suing McNamara but he was only awarded £10 and costs.

Morgan remained in court defending a slander case about a council meeting[11] and even then, O'Kane injected himself into the case as part of it debated whether municipal money should be used to advertise solely in the *Northern Miner* or an equal number of the same adverts be placed in other publications. When writing about the case, O'Kane's editorial annoyed the judge so much that he warned Morgan he did not want to see any comments that could prejudice the jury. Morgan lost.

By 1881 the relationship between O'Kane and Morgan was becoming strained. O'Kane voiced, on several occasions, that he suspected Morgan was writing for the *Townsville Herald*, however, this has never been proved. One difficulty with O'Kane's puritanical obsession is that he would often print articles without supporting evidence, thereby turning those not doing bad deals, as well as those who were, against him. An anonymous writer, 'Endymion', wrote in the *Queenslander* that O'Kane 'has lived all the time with spear and tomahawk in hand, has smitten and prodded with rigid impartiality all round.'[12]

Morgan's perceived desertion, along with the efforts of others, convinced O'Kane that there was a conspiracy to wipe out the *Northern Miner*. He wrote, 'the conspiracy is cunningly laid... Morgan "head centre" and promoter-general,' and he kept up a barrage of criticism of Morgan describing his actions in court as bullying, and claiming he had numerous 'bogus companies'; in almost every issue, there were claims that Morgan was quarrelling with other local lawyers.

The close friendship and confidence that had existed between Morgan and O'Kane was 'only now surpassed by their enmity and hatred of each other; in fact they are at "daggers drawn"' and from February 1882, O'Kane kept attacking his former friend, particularly his reputation in court.[13] One tactic guaranteed to cause as much trouble as possible was to set the huge population of miners against an individual, and the *Northern Miner* set out to drive that wedge between Morgan by claiming he was working against the miner's interests.

In Australia, a number of courts at this time were 'warden courts', set up to deal with mining matters. Articles in the *Northern Miner* implied corruption, carrying accusations that the Warden of the local court was in league with Morgan. In one, from 1882, the *Northern Miner* advised the Warden to keep 'decent order in his court' and not to allow 'a chimpanzee attorney to scatter insinuations against persons in no way concerned with the business before the Court.' Morgan was accused of bullying a witness in one case and that the Warden was being controlled by Morgan who

> like, one of those ugly little Indian gods, he screamed out, 'the administration of the law is all wrong, there is only one authority on the field, the great I Am' ... Morgan is constantly 'sitting on' the Warden in his own Court, everyone sees it but the Warden. He is trying to terrorise others, and he uses his right to sit at the Court to intimidate all. The Warden should put this crueliged Indian god on the logs if he does not conduct himself in the Court. He has been warned repeatedly, but he laughs at the warning, he walks into the Warden's private room as cheeky as possible the next minute and talks to him en grand sigueur. We can tell the Warden that this

association is rapidly losing him the confidence of the miners of this field, and we advise him to keep Morgan at arm's length, literally.[14]

Over the following days the *Northern Miner* printed yet more attacks, accusing Morgan of being in syndicates working against the interests of the miners, and of being corrupt in a case known as the 'Day Dawn'.

By May 1882, Morgan had had enough and sued O'Kane on the grounds that he had kept up an 'unmannerly and quarrelsome conduct towards him which was likely to lead to breach of the peace.'[15]

This charge had its basis in a statute Morgan had dredged up from the time of Edward III, which empowered magistrates to bind people over to good behaviour 'towards the sovereign and his people … wherever they be found, to the intent that the people be not troubled or endangered, nor the peace diminished.'[16] This was a tactic favoured by Morgan throughout his life and, years later, when he took on the UK government he would again resort to ancient laws.

The case generated a great deal of interest, not least due to Morgan's tactics of using a 522-year-old law, and the courts were crowded. Morgan explained that articles in the *Northern Miner* caused him 'the greatest annoyance' and he believed that a breach of the peace would be committed unless O'Kane was restrained, so he wanted the editor bound over in substantial securities for his good behaviour. Morgan claimed that he had never given any provocation for the articles and not a shred of proof had been produced. Morgan's argument was that the accusations would drive him to violence and that he would split O'Kane's skull open if the man was not restrained. He brought in a Fred Hamilton to attest that O'Kane's articles, which accused him of being a murderer, had also driven him to want to kill O'Kane.[17]

As Morgan stood in court examining extracts from the *Northern Miner*, he 'became highly excited when reading the paper of 9th May'[18], later apologising for his language, but that the case had caused him great stress, both professionally and personally. Morgan's wife Harriet had been drawn into the article and this had caused 'domestic trouble.' Various witnesses were brought in to attest that they believed the article to be about Morgan but O'Kane brought in no witnesses, content instead to champion the freedom of the press. It was the abuse of that freedom that was argued by Morgan, especially when it stepped into domestic life.

The article he had been so upset about was:

'Samival, beware of vidders,' he heeded not the words of wisdom. It was in a far Northern town in Queensland, she was a widow, soft and fair, and skilled in all the arts of coquetry. She dispensed smiles and nobblers with crushing grace. He – an offensive celebrity, blasé, unprincipled, an unbeliever in man's honesty or woman's virtue, a salacious Limb he yielded to the fascinations of that widow. She suited him, they were on a common level, and knew it. His schemes had all failed, his traps been broken and he came to the 'vidder' for comfort. She comforted him with deep draughts of Hennessy and other thing. At his house a pale-faced sad-eyed woman, sits and waits for her beloved who is so buried in business and the 'vidder'. Strange! that woman still believe in him and yet he outrages her every womanly feeling, makes love to other men's wives before her very face, and she sees it not. That Limb got drunk, but the 'vidder' was still by his side, she chafed his burning brow and gave him a 'stiff un' in the morning. He called for tea to recruit jaded Nature, and that 'vidder' was equal to the occasion. She procured a whole pot of Liebeg's Extract of Meat into one dose and poured it down the throat of that Limb. She very nearly killed him with that final meaty touch. He swears against 'vidders' now, and thinks of returning to the sober joys of domestic humdrum.[19]

Morgan believed he was the 'Limb' and the 'vidder' was an attractive young widow he was supposed to have kept at a hotel. He swore it was all a lie; a gross libel on his private character and the cause of great trouble with Harriet. He argued that pieces about such domestic issues would result in violence as people would seek their own justice against O'Kane if the court did not stop him. The court was duly convinced because O'Kane was bound over to be of good behaviour for 12 months, with sureties of £250 towards Morgan and anyone else and, if in default, he would be imprisoned for the same term.[20]

The *Northern Miner* published its next issue in mourning colours, declaring the freedom of the press to be dead and their intention to appeal.[21] Back in court that September, O'Kane cited not only Morgan but the magistrate and various justices of the peace who had made the ruling

– certainly a novel case, suing the court itself. O'Kane's argument hinged on the wording of the Edward III ruling, and that rather than being told to 'behave', a specific charge should have been made against him – which was true. No charge had been cited, only that Morgan had complained that *he* would be pushed into violence. O'Kane and his supporters believed the ruling was a result of the corrupt relationship between Morgan and the court, without considering how O'Kane's constant attacks on the people who ran the courts could have played a part.

O'Kane argued that, without a specific charge, he had not been able to provide a defence and added that the court could not rely on an ancient case in place of modern laws. But the defence countered that 'laws do not die of old age' and only cease when the offence is removed from the statute books. However, the court did agree that there was no real need to recourse to such an old law and found for O'Kane, but awarded him no costs and Morgan could not appeal.[22]

O'Kane had earned the unenviable reputation of having been forced to defend more libel actions and made more public apologies than almost all the newspaper owners in the colony. Two months after O'Kane won his appeal, Morgan was again criticising the *Northern Miner* for not adequately covering court cases. Philip Frederic Sellheim (1832–1899), who became Warden in 1874, said he would check the case records against the article and having done so, agreed with Morgan. Sellheim then wanted to bar O'Kane from reporting on any further cases. O'Kane retorted that he had beaten Morgan in the past and would do so again, adding, 'We give what we think material to the case. We suppress nothing, of interest to the public, and we distort nothing … we certainly do not yearn to publish all the twaddle uttered in the court … the editor of the *Northern Miner* fears neither Morgan … nor Sellheim' and further stated that Morgan's name would 'never appear in the columns of the *Northern Miner*.'[23]

Sellheim was in charge of the new, remote and turbulent Palmer goldfield, which attracted at its height about 15,000 European and 20,000 Chinese diggers. There was a great deal of racial and social tension and Sellheim advocated more orderly and systematic mining practices, doing a significant amount to improve working conditions and earning a reputation as an honest man. However, his rules drew animosity from mine owners and miners alike which was reflected in newspapers such as the *Northern Miner* that relied on the mining business. Morgan and Sellheim were considered to be working together and in Sellheim's court, 'Mr Morgan would get whatever he asked for,'[24] wrote the *Queensland Figaro*.

The struggle to control such a massive mining district is too complex to go into here and the dominance of personalities is a challenge to unravel. Morgan was obviously an exuberant character, and something of a Marmite character – people either loved or loathed him – and he fought to get his own way but the accusations of dishonesty need to be put into context. Even those papers who opposed him admitted he was very clever in court and would examine every single detail minutely. They agreed he could argue his cases well but when he won, they would often claim it was all a fix and that he was in cahoots with Sellheim.

In November 1882, Morgan appeared for John Deane, the man who had given up his seat for Macrossan, in a libel action against the *Northern Miner* when Deane was implicated in fraudulently and dishonestly obtaining gold by 'picking the stampers of the Defiance Mill,' of which he was at one time the owner. O'Kane conducted his own defence and at the opening of the case, a 'scene' took place when O'Kane complained to the judge that Morgan had been retained by him for the year, and produced a receipt for a £5 5 shillings retaining fee. Morgan replied that even if he held a dozen retainers, he would not allow any man to call him a 'day light robber' and 'swindler', and then appear for him to get him out of his difficulties. The judge agreed it was in bad taste but said he could not interfere and if Morgan had not acted fairly towards O'Kane, the latter had his remedy at law.

A man named John Hoolahan was brought in as O'Kane's witness and confessed that he had written the article, but the judge declared that he did not believe a word of it and declined the application made by Morgan to put him on trial for perjury.[25] The judge, in summing up, was very critical of O'Kane and the jury found for Deane – O'Kane was furious.

Although he won the case, Deane was awarded only the traditional farthing in damages. O'Kane placed an advertisement in the *Townsville Bulletin* offering a shilling in return for the coin and people flocked to give O'Kane a farthing, not surprising as there were 48 farthings to a shilling. At 10.00 am on 13 November in the Townsville Court House, a letter along with the farthing was presented to Morgan:

The barristers and solicitors present in Court, the reporters, and many others, were cognisant of the nature of the presentation and of the torpedo in the letter. Morgan took the document and with a look round at the expectant faces as much as to say, 'I'm not to be had,' opened the letter and when his eyes lightened on the farthing, he turned livid and green. The Bar, superior and inferior, smiled broadly, and we fancy the Judge himself got an inkling of the joke. That was how the verdict was paid.[26]

It does seem unlikely that, given the enormous turnout, according to the papers, and the wording of the advert placed, that Morgan did not know what was going to happen.

Throughout the remainder of Morgan's time in Australia, he and O'Kane continued their rivalry.

No evidence has been found to support accusations of corruption against Morgan but he was a very feisty character and more than willing to fight back, and if necessary, to fight dirty. The stories of Morgan's public and private contests in Australia could fill a book but he was no more excessive than many others of his time in an area that was known to be quite rough. However, his willingness to enter an affray, particularly a verbal one, did not always go down well after he returned to the UK where such behaviour was less acceptable.

In addition to his legal and political career, Morgan was also interested in mining – living in the middle of a goldfield, it would be hard not to be interested. Indeed, in one court case in 1882, Morgan said that he had been a solicitor for ten years but that he was largely interested in mining. This was the first time he had openly stated this, that his efforts had been moving away from his legal practice and he was investing heavily, financially and personally, in many aspects of gold-mining.

Back in May 1876, Morgan had secured interests in a gold mine known as Monoghan's St Patrick's Prospectors' Claim[27] and specimens were placed on show at the Criterion Hotel because of their 'extraordinary richness' that 'excited the admiration of all who inspected them.'[28] One feature throughout his life was that anything Morgan was involved in, he would spin it as the greatest or the best and his boasting was evident from the start – having invested in one mine it was, he claimed, 'the best gold mine in Queensland.' However, Morgan's managing clerk told

Vagabond that the proceeds of the mine were swallowed up in other mines that never paid any returns. 'Mining owes me £30,000,' Morgan once said, 'but I shall strike it some day.'[29] In his investments he was a spendthrift, described as 'brilliant, woefully extravagant and he dearly loved a gamble;'[30] his friend Stirling, in *The Never, Never Land*, writing that his investments were 'sure to draw a blank' adding:

> One often meets strange mixtures of genius, wit, and recklessness, in wandering about the world, but M was the strangest, the most amusing, and the most daring, I ever saw. He would work for a week to earn a couple of hundred pounds, and invest the whole of it in the first mine that anybody recommended the next day. He would say the smartest things on the spur of the moment, yet was incapable of even remembering the names of the mines he was interested in. He could hob-nob with a host of working miners on terms of the closest friendship in the afternoon, and come to a select party of ladies like a "man to the manner born," in the evening … Every one at Charters Towers, including M himself, has some amusing story to tell about the little man.'[31]

'Sam' of *The Queensland Figaro* did not approve of Morgan's inclusion in Stirling's book: 'Santa Maria! How Morgan is coming it over the English fellows. No one in the old country would suspect that W. P. M. was only a solicitor …

> For 'puff,' and pride, and posing guise,
> And blowing his own organ,
> There's none I know will take the prize
> From William Pritchard Morgan.[32]

In the same issue of the paper 'Sam' took another swipe at Morgan, writing 'Willie Morgan at Charters Towers, Solicitor, has been elected a fellow of the Royal Geographical Society of England. Great Heavens, only fancy – Morgan knows as much about Geography and Exploration as Moffatt's four-horned cow. What next, old fellow?'[33]

What is important when considering Morgan's later success with Welsh gold is his experience in quartz reef mining, where the gold lies within the quartz and has to be crushed out. Machinery in the early days was lacking and on 'a hitherto neglected reefing field', Morgan equipped the Normandy mine with a ten-stamper battery, one of the 'best of its kind' and in 1876, it was the largest in the district.[34]

Morgan bought into numerous mines and mining equipment patents; was a director in several; and was cited in many advertisements for shareholders to pay up late fees, many of his shares being forfeited for non-payment.

In 1881, Morgan was involved in a court case known as the Day Dawn, which captivated the local population as the outcome could affect every mine. The case examined the very nature of how most mines were financed, and shareholders eagerly awaited the result.

Robert Russell, the plaintiff, was an auctioneer and commissioning agent, as well as a book and stationery seller, and he had been investing in the Day Dawn mine for about two years. Fred Banholtz was a shareholder in the same mine as the defendant. Russell held a one-eighth interest and Banholtz, a one-sixteenth interest with Russell backing Banholtz in his claim.[35]

The substance of the case was that on 1 May 1878, Banholtz was working as a braceman (someone who supervised the loading and unloading of men and materials in a shaft conveyance) and became aware that the stone being brought up was rich in gold. Banholtz withheld this information from Russell and hid large and valuable specimens. He intended to defraud Russell by getting a man called William R. Hardwicke to buy out Russell's shares and give half to him. He would then declare the rich finds and make a handsome profit with Hardwicke.[36]

Russell's case was that he wanted the purchase of the shares and transfer to be declared void and to be awarded the profits, the interest and the court costs, which came to £15,000 in damages.

Banholtz countered by claiming that as a braceman, there was no way he could have known about the value of the stone; that he had not hidden any; and that there was no increase in the value of the mine when Russell sold his shares.[37]

Morgan represented Russell in the case. The Northern Supreme Court house, both inside and out, was crowded. There were thirty-two witnesses, several claiming they knew Russell had been swindled.

As usual, O'Kane injected himself into the case and published two articles claiming corruption, while the case was still pending, forcing Morgan to ask that O'Kane be sued for contempt of court – but the judge simply warned a 'certain journal' not to misrepresent the case.

The *Brisbane Courier* described Morgan's defence as 'able, searching, and exhaustive, the evidence of all the important witnesses being seriously damaged or shaken'.[38] Morgan began his summing up at 10.00 am going through the evidence on both sides exhaustively, carefully and clearly pointing out every word in his favour, and skilfully dissecting the evidence for the defence. By 5.00 pm, he had still not finished and so began again the following afternoon when 'he concluded one of the ablest addresses ever delivered here in a warden's court.'

However, despite his skilful oration, he lost the case. That evening, the victors celebrated by hiring a band and parading effigies of Morgan and Russell down Mosman Street.[39] Banholtz's defence lawyer was carried in a chair, a pipe in his mouth and his arms folded, obviously enjoying himself, alongside the effigies.

This was the last major legal case in Australia that Morgan would be involved in. In February 1883, Morgan took on a partner in his legal firm, George Edward Cooper, and the company was renamed Morgan and Cooper[40] in preparation for Morgan's seven-month absence in the UK.[41] He left on the R.M.S. *Dorunda* in March 1883[42] and later, those who travelled with him recalled that with his guitar, he was 'the life and soul of the ship.'[43]

He shared a cabin with a Charles Wodehouse who unfortunately died during the voyage and so, on reaching the UK, Morgan wrote to the man's cousin, John Wodehouse, the first Earl of Kimberley, to inform him of the death.[44] Morgan was known for his generosity and kindness, but he certainly would not have missed the opportunity to write to an earl.

Morgan travelled to Britain to represent a syndicate who wished to secure the rights to the Holloway-Longridge Process for extracting gold from complex 'auriferous antimony' ores. Extracting useless pyrites from gold ore was a difficult task and various methods were being developed to make the process easier and cheaper. Morgan had been involved in several experiments in London and Swansea on samples sent from Northern Australia[45] and, in 1884, Charles S. Dicken, the British Agent-General for Queensland, delivered his paper on *The Mineral Wealth of Queensland* which included an outline of Morgan's new process.[46]

Flushed with the success of his new contacts and the progress he was making, Morgan gave himself a bonus of £500 (about £60,000 today) and appointed himself managing director of the syndicate on an annual salary of £500.[47] He also took on a flash new office at 1 Queen Victoria Street, now the City of London Magistrate's Court, complete with brass plate reading 'W. Pritchard Morgan and Co., first floor, gold ores dry; corporation limited.'[48]

In March 1884, the *Brisbane Courier* reported, 'In the local papers a warm controversy is appearing on the subject of the application of metallurgy for the extraction of gold from the quartz. The return of Mr W.P. Morgan with his process is looked for with interest.'[49] The interest was due to the fact that at least half the gold brought to surface in Queensland was being lost in poor processes. Previous experiments in extraction had involved pulverising the ore and passing it through heated mercury, but this required some water which reduced the ore to a pulp and prevented the gold adhering to the mercury. A dry process was needed and Morgan's experiments, known as dry amalgamation, were going well.

Morgan was eager to demonstrate the new machine he and the syndicate had invested in and invited a number of people to view the crushing of ore at the Adelaide Engineering Works. Crammed into the small shop was the machine; Morgan as master of ceremonies; along with Stirling, the author of *The Never Never Land*; Admiral Selwyn, Judge Paul of Brisbane; Sir Julius Vogel (who went on to become the eighth Premier of New Zealand); James Needham Longden from London, whose great help Morgan acknowledged; Charles S. Dicken and people from Canada, America and Venezuela.[50]

The machine, known as a Jordan's pulveriser, was relatively simple. Morgan enthused 'why the whole thing can be put up in an ordinary store in Brisbane', with Sir Julius Vogel adding that a great benefit was that it could be placed under lock and key therefore saving all useless and expensive watching. The pulveriser consisted of two discs that revolved in opposite directions until the ore was as fine as dust. The waste was blown outside in 'so fine a condition that it ascends of its own gravity, or rather want of gravity, and one-third goes away in smoke.' The process had been banned in London for creating pollution, and it had been necessary at the shop to have a settling chamber by which the dust was prevented from becoming a nuisance.[51]

The practical result of Morgan's experiment was that, it was claimed, 85.5 per cent of the gold was extracted from ore brought from the Disraeli mine, owned by Morgan, Sterling, and three others. Before treatment, the assay contents were 4oz. 10dwt. 3gr (about 128 grams or a cup full), and after treatment, 14dwt. 2gr (about 21 grams). The *Courier* reported that good results could be obtained at a cost not exceeding 7s. 6d per ton, or about half the current cost.

However, despite the great show, and like so many of Morgan's enterprises, it was doomed to be a failure as so many variants of pulverisers were, and he was faced with the decision of resuming his life as a lawyer or trying something new.

Still, there was another idea – one that had apparently occurred to him while visiting relatives in Newport.[52] Morgan thought he could investigate Welsh gold. He had spent all his money on the failed extraction process and was a relatively poor man again. Nonetheless, he began to examine the possibilities of looking for gold in the Welsh mountains and borrowed money to engage William Crookes, the great chemist and physicist, to do some preliminary prospecting.

Even then, it seems he had not settled on the idea of permanent residence in Britain. The year after he left Australia, Morgan had sent £500 to the Patriotic Fund and pledged a similar sum[53] as long as a military contingent from Queensland was in the field for the Soudan War (1885) (one part of the Mahdist War (1881–99) also known as the Sudan campaign). He started his letter:

> Though temporarily absent from my Queensland home, my sympathies and heartfelt wishes are for the welfare of that country. I am indeed proud to find that, although the youngest of the Australias, our Government had not been backward in proffering assistance to the Mother Country.[54]

The idea of a temporary absence changed when, suddenly, several of his mining investments proved successful and Morgan was once again a rich man.

Chapter 3

Finding Welsh Gold

Now he had new ideas, Morgan decided to leave Australia for good. Dissolving his partnership with Cooper, Morgan travelled back to Britain in late 1884 while Harriet, left with the three children, packed up the house and auctioned the contents in one of 'the largest sale of furniture ever held on Charters Towers',[1] a testimony to how rich Morgan had become.

Once in Britain, Morgan flung himself into any project he could – including launching Australian gold mines on the British market, supposedly the first person to do so. Indeed, so great was the excitement, brokers 'clamoured' for shares.[2] Morgan, however, seemed incapable of settling on any one of his myriad schemes.

He extended his network of contacts and joined numerous social clubs including the Savage Club, a Bohemian gentleman's club in London when, on a trip down the Thames, he had the opportunity to meet fellow Welshman, Henry Morton Stanley (1841–1904), the African traveller.[3] Stanley had already risen to fame when he 'found' Livingstone in 1871 and, while it is not known if the two men had any chance to converse, Morgan would not have been slow in introducing himself to anyone with the sort of fame Stanley was enjoying. Morgan had yet to find his own fame and it was likely that Stanley did not know who he was, but they could have chatted about Stanley's experiences as a Californian gold prospector in the late 1860s. There was obviously some connection in Morgan's mind because four years later, he was to use Welsh gold to mark Stanley's achievements.[4]

Despite the myriad projects Morgan was involved in, such as applying for a new patent to separate silver from lead,[5] sending a floating exhibition round the UK ports,[6] newspaper proprietorship,[7] and others, he was paying serious attention to one: gold in Wales.

Forty years earlier, in 1844, a little-known engineer named Arthur Dean announced that he had discovered gold in Wales. Geology was a relatively young science but the news generated a great deal of public interest – it had only been twenty-three years earlier that William Smith (1769–1839) had published his massive map *A Delineation of the Strata of England and Wales with part of Scotland* (1815), which for the first time outlined the geology of Great Britain. He was followed by other great men, including Roderick Murchison (1792–1871) who wrote extensively on, and revolutionised, the understanding of British and Continental geology. In 1839, he published his findings in *The Silurian System,* enabling for the first time a stratum of rock to be identified by its embedded remains.

Despite the positive responses to Dean's paper, there were many in Wales who were angered by his claim that he was the first to 'discover' gold in North Wales. Locals pointed out that they had been constructing buildings from local rocks for generations and, of course, they had seen the occasional small veins of gold. Geologists loftily claimed that they had long known about the gold but as it was difficult to mine, they simply had not bothered with it. The pages of the *Mining Journal* included heated letters from several men claiming it was they who had discovered the gold, with geologist Andrew Ramsay (1814–1891) insisting that the earliest recorded attempt was that of Frederick Walpole and Sir Augustus Webster panning in the River Mawddach when they obtained 'an appreciable quantity'[8] in 1852.

All these claims however were empty for there is one piece of evidence which refutes them all: in the Swansea Waterfront Museum, there is a painting entitled *Panning for gold in the Mawddach* from the 1790s by John Glover (1767–1849), long before the claims of the correspondents to the *Mining Journal*.

Irrespective of who was the first to discover gold in North Wales, it was during the 1860s that a number of people attempted to mine in the area, resulting in what became known as the Little Gold Rush of Wales. Numerous mines were opened, including those that were to become famous such as Clogau and Gwynfynydd. Droves of miners flooded into the area; companies, both legal and fraudulent, sprang up in their hundreds; prominent individuals invested; and a few men made their names and fortunes before the rush died out.

One of the men who gained fame was Thomas Allison Readwin (1811–1889), an experienced engineer in both mining and railways who had held prominent positions in mines across the world. He also wrote a prize-winning essay on the 'cost book' principles of mining and a book on British geology.

Readwin's interest in Welsh gold began in London when a man showed him a medicine bottle nearly full of water-worn gold grains – sixty or more pounds. The man had walked all the way from Dolgelly (Anglicised spelling of Dolgellau), some 250 miles, with his panned Mawddach gold and had done so annually for several years.

From this casual encounter, Readwin became fascinated by Welsh gold and in 1853, he invested in the mines Tynycae, Ystrad Einion and Llaingoch. By July, he declared bankruptcy, predominantly because of his £3,000 investment in Berdan's Gold Quartz Crushing and Amalgamating Company – a machine similar to the one that had bankrupted Morgan.

By 1857, Readwin's finances had recovered enough for him to buy several mine sites in Merioneth, including Vigra and Clogau,[9] two names which were to dominate Welsh gold-mining. Two years later, having discovered gold at Clogau, he began successful operations which sparked off the formation of several rival mining companies and considerable investment in the area. Three years later, when he was poised to read his paper *The Gold Discoveries in Merionethshire* before the Manchester Geological Society, he was suddenly summonsed to London by the Commissioners of Woods and Forests. After reading a draft of Readwin's paper, they were concerned about his failure to pay Crown royalties and had confiscated his most important specimens. 'I had no alternative,' said Readwin, 'in self-defence, but to refrain from the publicity of the facts.'[10] It was not until eight months later that he was able to present his paper.

Just as the Commissioners of Woods and Forests feared, Readwin's paper encouraged people to flock to the area but these were Crown Lands and individuals could not stake a claim. However, after reading so much about the goldfields of California and Australia, people believed they could simply turn up and start panning or mining.

During the 1860s, Readwin continued to explore gold in Wales and although he found some at Gwynfynydd in 1863, he had to shut down just two years later. By 1867, he owed the Crown six years' back royalties (roughly £20,000 today) so he had to reach a compromise in order to pay it off.[11]

By the end of the 1860s, the Little Gold Rush in Wales waned. As with many rushes, some people made money but most did not.

In 1869, Readwin sold Gwynfynydd and it was taken over by William Rickford Collett, MP, and others, including George W. Hall, a prominent name in Welsh gold. At immense cost, an enormous waterwheel was erected, with twenty stamps for crushing the ore, but after twelve months it was found that the assays were delusions, the quartz only yielding a fraction of gold. The mine was sold for a song and the investors lost their money.[12] One unidentified shareholder wrote, 'If I am not much mistaken, gold-mining in Wales, if repeated, will end in a similar, though possibly a much more serious disaster.'[13]

Ignoring that advice, Readwin regained control of Gwynfynydd in 1883 and while he had big plans, he had little money. The Welsh goldfields had been quiet since the Little Gold Rush of the 1860s. Fortunes had not been made, reputations had suffered and the hills had settled back into the obscurity from which they had been dragged. The first hint of a change was on 24 April 1885 when a journalist for the *Brisbane Courier* heard of Morgan 'travelling with a number of friends last week, in a special saloon carriage, into Wales to inspect a gold mine near Dogelly [sic].'[14]

Morgan would have been very aware of the Welsh gold rush. Extracts of Readwin's reports were widely published in the Australian press alongside abundant articles following the fortunes of mines and their owners. It was something which had obviously played on his mind as he told the press in 1887 that four years previously, he had 'formed the impression that gold probably existed in the place where it has now been found'[15] and that he had recognised the geological conditions in North Wales were similar to that in Queensland,[16] but he did not say when that recognition took place. According to George Hall in *The Gold Mines of Merioneth*, Morgan had been making general enquiries and buying geological maps in 1884;[17] his sources are not named but years later, at Morgan's 1888 Crown court case, James R. Roberts said he had been employed by Morgan since 1884. An anonymous writer in the *Cardigan Observer* of 1887 recalled, 'Four years ago he [Morgan] told me he intended to make a fortune out of gold-mining in North Wales. I laughed at him; all the friends to whom he confided his faith laughed at him.'[18] Their laughter was premature, however, as Morgan had an advantage – he had money, and plenty of it.

Morgan quietly established an office in Dolgelly opposite the Ship Hotel[19], from which he made his excursions into the mountains. The small town of Dolgelly may have had only about 3,000 inhabitants but it had long been important in Welsh history: in 1404, it was the location of a council of chiefs under the iconic Welsh freedom fighter, Owain Glyndŵr (1359–c.1415), and parts of his Parliament House still stand. The town had a haphazard appearance; a local joke was to throw nuts on a table and however they fell gave an idea of how Dolgelly looked. One detail often repeated by the media was that the houses of Dolgelly were built of gold. Many had examined the walls and stated that the building material contained gold visible to the naked eye – a story that was to flourish during the gold crazes, so much so that the *Cambrian News* complained, 'If this thing goes on we shall have all the houses and other buildings in Merionethshire crushed for the gold contained in the stones, and then what will people do for homes.'[20]

The railway had arrived in 1867, bringing tourists in their droves to explore the stunning scenery. The Torrent Walk was a popular route to see the waterfalls and another, the Precipice Walk, was about three miles with panoramic views across the town and estuary.

Morgan bought Bryntirion, a stone-built Gothic mansion where he held court and ran his empire. It was an impressive building situated on the Mawddach estuary about half an hour's drive from both Barmouth and Dolgelly. A journalist who interviewed Morgan there described the house as 'about the most compact and charming country residence anyone could desire. From every window is obtained a delightful view, whilst in the enclosed verandah [*sic*] in front of the house oranges and other exotics are thriving luxuriously. Mr Morgan has purchased Bryntirion as his permanent residence, and intends to acclimatise kangaroos in the swampy land skirting the river.'[21] No kangaroos ever appeared.

Despite settling his family in Dolgelly, Morgan maintained a magnificent London office that 'would not disgrace a colonial bank'[22] and was 'a veritable geological museum' covered with Welsh quartz.[23]

However, Morgan did spend most of his time in North Wales and threw himself into local life, entering horse-riding competitions; showing his livestock and vegetables at village fetes; and supporting the local eisteddfodau, a passion he retained for the rest of his life. This quintessential annual Welsh arts and culture show enjoyed massive audiences during the late nineteenth century and Morgan was often involved, although he did not avoid controversy. When he endowed a pure gold baton (the only completely gold baton in the world) as a prize in the Welsh Choral Contest between 1888 and 1891, it created havoc with choirs pitted against each other, finally ending in a court case. The story is too long to include here but is covered in the book *The Curious Case of the Eisteddfod Baton*.[24] Morgan also kept up his own singing and playing the piano and would often enliven official dinners by singing songs about gold mines accompanied by his son, Herbert.[25]

In the meantime, Morgan was quietly buying up land and mines in North Wales, putting some in his wife Harriet's name, and investing in others, such as Gwynfynydd.

Readwin had formed the Mawddach Gold Mining Company to run the mine and he was anxious to push on, so he commissioned Morgan to install his Gold Ores Dry Reduction process[26] and lay a tramway in the level popularly known as the Chidlaw Lode.[27] Morgan, never one to miss an opportunity, increased his involvement by taking out a number of shares and influenced his friend Richard 'Dick' Wingfield Stuart to do the same.

Morgan's presence was probably very welcome and his wealth something of a saviour as little money had been generated by the shareholders. Readwin did manage to recover some gold but the money he raised soon ran out, with little to show for his efforts. The shareholders grew uneasy and decided not to invest any further – a decision that infuriated Morgan, who liked to throw money at a problem. He failed to persuade the shareholders and to make matters worse, fell out with Readwin over the exact amount of money owed for the tramway and other work.[28] Unable to reach an agreement, Morgan went to arbitration where the court found in his favour and ordered Readwin to pay £2,250.[29] By this time, however, the company was broke and Readwin could do nothing but watch as Morgan took over his holdings.

Now in charge, Morgan rushed forward, spending huge amounts of money in his search for the gold that he was convinced was there. He went back to the shareholders for more money but exasperated with their continued refusal to invest in their own mine, he took out another court order forcing the Mawddach Gold Mining Company into liquidation. The order appeared before the London High Court of Justice in August 1887, petitioning to wind up the company.[30]

Not wanting to shoulder all the costs himself, Morgan offered the shareholders an olive branch – sending them a circular outlining his plans and offering them easy terms,[31] but none accepted. Morgan had taken over Gwynfynydd but nobody, it seemed, wanted to work with him.

Still, being left on his own allowed Morgan to mine the way he wanted, and he set up the Morgan Gold Mine with stamps to crush the ore day and night. He drove shafts down 600–700ft (182–213m),[32] deeper than ever before, spending around £33,000. With a hundred men working for him,[33] they laboured on without seeing a grain of gold until they returned to the Chidlaw Lode where Readwin had commissioned Morgan to lay the tramway. Here, gold had been found previously and they relentlessly drove forward.[34] Finally, on 11 July 1887, Morgan received a three-word telegram from his manager – 'Struck heavy gold.'

For the next three months, Morgan managed to keep his triumph a secret before it was finally leaked in mid-November when Readwin sent a letter to the editor of *Gwalia*. Morgan spoke no Welsh so it is interesting that Readwin chose a Welsh-language newspaper to write to. He may have been using the gold discovery to promote his own theory that seventeenth-century mining engineer Thomas Bushell (c.1593–1674) had made coins of Welsh gold at Aberystwyth. Readwin had been out of the press for many years and so needed a means to remind people that he was the authority on Welsh gold. By using Morgan's find and ambiguous wording in his letter, it sounded as though he was still involved while giving him the opportunity to publicise himself. Ten days later, the *North Wales Chronicle* duly reprinted Readwin's letter in English:

> The discovery of valuable gold has been made in the parish of Trawsfynydd, in a place called Gwynfynydd, close to Pistyll Cain and Rhaidr Mawddach. It is said that this discovery is better than the one that was carried out in 1862 at the Mountain Clogau, half way between Dolgellau and Barmouth, when it sold £60,000 or £70,000 gold to the Bank of England. We will have further to say on this matter in due course, as soon as more facts are made known.[35]

Soon after, *The Times* wrote five lines on the 'important discovery of gold … reported by Mr T.A. Readwin'[36] and the floodgates opened.

In just one month, hundreds of articles appeared in the UK and international press. If Readwin had intended to annoy Morgan with his leak, it certainly worked. Gwynfynydd, and a very unhappy Morgan, were besieged by hundreds of people anxious to write about or view the new Welsh El Dorado.

For months, Morgan had been quietly working to crush the ore, collecting his gold and planning his great announcement. He had organised a number of experts to look at the ore and to run experiments while he carefully bought up as much local land as he could. He later explained his silence as a concern that if the news became common knowledge, speculators and individuals would rush to the area. His experience, he said, of the goldfields of Australia was one he wanted to avoid in Wales,[37] but Morgan's silence may have been for other reasons. Certainly, he wanted to secure as much land as he could but with the liquidation of Readwin's company, the mine needed a new lease and he had not signed one. Despite the fact that Morgan had hit gold in July, it was not until 20 October (by which time his gold had realised about £14,000[38]) that he signed a lease with Chidlaw Roberts, the owner of the Gwynfynydd farm.[39] Obviously, until this was signed, Morgan did not want anything to jeopardise that lease. Equally, he had not acquired a Crown lease – all precious metals in the UK belong to the Crown – but he seemed to be conveniently ignoring that fact; and Alwyn Evans, in a dissertation on Morgan's friend George Hall, suggested in the meantime 'much of the gold was probably spirited away.'[40]

Morgan admitted that he had been 'much annoyed by the premature announcement of this success.' He had wanted, he said with his usual style for the grandiose, to wait until he could present the first bar of gold to the Queen at Windsor,[41] but it was not the sort of news that could have been kept quiet for long, for the miners had been gossiping and rumours were flying about.

For several months, Morgan stubbornly kept his silence and refused to talk about, or admit visitors to, his mine. Reporters, anxious to write anything about the gold, turned to anyone who had a view until wild claims and speculations were being flung around by people with no connection to Gwynfynydd. Morgan was grudgingly forced into writing and sent a statement to *The Times* via his solicitor J.H. Davidson. Morgan had been stung, Davidson wrote, by the 'flickering rumours of an indicrously [sic] imperfect character' and had considered it better to reveal 'the true character of his undertaking.' Morgan believed, Davidson continued, that he would succeed because, until now, no systematic efforts have been made to penetrate the deeper-seated deposits. Over a hundred men had been working for several months and had raised about 2,500 tons of stone, 'richly laden with gold', ready to be crushed. Morgan enthused, 'what may be the ultimate annual yield of Welsh gold-mining, when the whole resources of the Principality come under development, it is as yet impossible to conjecture; but the mine now in operation is, without doubt, one of the richest in the world, and there are 50 other sites in Wales alone where there is reason to believe that gold will be found in large quantities.'[42]

Unfortunately, Morgan's letter, rather than defuse attention, made matters worse. The 'real facts' were confusing and the riches in Morgan's letter quickly came in for fierce controversy in the columns of the international press. On the one hand, he quite reasonably declared that he wanted to withhold declarations of yields until bars of gold could give a practical demonstration of their value, but then quoted the gold 'has been estimated to yield six ounces (170g) to the ton' while elsewhere stated that it was 2oz to the ton – this was at a time when a few pennyweights would have allowed a good profit. Experts around the world immediately challenged what the *Brisbane Courier*, Morgan's old adversary, called 'ludicrous proclamations.'[43]

Since the first gold rushes of the 1840s, people around the world had spent a great deal of time and money attempting to increase the yield of gold when separating it from its surrounding matrix. The current method was to ground the quartz to a dust and then separate the gold particles, a difficult and expensive job. Various machines had been invented to increase yield, including Morgan's own, and there was a great deal of interest in who could extract the largest amount. Newspapers vied with each other to provide proof of an average yield, and figures ranged from half an ounce (15g) per ton (a British pound coin weighs 9.5 grams) to one and a half ounces (45g). Morgan's 2oz would be 56 grams and his 6oz would be 170 grams, an astonishing amount by anyone's calculations.

Why, then, had Morgan fuelled such controversy? To justify his estimates, Morgan quoted the experts who had backed research into Gwynfynydd: William Crookes (1832–1919), the great chemist and physicist; and Readwin, whose figures must have been attained prior to his departure. Morgan stated, 'the figures I have quoted are drawn in accordance with their researches as to the value of the stone' and by doing his own experiments. William Crookes' son Henry was also working for Morgan as an assayer, thereby deepening the association between Morgan and the experts.[44] It was Crookes' and Readwin's names which kept the press comments reasonably deferential. The *Liverpool Mercury* wrote:

> If this estimate is anything like correct – and there appears to be no reason for doubting it, for Professor Crookes and Mr T.A. Readwin have given their assistance in the experiments made – it follows that Mr Morgan is in the enviable position of owning one of the richest gold mines in the world.[45]

However, there were plenty of other people who urged caution: 'many persons,' continued the *Liverpool Mercury*, 'have had unpleasant experiences of gold seeking in the Principality in past years will receive the statements made with considerable incredulity. Vast sums of money have been spent in mining for gold in more than one district, but the returns have been very small, and only achieved at a cost which involved ruinous loss.'

Despite this, the *Liverpool Mercury* could not shake off its respect for Cooke and Readwin, 'The statements now published, however, may be said to be made on "authority" and they do not appear to be open to much doubt.'

The *Leeds Mercury* was also cautious, 'We hope for his [Morgan's] own sake, and for that of the Principality, that his "convictions" have so fully established their value that no reason for further hesitation really exists. Certainly, the facts reported – if they may be accepted as facts – are full of amazing promise.'[46]

John Calvert, taking advantage of the publicity to advertise his book *The Gold Rocks of Great Britain and Ireland*, reminded people that gold was found in small amounts that had a tendency to disappear as quickly as they appeared. Also, while laboratory testing of a small sample might indicate large deposits, the machinery used at mines was not efficient enough to extract it all and much could be left behind in the tailings and dumps. Samuel Pope, a resident of Dolgelly for 20 years and well experienced in mining in the area, noted that 'Welsh ores are what miners term "intractable" that is, the gold, though undoubtedly present, exists in combination which cannot be separated at a less cost than the value of the results ... Most miners have had bitter experiences of the difference between a laboratory assay and a practical result in testing large bodies of ore.'[47]

Assay results were notoriously unreliable as miners would often send the best pieces for analysis which did not reflect the real yield of all the ore produced. In all probability, Morgan used the 6oz figure for publicity purposes – but did he believe in the 2oz figure? Probably yes. He, too, was seduced by the 'expert's' figures and nobody but a fool would have promised to pay off the national debt, as he did when the first announcement of his find was made, if they were not that convinced.

Morgan's knowledge of the press, particularly his experiences with O'Kane, made him anxious to keep on good terms with the *Mining Journal*, the most powerful voice in Britain in the field of mining, and that other powerful newspaper, *The Times*. With other publications, his relationship was more complex, often alternating between embracing them and keeping at arm's length. He was frequently annoyed that some of the media did not research claims about the gold and when repeating his own statements, aggrandised them. As a result, he could be tetchy with journalists, such as ending an interview with the *Glasgow Herald* when he thought he was being quizzed too deeply, saying that as it was his own money and not 'a shilling of anyone else's ... he didn't see why he should be interrogated further.'[48]

Morgan, worried about the headlong press rush, wrote to various publications urging caution and while promising money and jobs in the future, he urged people to stay away from the area.

A week after the news had broken, Morgan, in a more magnanimous mood, granted the *Birmingham Daily Post* an interview. 'The lode,' he told them, 'was 20ft (6m) in width, and since that I have had men working at it night and day.' Never one to resist an opportunity to boast, he added:

> There are lodes in the hills on my property from 20ft to 60ft wide, and, as I have already said, I consider Wales to be as rich in gold as any country on the map. My operations have exposed hundreds of thousands, if not millions of pounds' worth of ore, and the gold is of

an exceptionally good quality realising £3 12s 6d per ounce. I have 300 acres around the house; but at the mines I own either in freehold or leasehold something like 4,000. The whole of the neighbouring land has been taken up by a syndicate over which, however, I have a controlling power. At the back of this ring is the strongest living financier... With the perfected machinery which I will and have already put in operation, the property should produce a million a year.[49]

Morgan was quietly allying with mining experts with the aim of working an area as a syndicate. If the area became profitable, he planned to form a company, pay off the syndicate, and continue to the next likely site.

Readwin, the man who had done so much for Welsh gold, and who had been quoted by Morgan as one of his 'experts', was noticeably left out. Throughout many of the press articles, Morgan claimed some of the greatest financial houses in the City were either in, or enquiring about, his syndicate and that the required subscription had been reached. Barings Bank was supposed to have come visiting[50] but the loudest and most persistent whisper, often repeated by Morgan himself, was that one of the greatest financiers had paid a visit to Dolgelly. It was a whisper he repeated to a *Birmingham Daily Post* journalist:

'At the back of this ring is the strongest living financier.' 'Baron Rothschild?' I hazarded.

'I did not say so,' he answered. It is, however, noteworthy here that a rumour prevails in Dolgelly that Baron Rothschild visited the town on Saturday.[51]

The Rothschild family, one of the richest and most powerful families in the world, had invested widely in mines, and mine owners all over the world sought their patronage. An unconvinced *Pall Mall Gazette* sniffed, 'Whenever anything is to be boomed in the City it is whispered about that the Rothschilds are at the back of it. Is it on the same principle that Mr Pritchard Morgan has dropped a hint to that effect?'[52] The *South Wales Daily News* seemed more informed, pointing out that the previous mine manager (under Readwin) was 'now employed by the financial ring which is supposed to be headed by Baron Rothschild in prospecting the neighbouring country.'[53] Throughout his life, Morgan would, in all his endeavours, imply he had the backing of important people – a character trait not hard to understand when bearing in mind his humble origins. He was a self-made man from a foreign country where the constrictions of Victorian society were less marked and on returning to Britain, he found his money was less influential than his contacts.

During the research for this book, letters were discovered in the Rothschild Archives that show someone connected to the City Bank N.M. Rothschild & Sons (although not Baron Rothschild) did, indeed, visit Dolgellau and invest in Welsh gold; while it is highly probable that Morgan met with them, what kept him quiet was that they invested not in Gwynfynydd, but in Clogau.

Nevertheless, the flurry of press speculation about Morgan's alliances continued unabated and numerous names of prominent mining engineers and financers were mentioned. What should be borne in mind is that despite Morgan's statements of syndicates and VIP investors, he actually owned everything – a contradiction the press was already picking up on. The *Western Mail* reminded readers that, 'the whole of the mine belongs to Mr Morgan.'[54] It was Morgan who decided what happened at Gwynfynydd and no opportunities would be open to anyone without his agreement – certainly no members of the public would be allowed subscriptions.[55]

Visitors of all classes were flocking to the mine, some wishing to get involved, others just to look, such as the locals who regularly climbed the mountain until Morgan was forced to fence off the property. On one particular evening, a great crowd of Barmouth sailors and fishermen besieged the site causing the mine managers some concern but, impressed with the men's good humour and genuine interest, they received them and gave them a guided tour.

Throughout December 1887, Morgan was inundated with requests from the press but he was choosy about whom he met with personally. Important journalists and editors from influential publications visited by special invitation, while the rest were left to be shown around by his staff. Many journalists mangled Welsh names, one wryly noting, 'there are several lodes with unpronounceable names so Morgan lumped them all together as Mount Morgan.'[56]

Those who did make the journey had an uncomfortable time in the depths of a Welsh mountain winter. One anonymous journalist had a difficult journey to Bryntirion but wrote of the spectacular scenery on the way. He arrived cold and freezing and was shown into the library where he met Morgan, later describing him as:

> a man of about five feet six inches in height, with a strong, symmetrical framework, he appears to be about 40 years of age, and has a genuinely Welsh countenance, brightened by dark, expressive eyes. A somewhat nervous and excitable temperament is evidenced by his restlessness, for he paces the room constantly while conversing, and though he is outwardly nonchalant about it, there can be no doubt that the gigantic dream – or it may be the reality – with which he has startled the community permeates his whole being.[57]

After the interview, the journalist was left to make his own way to the mine but with others, Morgan took a more personal approach.

Early one morning in early December, some of those people Morgan considered suitably influential were waiting in Dolgelly for him to show them the mine. In the group was Owen Morgan (1836–1921), better known as 'Morien', one of the most well-known journalists in Wales, who described Morgan's arrival,

> I observed a sharp looking gentleman, rather small in stature and slight of frame, and wearing a thick drab overcoat of fashionable make, walking smartly into the bar... He was followed by eight or nine other gentlemen, all visitors, and I noticed that some of them addressed the leader familiarly as 'Morgan' without troubling themselves about prefixes of any sort.[58]

Morien was received with great cordiality by Morgan who introduced the journalist to his Australian friends with whom he had 'roughed it' in the bush and gold reefs of Australia. 'There was an air of Colonial freedom about the whole company,' continued Morien, 'which was very pleasing. The presence of some … who had made large fortunes at gold diggings at Gimpy, Queensland, and elsewhere, gave an air of reality to the subject.'

At ten in the morning, Morgan's group left the hotel in three horse-drawn carriages heading for the mine some eight miles away. The *South Wales Daily News* journalist noted, 'It is a much more picturesque and romantic kind of thing when the tyro is arrayed in all the glory of a bushranger's costume, sombrero hat, red shirt, top boots, and brace of revolvers; but there is something incongruous in a departure for the goldfield accoutred with a topcoat and a portmanteau and armed only with a ticket and a luncheon basket.'[59]

The route to Gwynfynydd was along narrow paths alarmingly near the edge of a ravine with a thundering river as it 'foamed from ledge to ledge'. The *Daily News* journalist was clearly nervous, 'on one side a wall of rock and on the other a precipice, whilst here and there two vehicles could not pass, so that a stranger in the locality did not feel altogether happy when the dog-cart gave an extra jolt over a frozen rut.'

Morgan enjoyed playing tour guide, entertaining his guests by pointing out features of old mines from the Little Gold Rush and at Gwynfynydd, leading them to the edge to look over at the majestic waterfalls, the Pistyll Cain (Cain's waterspout) and the Rhaeadr Mawddach (Mawddach waterfall). Below, the visitors could see the machinery and buildings Morgan was erecting as part of the extensive mine complex. In the fork of land between the waterfalls, men were busy erecting machinery to be worked by the water power for crushing the quartz and extracting the gold.[60] A huge waterwheel, not yet working, overhung the steep bank, the summit of which was in line with the top of the Mawddach waterfall. Between the back of the two falls was a hill on the top of which was a huge drum controlling a rope which worked a steep tramway. The ore was to be moved up and down the mountain by means of this narrow double tramway with an incline of about 1 in 2.[61]

The number of men employed at the mine varied widely in the press from 10 to 150, but we rarely hear from them with the exception of the mine's foreman, Hugh Pugh, who left a diary:

> I started work in 1888 with a lot of boys under 15. We used to meet on the bridge at 3 am on Monday with a week's rations in our white wallets, including a big homemade loaf. We would walk 8½ miles to start at 7 o'clock and we used to have a few minutes rest halfway. Once we found a donkey meeting us on his own and found that

3 miners had taken the donkey to carry their wallets halfway and turned him back on his own.⁶²

From the numerous articles written that December, many include extensive descriptions of the picturesque and romantic journey and the workings, leaving us with the most comprehensive account of a Welsh gold mine, but while fascinating, they are too extensive to publish here.

Morgan had shown off his mine, the journalists had written extensively and just twenty-three days after the first article was published, he was dubbed the 'Welsh Gold King'.⁶³

Chapter 4

Entitled to a Seat in Parliament

As the media debated his finds, Morgan enjoyed the attention. He was invited everywhere: playing the piano at the Queensland dinner in London to joining the Dolgelly Rowing Team annual banquet where he prophesised a very bright future for the district.[1]

Morgan's confidence in himself was one of the most positive driving forces in his life but it could also be detrimental. He rarely sought help or advice, instead pushing relentlessly forward on his own convictions, often acting first and thinking second, a policy that was to trip him up on more than one occasion in the years to come. His brash attitude, forged in Australian politics which did not conform to the more traditional British respect for class and authority, got him into trouble in the more refined UK. Never was his drive more evident than in his pursuit of political office. His friend Stirling supported him, writing, 'if he gets in he will make his mark in the Imperial Parliament.' Referring to Morgan's famed eloquence, he added, 'I should very much like to hear him tackle Lord Randolph Churchill. They would be well matched.'[2] Few others, however, seemed willing to follow Stirling's example.

Undaunted, Morgan planned to use his new-found fame to further his ambitions. To pave the way, he would donate a bar of gold to the Queen, he said, and offered to pay off the national debt. Comfortable with people from all classes, the levelling effects of life in Australia made him able to mix with gentry or the poorest of people, and the press admired him for this. So, a month later, when Morgan was publicly confessing his great ambition to be an MP, the press was generally supportive.

It was rumoured he would stand for Dover[3] but nothing came of it. He also claimed he had been nominated by London's Lord Mayor to be Sheriff of London and Middlesex[4] but this never came about because his work, he said, commanded so much of his time as to 'necessitate his withdrawal from seeking to fill the high office.'[5] The irony of his statement seemed to have escaped him and he gave no explanation on how he was then going to have time to be an MP.

New rumours began to fly that he would stand as a Conservative for Boston, Lincolnshire but that 'in deference to the wishes of the party he subsequently withdrew in favour of a local man.'[6] For most of his political life, the media presented Morgan as something of an apostate, changing his political beliefs whenever it was convenient. But in reality, he did not share Conservative beliefs, although he was not averse to brushing shoulders with them when he felt the need.

Having failed to find a suitable seat, Morgan decided to approach the Liberal Association (LA) of Newport and sent them a letter expressing his willingness to oppose the Conservative Sir George Elliot (1814–1893) at the next election.[7] His interest in Newport was genuine – many of his family were still living there and he had regularly sent money home to support them but the incumbent Englishman would be tough to beat. Elliott was a self-made man who had begun life as a collier and worked his way up to owning several mines; he was ennobled in 1874 in recognition of his public works. Originally an MP for North Durham, he lost his seat due to a reorganisation so stood instead for Newport in 1886 and won. Morgan thought he could prevent Elliott from being re-elected.

The secretary of the LA replied to Morgan, asking him to submit his views. Morgan's reply described his pride in being nominated as Sheriff of London and Middlesex, but continued,

> My greatest ambition in life always has been, and always will be, to represent in Parliament the town with which my early associations are connected. I had watched closely ever since I had been in England the politics of Newport, and I had fully determined, before I had your letter, to contest the seat whenever a vacancy occurred. But even that ambition has been intensified by being asked to express my opinions with a view to being requested to contest the seat for the district. However, sentiment must be set aside, and I know I shall be subjected to a very severe test, and I shall have to prove myself worthy of your confidence before I can obtain the honour of representing you. I have ideas and ambition far beyond the acquisition of wealth and as a matter of fact could have become an idle country gentleman years ago if I had any desire to do so.

Despite acknowledging that he had to prove himself, Morgan certainly felt he was owed, writing, 'I consider the important discovery which I have made in the United Kingdom entitles me to a seat in Parliament', compounding this conceit by adding, 'I may say, without fear of contradiction, that Newport is not the only place I have been asked to represent but as I have before stated, my greatest ambition in life would be to represent your borough.' Perhaps not the best start to a letter seeking support.

Morgan outlined his political views for the LA, explaining he was not, he said, Conservative, Liberal or a Liberal Unionist in 'the ordinary acceptance of those terms', seemingly unaware that this admission would not endear him to the Liberals. Instead, he seemed proud of the fact he was a political magpie, picking those bits he liked best from the various parties. 'There are many features in the programme of Mr Gladstone which I have in times past sincerely admired,' he continued, 'and there are still some left for which I have sympathy; and there are many features in the programme of the Conservative party with which I sympathise and which may receive my support.' Morgan was hedging his bets; the Liberals had dominated British politics and had won five of the six elections since 1859 but in 1886, the Conservatives had gained power – but only in a partnership with the Liberal Unionists.

In his letter to the LA, Morgan outlined his position on some of the key issues of the day but was careful not to give too much away. He was in favour of the disestablishment of the Church of England in Wales, 'for reasons which I will fully explain when the time arrives' but he was not necessarily in favour of disendowment (taking property and money away from Church of England centres in Wales).

He also favoured Home Rule for Ireland, Scotland and Wales – a form of local government similar to the way those countries are run today – perhaps due to spending most of his adult life in the relative freedom of colonial Australia. 'I consider it,' he said 'an absurd thing, with all our possessions, that an Imperial Parliament should have its time occupied by the consideration whether or not a railway two miles long should be made in Wales or in Scotland.'

Similarly, he wanted colonial countries to have more federal power and more representation in Parliament, with more colonial and Irish peers. Throughout his life, he spoke against hereditary legislators in the House of Lords, 'and for that reason would use my influence to oppose an hereditary peerage, but I am strongly in favour of life peerages, to be given to men who have earned distinction.' 110 years later, in 1999, the government began the process of ending the automatic right of hereditary peers to sit in the House of Lords.

Morgan supported the monarchy as opposed to a republic but did feel that existing royal marriage laws should be done away with, 'because I consider that there is blood in our possessions quite worthy of being infused into the Royal.' By the abolition of these laws, he believed, the monarchy would be cemented to the people and the people to the monarch, and the introduction of foreign princely paupers would be obviated. He never saw this happen – the first modern, 'common' blood was that of Antony Armstrong-Jones when he and Princess Margaret married in 1960.

He also supported female suffrage, 'I have seen women with brains equal to most men; and as they are now allowed to hold property, and even, although under marriage ties, are allowed all the legal rights of individuals. I consider that their influence should be extended and that they should be allowed to exercise a voice in the government of the country.' Morgan did not live long enough to see the partial suffrage of women in 1928 but he did see Constance Markievicz, an Irish Nationalist, become the first woman to win a seat in the UK Parliament in 1918 when women were permitted to stand for the first time.

Some of Morgan's other policies were state-funded emigration and tackling drunkenness with legislation:

> I am convinced that the number of public houses is far in excess of what it ought to be, and should support any measure calculated in the first instance to give men or women, if they want it, something more than poison to drink. We have inspectors of food and milk, and we allow publicans to sell poison without interference. This should be rectified at once; and when that has been done and the best price of intoxicating liquors not injurious necessarily increased by their quality, drunkenness would receive a severe blow, and then it would be time to educate the people in the principals of temperance.

Morgan wanted to see a change in land laws and the enormous fees charged which debarred anyone but the rich from owning land, 'I consider the lands are the lands of the people, and on the first principles of the laws of God and man every person should be enabled to have at any rate the sentiment of being the owner of the fee simple upon which his dwelling house rests.'

Morgan ended his long letter to the Newport LA by stressing his affection for the place, 'I have no ambition to be a mere delegate and until I can achieve the former proud position – and that pride will be intensified by representing the town where I received my early training – I will never enter political life. Trusting my views may be in accordance with – as I hope they will be and as I feel they should be acceptable to – the majority of the electors of your district, believe me, dear sir, yours obediently.'[8]

Having published his beliefs, Morgan did not stand out either as a dedicated party man or as someone with original thoughts. Unsurprisingly, the Newport Liberals turned him down.

Morgan had written to the Newport LA on 19 December and it probably took several days before he received a reply, his letter not being published until the end of the month. However, despite insisting Newport held his loyalty, he was already looking at Merthyr Tydfil as a possible seat and by 31 December, he was campaigning there too.

His first appearance was at a large meeting in the Drill Hall and his opening comments were perhaps not the wisest. Complaining he had been viewed by many as nothing more than an 'adventurer', he argued that he had spent £80,000 of his money in the development of the gold mines in North Wales and if any man were entitled to represent a constituency of Wales in Parliament, it should be one who had done something for the country. His sense of entitlement before an electorate who would not benefit directly from his actions was a curious way to try and appeal to them.

Nevertheless, Morgan must have presented a decent enough argument because he was voted a 'fit and proper person to represent the constituency.'[9]

In the meantime, Welsh gold had entered the public consciousness; jokes abounded in the papers, 'Gold in Wales! Here's a discovery. Whoever thought of W(h)ales being gold fish?'[10], novels referred to characters losing money and even the Christmas pantomime *Cinderella* at Leeds contained a reference to a man who invested in Welsh gold.[11]

Amid the levity, there was growing scepticism of Morgan's find. Much had been spoken but little had been produced so, in early December, John O. Grant, editor of the *Mining Journal,* returned to Gwynfynydd with a mining expert. What he saw convinced him:

> I am compelled to think from my inquiries in London and on the spot, that the failure which has hitherto attended the development of this important enterprise is explained by the fact that it has never hitherto been prosecuted with mining intelligence, continuity, and financial enterprise.
>
> My knowledge of Mr Pritchard Morgan and the vast experience he has had both as an advocate for gold miners and as a gold miner himself for 20 years at Charters Towers impels me to think that he would not rashly risk his capital so lavishly as he has done in Wales were he not thoroughly well advised by practical, responsible, and disinterested mining authorities. I have reason to know that these share Mr Pritchard Morgan's hopeful views for Welsh gold-mining.[12]

Morgan, however, was feeling the pressure of the constant media barrage and, just before Christmas, he wrote to *The Times* complaining that he was not responsible for everything that had appeared in print and could not be held accountable for the stream of daily inaccuracies. While he appreciated the congratulations that were flooding in, it was almost impossible for him and his two secretaries to keep up. Men in their hundreds had been applying to him for jobs, and charities were appealing for money.

Morgan told *The Times* readers that he was convinced there was untold wealth in the Welsh mountains and during the festive period, all classes should feel the possibilities of the discovery 'doing good to the whole community'. He sincerely hoped it would be of national importance 'and in answer to those who appeal to me to assist them in their various desires to relieve suffering humanity, I pledge myself publicly to settle the whole of this wealth, except what may be sufficient for my family, to a national purpose.' A fitting termination for the close of Her Majesty's jubilee year.[13]

However, at that point only three bars of gold had been completed and sent to analysts to ascertain the quality of the gold, even though 150 miners were employed and 500ft (152m) of gold reef had been stripped.[14]

Kenneth Ffarington Bellairs (1846–1914), editor of the *Weekly Bulletin*, author of *The Witwatersrand Goldfields* (1856), and someone who described himself as a person who 'will advise as to investments or things generally of every nature or description,'[15] had begun a series of letters in

The Times, explaining the layout of the gold in the Dolgelly area with a comparison of how other mines in the area were doing.

When visiting the area with colleagues, Bellairs had taken extensive notes as they traced the main lodes of gold over a distance of 6 to 8 miles. One lode reached the main road a little west of Halfway House, now a hotel, and Bellairs speculated that gold-bearing ore should continue to run under the estuary of Penmaenpool across to Arthog, a distance of some 7 miles.

The area was divided into 'setts' and the government (if they owned the land) or other landowners, would offer 'take notes', usually about 200 acres, for an annual fee. Bellairs expressed his concern that someone would get hurt in 'the coming Welsh gold mania' because most of the more profitable mines had already been taken. The most valuable lode, he argued, was that at Cefn Coch and Clogau, which crossed a stream near Vigra, where it turned more to copper than gold. It was this lode that had been worked periodically during the Little Gold Rush and it was here that Readwin found gold in 1854.

In all, twenty-four sites had yielded the precious metal between 1845 and 1875, the latter years seeing more failures despite large amounts of money being invested. Bellairs claimed these failures were due to insufficient machinery and want of knowledge, and complimented Morgan for his operation and for targeting areas Bellairs knew to hold gold. He hoped Morgan would do well but cautioned that until the returns from the large-scale crushing, of around 3,000–4,000 tons, had been assessed, it would be best not to speculate on the average yield and not to 'lose our heads', adding that 'Welsh deposits are different from any others in the known world.' He also cautioned the public not to travel to Dolgelly in the hope of getting setts as Morgan had 'scooped' the best available ones for himself, and what he had not taken was owned by the syndicate he was a part of. He doubted if there would be any useful ones left and believed that only large capital and 'complete scientific knowledge' were vital for success. Anything less would result in failure.[16]

In the interim, Readwin was still lecturing and appeared for the Geologist's Association at University College, London before a large audience on the topic of 'Gold in North Wales',[17] mostly repeating his earlier paper.

Readwin began by reminding his audience that ancient Britons' knowledge and working of gold went 'almost without saying' – something that has been more difficult to prove in modern times. Readwin referenced the Mold cape to prove his point (one of the most spectacular examples of prehistoric sheet-gold made c. 1900–1600 BC and found in Flintshire in 1833) – but it must be remembered that simply because something was found in Wales did not mean it was made in Wales. He also speculated that when the Romans arrived 'it was more than probable' that they found the gold in South Wales themselves, however, it is now accepted that Bronze Age people were already recovering gold from the Ogofau (Dolaucothi) and drew the attention of the Romans. It is the only known area of Welsh gold outside the Dolgelly belt.

Readwin continued to push forward his theory about Bushell and showed the audience a £3 coin made by Bushell at the Welsh Mint, dated 1644, containing 411 grains of gold[18] with the Welsh plume on it and he said that 'without doubt' this gold came from the Mawddach Valley.

His listeners, however, wanted to hear more about the current situation and after relating some highlights, he said, notwithstanding recent exaggerations, there was plenty of gold at Gwynfynydd; Old Vigra and Clogau; the Prince of Wales; Cefn Coch; Berkllwydd [*sic*]; Cefndenddwr [Cefn-Deuddwr]; and noted that other mines were destined in the near future to yield on large quantities, nearly an ounce of gold to the ton of mineral,[19] when only a 'quarter of an ounce would cover all mining expenses.'

He added a note of caution:

It is sheer folly to attempt to lift gold-mining out of the range of adventure. It is said that nearly all the Crown lands are taken up. A large number of them, it would appear, are about to be put together in one big syndicate, with well backed up capital. The public, it seems, are not going to be asked for subscriptions. Peddling little companies are not to be tolerated in their midst; the most able management possible is to be adopted, and, under such circumstances, the proposition is to wait with patience a year or so until the commercial value of Her Majesty's gold ore is fully and fairly determined. I have advocated this mode of proceeding for a quarter of a century, but the time and circumstances have never been propitious until now. I rejoice over it, and do not see why people should go off their heads about it, or lose much of their money in the adventure. Besides, it should be remembered that every £1,000 worth of fresh gold brought to the surface enriches the nation just by that much, no matter what it costs to get it, for the amount of costs is not thrown into the hole out of which the ore is taken. It only changes hands.[20]

John Calvert, author of *The Gold Rocks of Great Britain and Ireland*, immediately took issue with Readwin's statements and, two days later, his challenge appeared in *The Times* and noting that, as he considered himself an 'authority of 25 years' standing', he believed Readwin's statements were misleading. He said that he was a 'pupil upon this subject' but unlike Readwin, who had restricted himself to only one Welsh school, he, Calvert, had travelled 'every quarter of the globe' to learn about gold:

> One of Mr Readwin's mines has several rich and valuable gold bunches in it, but he evidently cannot see an inch beyond his pick, or why should they remain rock-bound? Perhaps he is to be pitied, as in his paper, speaking of the Welsh gold locale he says the district geologically was a perfect puzzle. During my researches in Wales I never found any formation out of place; there were the conditions in natural order, as a consequent result of the causes governing the situation.

Either Calvert knew little about Readwin or he was putting up smokescreens because Readwin had held prominent positions in mines across the world. He also called Readwin's analysis of the Bushell question into doubt. Calvert claimed he owned manuscripts from Bacon and Bushell which contained grants, patents and letters from royalty and the Lord Protector; a paper by Bacon on winning gold from ores; and a letter from King Charles I to Bushell, which he said showed that Bushell did not find any gold mines in Wales and died deeply in debt.[21]

Four days later, Readwin replied to Calvert by repeating a letter he had published in the *Mining Journal* in 1881 where he quoted all the monies and supplies Bushell gave to Charles. He argued that Bushell's contributions amounted to half a million pounds sterling, showing he must have been very wealthy.[22] However, it is now accepted Bushell probably did have money problems at the end of his life.

Although Bushell's gold coins, complete with Welsh feathers, do exist, they are rare because most were melted down after the war. There is documentation to show that silver Charles I coins came from Wales but the same had not been achieved with regard to the gold.

While Readwin, Calvert and others argued about history in various publications, Morgan rarely responded and carried on in his own way. His historic knowledge of Welsh gold may have been limited and he probably thought it prudent to remain outside of historic arguments. Instead, he was enjoying his celebrity status and the numerous invitations to speak – being careful to restrict himself to those he considered most useful. He spoke in detail about depths of shafts, lengths of tunnels, tons of ores and percentages of gold; and complained about landowners raising rents: 'If the landlords would not come to fair and reasonable terms,' he said, he was convinced that the Crown would step in and regulate their powers. 'If they would but exercise their prerogatives in a just and reasonable manner gold-mining might become, as he firmly believed it would become, a great and paying industry in England.'[23]

With visitors streaming up the mountain to view Gwynfynydd, Morgan was becoming concerned about possible thefts and in January 1888, he wrote a letter to Mayor Best, the local chief constable, asking for two policemen to be stationed at his gold mines. 'There are 100 men employed there now and I hope that number may be doubled or trebled very shortly. The amount of property at stake in the district is,' he argued, 'very great, and nothing is easier to remove and nothing more tempting than precious metal.' The week previously, he said, a large piece of rock was knocked off and carried away.[24] The matter went to court and Samuel Pope QC (1826–1901), opposing, said Morgan had to protect his own property as other people did, and as a private undertaking it was not entitled to special police protection. 'There are a good many more at work at Ffestiniog Slate Quarries,' he pointed out.

'But,' countered Morgan, 'with all respect … people don't steal slates,' to laughter from the court.

Pope was not convinced, 'I think the duty of the magistrates would be the protection of the public peace; and you would have to protect your private property, as we all have to do.'

Morgan answered, 'the presence of one or two constables would to a great extent protect my property, and inasmuch, this would necessarily be a benefit to the country. Suppose,' he continued 'after this argument and after this application a couple of bars of gold are stolen, would I have any claim against the county?'

'Certainly not,' snapped Pope.

A disgruntled Morgan said that in Australia, they had certain ways and means of protecting their gold and that he would take every means possible to do the same if not protected legally. Pope took that as a threat and warned him that if he did protect himself, it should be in legal ways.[25]

Realising he was losing, Morgan offered that if the magistrates 'do not feel disposed or justified in doing so at the expense of the county, I have no other alternative but to ask that this application be granted, and I will pay the expenses of the constables myself.'

A number of the magistrates agreed with Pope and wanted to refuse the application but in the end, after being put to the vote, fifteen were in favour with eight against, on the condition that Morgan paid all expenses and clothed the police as well.[26]

In March 1888, Morgan's fear of theft from his mine was realised when four miners were arrested on charges of stealing gold ore. Morgan was adamant that he would press for a heavy penalty, as it was believed that pilfering has been going on for years.[27] He had done all he could to stop robberies – putting up printed notices around the site, getting miners to sign a declaration that they would not steal, and securing the two special constables stationed permanently at the mine.[28] In spite of this, there was more pilfering and on 23 April, Captain William Richards, aged 60, an underground manager at Gwynfynydd, was arrested and later found guilty of theft and sentenced to six months' hard labour. Morgan went to see Richards in jail and the man told him, 'I am very sorry that I have betrayed your trust.'

'Yes, you beggar,' replied Morgan, 'I am sorry for you. If I had my own way with you I would give you 50 lashes and let you go.'[29]

After another case in April, Morgan complained,

> My men steal the gold, and in one instance the magistrate fined a man £2 for stealing £10 worth of gold, although I had issued a reward of £20 for information to lead to the conviction, and I now see by the *Law Journal* that this man ought to have been discharged, as he had committed no crime – first, because the property savoured

of the freehold; and secondly, that it could not belong to anybody, inasmuch as the Crown had an inchoate right to it, but, as they had not taken possession of it, it did not belong to anybody, and larceny could not be committed respecting it. My manager – and as he has admitted the theft there is no question about it – removed £300 or £400 worth of gold immediately following the conviction of the man (probably knowing the law as well as the *Law Journal*), and commenced building it up in the chimney of an empty house. I had to go, in company with numerous constables and witnesses, the other day from a town called Dolgelly, situated close to the mine, where there were eight or ten magistrates existed, to try the prisoner. The witness and myself arrived about 10.30 am, while the prisoner, with two constables, arrived by another train and another line about 12.30 and by 3 pm one of the magistrates having completed the vaccination of quite a small colony of children before taking his seat on the bench, we proceeded to try the prisoner. There only being one train from this place in the day, a drive home of 26 miles along the coast of North Wales, in an empty break, with a blank easterly wind, arriving at 2 o'clock in the morning, was a pleasant termination to a chase after a gold thief. I applied to the Justice in the Court of Sessions for constables to be located where I had put down a large population. This they refused, but ultimately granted by a large majority, on the simple condition that I paid the constables and clothed them; in fact, they allowed me at my own expense to protect my property, or rather, what appears now to be the property of the Crown. I have also asked the Crown to provide me with an escort to bring the gold down from the goldfield. This they say I must do my own way.[30]

Meanwhile, Morgan was continuing with his developments. By the end of January, he had erected ten heads of stamps at what was now being nicknamed 'Mount Morgan' and operations to start crushing the ore that had been sitting in the paddock began, with initial results pronounced to be highly satisfactory. Amongst those present at the early experiments were Sir Warrington Smyth, chief inspector of Crown Mines; George Culley, Commissioner of Her Majesty's Woods and Forests; Mr Lowray, secretary of the Commissioners; and Le Neve Foster, government inspector of mines. The general manager of Gwynfynydd later announced that the result of the first trial on 625lb of ore produced 18 ounces of gold which was cast into a bar and presented to Morgan. In another test, 1,354lb ore was crushed which produced two bars of gold equal to 45oz, or an average rate of a little over 67oz of gold to the ton. While the tests were deemed to be satisfactory, they were too small to get a real test of the value of the mine[31] and these very high returns were certainly not average. It is most likely that the choicest samples of rock were selected to give such a high ounce rate to tonnage. Soon after these tests were done, Morgan had to break work for a few days due to severe weather and accumulations of ice, a frequent problem during winter when dependent on water power.

Despite the positive news coming from Mount Morgan, sentiment both for and against Morgan was increasing in the press, particularly about his limited release of detailed accounts for those experienced in mining to review. New Zealand's *The Mercury* noted,

> Last week Mr Morgan took a select party down to Dolgelly to see his gold, but he does not appear to have shown them much, for the account of the visit which appeared in the *Daily News* did not add greatly to our information. At the Queensland dinner last October, Mr Morgan was showing a few specimens of his newly discovered gold quartz, which he carried about with him in a small box, but he was very solicitous that they should not be taken out of the box. The best evidence in support of the theory that paying gold can be extracted from the Welsh quartz lies in the favourable opinion expressed by Mr W. Crookes, the eminent metallurgist. One thing can be asserted positively, and that is that Mr Morgan keeps very quiet upon such points of his discovery as the public would like most to learn about.'[32]

This disquiet increased when Morgan did not address the concerns, but attempted to mollify journalists with visits to his 'veritable geological museum' London office where lumps of gold ore ranging in size were strewn across tables and cupboards.

Those journalists who were allowed such access were strictly controlled by Morgan but he allowed one group from his old adversary, the *Brisbane Courier*, to meet with him (probably through the influence of his writer friend Stirling who was known to occasionally write for the paper). When they met, Morgan acted 'the part of liberal and jovial host,' relating how he had almost been made High Sheriff of London and Middlesex; that he was soon going to be MP for Merionethshire; was expecting a baronetcy; and that before long, he would be a millionaire.

The party drove up the mountain to where the 'first crushing mill was built on a peninsula formed by two rapid strong mountain-born rivers, two of the finest waterfalls in North Wales within 300 yards of the mill.'[33] After giving a detailed description of the mine and workings, they did caution readers to wait until more gold bars had been produced to allow more accurate yield figures.

Over the following months, the press reported on the amounts of gold going from Gwynfynydd to London, its weight and values, and expectations were high. Still, in July, Morgan sold his interest to a new venture, the Morgan Gold Mining Company – this is something he would do throughout his life, setting up companies and quickly disposing of them. According to National Archives records, he received 70,000 £1 shares and £90,000 in cash[34] (although George Hall claims it was £45,000 cash and 145,000 shares).[35] In August, the newly formed company held its first meeting under the chair of the Earl of Winchelsea, who gave a glowing account of the company's prospects and what he saw as a bright future for Welsh gold.[36]

Morgan, meanwhile, was returning to what he claimed was his main ambition: political office.

Chapter 5

The Classes and the Masses

On 21 August 1888, Henry Richard, the hugely respected MP and 'apostle of peace' (1812–1888), died suddenly. Richard was widely respected and admired throughout the world, an ex-preacher who had resigned his ministry to work full time as Secretary to the Peace Society. During his career, he fought hard for the disestablishment and disendowment of the Anglican Church in Wales; was one of the most influential nonconformists in the House of Commons; and was highly critical of the gentry's influence in Welsh politics. Eighteen years after the 'Treachery of the Blue Books', the nickname given to the *Reports of the Commissioners of Enquiry into the State of Education in Wales* (which included wildly inaccurate and unfair portrayals of the Welsh), Richard wrote a series of letters to the *Morning and Evening Star* in an attempt to provide a more balanced view. The letters were so influential, even William Gladstone wrote,

> I will frankly own to you that I have shared at a former time, and before I had thus acquainted myself with the subject, the prejudices which prevail in England, and among the Englishmen, with respect to the Welsh language and antiquity; and I come here to tell you how and why I have changed my opinion. It is only fair that I should say that a countryman of yours, a most excellent Welshman, Mr Henry Richard, did a great deal to open my eyes to the true state.[1]

When Richard stood as MP for Merthyr in 1868, aged 56, almost the whole constituency voted for him. This was the first general election following the Reform Act (1867) enabling many more men to vote and which saw the Liberals, led by William Ewart Gladstone (1809–1898), increase their majority over the Tories to more than 100 seats. It has been argued that this general election marked a turning point in the political position of Wales. In the 1865 general election with thirty-two Welsh seats, the Liberals enjoyed a slim lead with 18 compared to 14 for the Tories but, in 1868, the Liberals made great gains in the now thirty-three seats available, securing twenty-three seats compared to the Tories' ten. This gave Wales a greater voice in parliament.

In Parliament, Richard was known as 'the member for Wales' as he worked hard to mould Welsh members into an organised body, and he was seen as important in bringing Welsh Liberalism to the fore. When he died aged 76, he left behind an honoured name – and enormous shoes to fill.

Even before Richard was buried, the fight for his seat began. The *Western Mail* was speculating about many possible candidates – but most attention was fixed on William Pritchard Morgan.

The *Western Mail* described Morgan as, with the exception of explorer Henry Morton Stanley (1841–1904), the most widely-known Welshman of the present time,' and continued

> There is scarcely a newspaper published in any part of the world or in any language in which his name has not been spoken of during the last few months. As having achieved such a great success in Welsh gold-mining, every Welshman, is naturally, proud of him, more especially as a South Welshman. Probably still more proud of him are the large number of miners of all descriptions earning their livelihood in the Principality beneath the bowels of the earth.[2]

Morgan's race to contest Richard's seat was, according to him, because he had received applications by 'one or more voters of Merthyr' urging him to stand. Yet, there is no record of who these were and it may simply have been the suggestion of John Vaughan, a Merthyr solicitor who was to become Morgan's political agent. Certainly, Vaughan was poking around just two days after Richard had died to see if there was any likelihood of success. The *Western Mail* seemed to think that likelihood existed: 'Morgan's views were Radical and his platform in thorough harmony with that of the Liberal Association... and would be as thorough-going as a labour candidate.'[3] The *Echo* was not so convinced, 'Mr Pritchard Morgan is an unknown quantity as a politician, and the Welsh want something more than a gold discoverer.'[4]

The staunchly conservative *Western Mail* had their reasons for supporting Morgan. It was highly unlikely that a Conservative candidate was going to come forward as Merthyr was 'one of the safest Liberal seats in the three kingdoms.'[5] Liberalism had dominated Wales since the 1868 election which had been seen as a great awakening of Welsh nationalism and they were campaigning on various issues, including fairer representation for the people. The Conservatives, who had held power for so long, were viewed as the architects of this poor representation and 'Tory' was a dirty word in Wales.

However, the Liberals were also not seen as fully representing working men and, since the election of the Liberal-Labour candidate William Abraham (1842–1922), popularly known as Mabon, in 1885 (one of twelve Lib-Lab men elected that year), more and more working men wanted someone similar to represent them. Liberals were viewed as upper/middle-class, unable to empathise with workers and it was resented when they swooped in from all over Britain to stand for an empty seat in Wales. One *Western Mail* correspondent wrote, 'It would surely be well to exhaust the list of eligible native Welshmen before applying to the gentlemen from England, who never trouble themselves about Wales, until and when a vacancy occurs they sweep down like ravens upon a dying sheep.'[6]

Morgan's Welsh background and his mines meant he avoided the accusation of swooping in for a vacant seat. He had obviously received a positive report from his agent Vaughan because on the evening of Richard's funeral, Morgan was addressing Merthyr voters – which made the *Western Mail* uneasy, 'The same enterprising spirit which enabled Mr Pritchard Morgan to successfully "prospect" and develop the mineral wealth of North Wales,' they wrote, 'is now observable in the speedy manner in which he has presented himself to the Merthyr electors.' They were equally unimpressed with his draft manifesto:

> The declaration of his political faith, as drafted, bears on the face of it evidence of haste. The reference to Home Rule – applicable to the three kingdoms – is singularly elastic … It would be premature as yet to offer any further comment on his candidature. This much is certain, however, that the discoverer of the Welsh gold mines is go-ahead, as colonists are apt to be, and there is no fact about him more unmistakable than his earnest desire to get a seat.[7]

Criticism for what seemed like Morgan's unseemly haste was growing. His address, thin as it was, had been written on the day of Richard's funeral, which did not sit well with many. Nevertheless, he ploughed on and telegraphed a journalist on the *South Wales Daily News* to meet with him at the King's Head Hotel, Newport. Morgan was accompanied by his old Australian friend, the journalist Vagabond, who had been on a visit to London when he read that Morgan was standing for Merthyr and had hurried down to testify as to his friend's worth.

Morgan anxiously pointed out to the journalist that he had only written his address on the day of Richard's funeral in order to show it to some people from South Wales who had travelled to London to attend the funeral (in his article, the journalist confirmed that Morgan had shown him the address around 5.30 on the platform at Paddington).[8] Morgan argued that he had been forced into doing so because *The Times* had prematurely brought up his name, claiming he would contest the seat. In fact, it had been the *Pall Mall Gazette*[9] who had first mentioned him two days after Richard died, though how they got his name is unknown, and this was followed by *The Times* and numerous other papers.

Having firmly placed the blame for his haste on the media, Morgan anxiously pressed home his suitability. 'Throughout my career I have always maintained my love for Wales, and it has been my constant ambition to do something for the benefit of my fellow-countrymen,' he said. This was confirmed by Vagabond who spoke of Morgan's patriotism in Australia which, he said, had been so strong that everywhere he had been known as 'the little Welshman'. In those days, he wrote, anxious to remind people of Morgan's labouring background, he 'appeared in his shirt and britches, and was then a much more picturesque object to look at than in his present fashionable attire.'[10]

Morgan's 'Welshness', however, could be flexible. At times, he was quite happy to identify himself as a Queenslander and while showing off a bar of Welsh gold at a dinner in 1888, he wrote on a board 'Got by a Queenslander out of Wales'.[11] His Welsh identity was, like many people of his time, complex. While he promoted a 'Welsh' persona, it was inexorably mixed with his identity as 'English' or, as we would say today, 'British'. Politically, despite his belief in 'home rule' in Wales rather than full independence, there is no evidence he connected in any meaningful way with the Cymru Fydd movement which promoted home rule and

Welsh cultural identity. He supported the eisteddfodau and the Welsh language but he did these in ways which were not part of his promotional strategy, so he seems to have had a genuine feeling for these. It is doubtful if he would ever have supported independence as he was an Imperialist and saw the Empire as a benign influence (as did other Welsh people such as T.E. Ellis MP, the leader of Cymru Fydd and David Lloyd George) – although Morgan did advocate for all Empire countries to have a seat in Parliament.

The *Daily News* journalist, sensitive to the importance of the Merthyr seat, cautiously replied, 'Sentiment cannot be allowed to interfere with politics … it is a constituency which has sent great men to Parliament and to represent which is a distinguished honour.' His concern, and that of others, was rooted in Morgan's political views that came across as somewhat 'weak-kneed', which would not commend him to Wales. 'Are you,' he asked, 'a Liberal or Conservative?' Always prickly when it came to criticism, Morgan resented the implication of 'feeble minded mediocrity' and declared, 'I am a Liberal to the backbone', conveniently forgetting that at Newport he had stated he was not Conservative, Liberal nor Liberal Unionist (Unionists were those opposed to splitting up the United Kingdom). Instead, he proceeded to illustrate his claim with examples from his Australian campaigns where he had stood for free and non-sectarian education and the disestablishment of the Established Church, all principles dear to a Liberal's heart. In fact, he said, in one of his oft-repeated stories, he would have got in on a Liberal ticket in Australia had he not been beaten by one vote and that was only because his opponents shot the man who was bringing the ballot box from a district known to be in his favour.

Despite the fact that Morgan did not mention the great issues of the day, the journalist was sufficiently impressed to recommend him as someone of the 'widest Radical views' but whose 'residence in England too short to enable him to thoroughly comprehend the complexities of the social system, or to master the aspirations of the people. That he has the will and sympathy there is no doubt,' and that he could indeed 'throw himself body and soul into the van of progressive national spirit which has awakened' in Wales.[12]

One of the most influential Conservative papers in Wales at the time, the *Western Mail*, also cautiously supported Morgan, precisely because his affiliations were so vague and they tried tempting him to the Unionist side. However, the *Western Mail* was sufficiently wary of him to tread carefully. If he did turn out to be 'a Liberal to the backbone', the paper would not want to support him, so they adopted a 'wait and watch' approach. They also hoped that Morgan would drive a wedge large enough to let a Unionist candidate slip in or that working men would find a labour man to represent them, causing a four-way contest that would favour the Tories.

The *Western Mail* did, however, admire him, 'Beyond a doubt Mr Morgan has carefully considered what his candidature involves. The pluck which carries him through two, if not three, Colonial contests, and pluck is all necessary to a candidate soliciting the suffrages of "the boys" of the Australian gold fields, may assist him greatly, for the "horny-handed" of Merthyr respect "grit" however manifested, and the other qualities of the "Gold King" which have ensured his success commercially, may prove not less efficacious when utilised politically.'[13] It was due to the *Western Mail*'s support that Morgan was frequently accused of being a secret Tory.

Despite the press chatter about him, Morgan still had the field alone and whether deliberate or not, he took rooms at the Castel Hotel, Merthyr as his campaign quarters, a building significant in local history as part of the Merthyr Rising (1831) when the working class had protested against the lowering of wages and unemployment. Fifty-three years after the rising, Morgan was at the hotel, amidst its long rambling passageways and dark steps, in an upstairs sitting-room from where soldiers had fired on the crowds below. Morgan and his secretary worked there along with his agent Vaughan, and Vagabond, constantly fending off a stream of journalists.

One reporter from the *Freeman* managed to secure an interview and found Morgan to be 'short and muscular, sunburnt, with hands browned and hardened by toil in early youth, and hair already streaked with grey' who 'would stride rapidly around the room dictating to a young secretary, a young man a cousin of the Vagabond. Another Australian journalist sits at another table writing his copy for the Australian papers where Morgan's candidature is being followed with great interest.'

A cable had arrived from Charters Towers wishing him well and Morgan was greatly touched by its contents more so than any other cable. Turning to the journalist, he said,

I wish you clever Pressmen would not call me the 'Welsh Gold King'. I am a man of the people. If I have made a fortune after thirty years of hard work, I do not wish to be thought a mere representative of money. It is not on account of that that my old mates in Australia sent me this cablegram. People laughed at my letter to *The Times* in which I said I would devote my wealth to national purposes. But if my mines turn out as I expect, I hope to astonish the House of Commons some day. I wish to leave my children well off. I like to live well, to give my friends who come to see me the best of everything; but beyond that I think no man ought to possess wealth which can only be hoarded and accumulated.... My public platform is that I am a nationalist and home ruler to the spinal marrow of my back bone. How can a Welshman help being a Nationalist? We have suffered and still suffer in Wales from evils forced on us by English Tories; from laws made by Parliament not in sympathy with the people; from an English Established Church which the majority dissent from; from a system of land tenure which must be altered. Justice to Ireland demands that it shall have Home Rule, either Mr Gladstone's measure or one more advanced. And justice to Wales and Scotland demands that Ireland will help us to a thorough system of Local Self-government when she has got what she wants. ... All my life my aspirations have been with the *Hen wlad fy nhadau* the land of my fathers, as we say here, and I hope to live to be no unworthy member of a national Welsh party, which, with the Irish and the Scotch Radicals will control English Tories. Good bye! Cymry am bydd![14]

In the meantime, various names were being pitched as possible candidates, including Sir Horace Davey (1833–1907), a QC from London. He had lost his seat in Christchurch in 1885 and was looking for a new one, but he had a poor reputation in South Wales due to a previous debacle in Gower. In the by-election of March, the West Glamorgan LA had selected Davey as their representative, much to the fury of the locals who, along with the Welsh Nationalist Party, refused to recognise the Londoner's candidature, arguing that he was not a local man and that the LA was not representative of workers. A local solicitor named David Randall (1854–1912) was invited by the workers to stand instead; Davey was 'frightened away'[15] and Randall subsequently won.

Morgan's decision to keep journalists at bay made the press turn their attention elsewhere and the most obvious choice was the local Liberal Association. The LA was a local branch of the British Liberal Federation that had branches across Britain, including two in Wales, one in the North and one in the South. The great days of the Liberals, however, were starting to fade as the LA was seen as a self-contained, non-elected, high and middle-class clique and, in the twenty years since more working-class men could vote, they wanted representatives who would work on their behalf.

The Merthyr and Aberdare Liberal Association, with about 500 members, was dominated by a handful of men. Henry Richard had been a key member along with David Alfred Thomas (1856–1918), a wealthy local coal magnate who had won his Parliamentary seat earlier in the year. However, relationships had not been good between the LA and the working men for some time. Thomas had been chosen as the sole candidate for Merthyr, much to the annoyance of many working men and also some members of the LA itself.

Morgan's speedy entry into the Merthyr election seems to have caught the LA napping, so confident had they been in their own power to decide the next candidate. Thomas had been down to Merthyr to discuss the situation with a large number of unnamed constituents[16] but apart from this, no meetings had been arranged and their slowness was puzzling to those anxiously watching proceedings. Instead, the LA seemed content merely to express their irritation at Morgan's unseemly rush. They believed that he, or his agent, should have presented Morgan's political principles for them to vet and several were indignant at Morgan's implication that he would be going forward with or without them. An unnamed 'friend' of Morgan's tried to smooth the waters by telling a *Western Mail* correspondent that he was sure Morgan would not go ahead without the LA and was certain he would be meeting with them soon – and so confident was he of Morgan's selection that he saw prominent men like MP Tom Ellis (1859–1899) coming out in support of him.[17]

Certainly, the *Western Mail* thought that Morgan had 'ignored' the LA and they were the first to make such a claim. Morgan's excuse was that he was unaccustomed to 'English' political life and that in Australia, there was no corresponding organisation,[18] but this seems a thin argument – he had lived in Wales for four years and had stated his devotion to politics so it seems unlikely he was ignorant of the way political organisations worked. Certainly, he had approached the Newport LA eight months earlier who had vetted, and found wanting, his political credentials.

There are a number of possibilities as to why Morgan ignored the LA. He was supremely self-confident and had been bemused by the Newport rejection. He had an almost obsessional belief that he was meant for political life and, indeed, since his gold discoveries felt he was 'owed' an office. Also, Morgan was not a 'team player' and even had he been adopted into the Liberal caucus, he would have found it difficult to tow a party line – especially as that particular party, according to his political agent Vaughan's research, was falling out of favour and Morgan may well have been reluctant to tie himself to a fading star.

Despite the slowness of an official response from the LA, names were filtering into the press as possible candidates, mostly rich and influential men. Many debated why Morgan, another rich outsider, should enjoy a better reception than others and a letter from a Dowlais man to the *Western Mail* summed it up:

> I am aware that Mr Pritchard Morgan's principles are not the same as yours, but I hope nevertheless, that you will, with your usual fairness, allow me to recommend him to my fellow-workmen. As there is no chance for a Tory, I hope you will open your columns to discuss the merits of the different candidates. There is one thing about Mr Morgan which commends the respect of everybody – he is a self-made man. He has made a fortune, and is willing to employ it for the good of the country. Who knows but that he may start some new industry in our midst that would give employment to hundreds and find bread for thousands. Some persons complain that Mr Morgan has issued his address without consulting the committee. I think nothing of that – I like him all the better for his independent spirit. Who are the committee? How many people do they employ? If we return Sir Horace Davey, as Mr Simmons recommends, what should we be the better? We want men who will spend their money among us. There are plenty of lawyers in the House of Commons already, and they are, most of them, looking out for the loaves and fishes. Thank you for allowing me to have my say, and hoping that Mr Morgan will be returned. I am a DOWLAIS MAN.[19]

The hope of Morgan investing in local industry was one which was to often resurface.

The LA announced they would not be making any decisions until the miners' meeting on 3 September when the working men would decide if they were going to put up a labour man.

Morgan took advantage of the LA's delay and threw himself into campaigning. On 21 August, he and his entourage were flitting from place to place including the offices of the Welsh-language papers, *Tarian y Gweithiwr* and *Gweithiser*[20] eliciting their support, however, they were coming out for the working man, both papers recommending a collier ran. It is not clear why, but the Welsh-language papers had an antipathy for Morgan which was to remain for many years.[21]

As calls for a labour man grew, Morgan suddenly changed tack: instead of pushing home his beliefs, he began declaring that on no account would he split the Liberal interest and if the electors found someone who suited them better, then he would quit. His inconsistency left the *Western Mail* puzzled: 'People could be excused asking why,' they wrote, 'he had come out at all and why he then continues to canvas.'[22]

Two days later on 3 September, the pits shut and the workmen in their best clothes streamed into Aberdare to assemble at the Market Place for the miners' meeting. They arrived early and filled the streets, collecting at corners and chatting with no apparent haste to get to the meeting. Many did not know exactly where it was taking place or what was to be discussed and, as the meeting began, only a few people surrounded the speaker's platform. But by 11.00 am, most had leisurely arrived and when the chairman rose to speak, there were between 3,000 and 4,000 men and boys present.

Morgan had been invited to speak, which must have infuriated the LA, and as he rose, he was enthusiastically received. He told the crowd that he regretted there was not unanimity among the Liberal electors and despite the large number of names that were being thrown around, none except he had come out. He confessed that he did not regard himself as the best man they could get to represent them and if, by a fair majority, they could choose a labour candidate from amongst themselves, then he would willingly withdraw in his favour – but otherwise not all the Horace Daveys that could be brought from London would frighten him. He explained that he was a 'thorough Welshman' and in entire accord with the sympathies of the Welsh people. He went on to say that he was born on the other side of the country, but that was not his fault, and in an attempt to curry favour, stated that if he had had a voice in the matter, he would have chosen the Merthyr boroughs as the *locale* of his birth – despite having previously describing Newport as his first love.

He did not, he reassured his audience, intend to set himself up against any labour candidate and he reiterated that he would withdraw in favour of such a man, even assisting in supporting him out of his own pocket, and the crowd roared their approval.[23]

When the miners' meeting finally started, there were five subjects on the agenda for the colliers to discuss. They had been getting fed up with discussions about Home Rule and Disestablishment, and believed that even if these were passed, there would be little benefit for ordinary people; instead, the agenda considered those matters directly affecting the miners – one day off every month; the movement to restrict work to eight hours a day; the Nantmelyn Colliery dispute (regarding the sliding scale, namely colliers were paid not on how much coal they mined but on the market price); the number of accidents in collieries; and the advisability or otherwise of sending a delegate to the Trades' Congress. The proceedings were held in Welsh and many of the Irish and others did not know what was going on. The apathy was noticeable and nobody objected to anything nor raised any questions, and no real discussions took place, which bothered the journalists. However, the miners reassured them that these meetings were not considered important; the real discussion would take place at the pits, and the only discussion that raised any interest was the question of securing a labour candidate.

The miners were worried about a working man becoming an MP. Without a wage, it would mean they would have to financially support them at a time of great difficulty when their wages were low. They would need to find the MP money for electioneering, travel and entertaining, and there was always the worry in discovering someone of sufficient education to hold their own with the highly educated MPs. There were about 16,000 workmen in the district and if they all paid between 6d and a 1s each, they could afford to send a member to Parliament for two years but this amount was beyond the pocket of most local men. Reluctantly, the meeting decided that they were not in a position to select a labour man.[24] These funding problems continued until 1911 when MPs were given a salary.

The miner's decision not to run a labour man gave Morgan the freedom he needed to move his campaign up a notch and he released a public letter continuing to press his credentials as a working-class man. 'I am of the opinion,' he said, 'that there is too wide a margin between the Classes and the Masses, between the men who watch and the men who work.'[25]

Morgan was in favour of disestablishment; he and his family were nonconformist and he did not see why he should be compelled in any way to pay for the maintenance of a Church in which he took no part or interest. He believed that while the Church of England had a great deal of property, acquired rightfully or wrongly, disendowment contained many problems; however, Liberals believed that as the tithes were collected from people who never attended the church, the money should be returned to them.[26] After the disestablishment and disendowment of the Irish Church in 1869, Watkin Williams (1828–1884), later Justice Williams, began a resolution on 24 May 1870 which stated 'That, in the opinion of this House, it is right that the Establishment of the Church and its Union with the State should cease to exist in the Dominion and Principality of Wales.' It was rejected by 209 to 45. Sixteen years later in 1886, Swansea MP, Lewis Llewelyn Dillwyn (1814–1892) took up the subject: 'That, as the Church of England in Wales has failed to fulfil its professed object as a means of promoting the religious interests of the Welsh people, and ministers only to a small minority of the population, its continuance as an Established Church in the Principality is an anomaly and an injustice which ought no longer to exist.' Again, it was rejected by 241 to 229.

Initially, Gladstone was not in favour of disestablishment but he did advocate for Welsh-speaking clergy – services, including burials, which were usually conducted in English despite many not speaking the language. Gladstone's 1873 speech at the Mold eisteddfod on the importance of nationality in the Welsh Church played an influential role in the disestablishment movement. At the 1885 general election, thirty-four MPs were returned. Thirty were Liberals, half of whom were nonconformists, and it was these Welsh MPs who provided Prime Minister Gladstone with support and emboldened them to push forward Welsh interests.

Back in Dowlais, Morgan's speech, delivered with his famous eloquence, had been hailed a victory which finally spurred the Merthyr LA to meet the following day to appoint new officers and to put a candidate into the field as quickly as possible. Morgan was invited to present his policies to party members which he did, saying 'although I may not have acted strictly in accordance with the legal and constitutional procedure of your organisation, I feel certain that you will not allow the electors on the one hand, or myself on the other to be prejudiced by the course I have taken.' He outlined his usual claims and ended, 'I sincerely trust that the Liberal Association will feel as I do, that nothing should be done whereby the possibility could arise of the splitting up of the party to the exclusion from the House of Commons of a Radical and National representative.'[27]

His words had no effect. The LA rejected him and the following day, the attacks began; both the chairman and the secretary sent openly critical letters to the *Western Mail*. They felt he had lied to them. The chairman, Thomas Williams, wrote to the *Western Mail* saying that he had explained to Morgan that the LA was going through some restructuring, but that Morgan then spoke of the organisation as being 'in disarray', which he objected to, declaring there was 'no disunity in the LA.'[28]

The secretary, Gwilym C. James, also complained about Morgan's supposed ignorance of the LA. He described how Morgan had called on him in London on the day of Richard's funeral, declaring his intention to contest the seat and asked James to be his agent. James had refused, saying that a Merthyr LA existed and that before Morgan had been accepted by them, James could not accept the job. He added that the chairman, Thomas Williams, was leaving by the evening train and Morgan could possibly catch him then. He later saw Morgan at Paddington who proceeded to tell him that there was nothing like being first in the field, and that he had sent his address to the South Wales newspapers.[29]

It would seem that Morgan had deliberately lied when he said he was not aware of the LA. While there was much criticism of the organisation, they do not appear to be overtly dishonest (Williams was a Justice of the Peace) and probably both the chairman and the secretary were telling the truth. What is more likely is that Morgan's application to be an LA candidate was not received warmly by the two men and Morgan, realising that he really had no chance going through the LA, decided to go it alone. He then tried to fudge the affair by denying he had spoken to either man.

Morgan did not reply to either letter. In the meantime, the LA was not making a decision but simply watching Morgan to see if his reception through the constituency would be as triumphant as that at Dowlais.

Additional rumours were talking of a split within the LA with members declaring their refusal to vote for certain names and, more worrying for those at the top, rumours that the rank and file were favourable to Morgan.[30]

Ignoring this, Morgan carried on campaigning to crowded audiences. He referred to the friction which had arisen between himself and the LA but asked why the constituency should lose their individuality and vote simply because of what the LA said? Why should 16,000 people follow 500, and a divided 500 at that? Or more accurately, why should they follow the five or more men at the head of the LA?

Eight days after the miners' meeting, working men from all industries, including colliers, met at Abernant to discuss the miners' resolutions. Unlike the miners, they overwhelmingly voted to keep trying to find a labour candidate. They had nothing against Morgan but wanted a member from their own ranks and to have more labour men in Parliament. If Merthyr, they argued, did not make a start, they could not expect other districts to do so.[31] The LA came in for fierce criticism for sitting back and letting the working men do all the work without any help,[32] and it was decided to wait for a report from the Merthyr and Aberdare Miners' Association to see if they had raised the £300 necessary to put a man in the field. If the money was not forthcoming, then it was all over and they would have to decide what to do. The meeting discussed the exact definition of a labour candidate but only came to a hazy conclusion; nevertheless, they nominated two candidates and referred the final decision back to the pits. However, the Dowlais and Mountain Ash men declined to support a labour man, saying the time was premature and without the support of these two huge constituencies, it was inevitable that the movement would collapse.[33]

At another meeting on 15 September, things became more confused when names were put forward and rejected.[34] It was not only the LA that was suffering from a division within ranks – the miners were suffering the same.

As the electorate waited for the miners to decide, the LA was coming in for more criticism. Like similar caucuses, it was seen as 'arbitrary and tyrannical' as it was in the hands of the non-labouring classes who would select a candidate to please Gladstone, not the people – and bring in people from London or elsewhere. Morgan was seen as an instrument to break their spell. Attempts made to discredit Morgan damaged the caucus and secured a certain amount of sympathy for him as an injured man: 'Every effort is made to prejudice the electors against Mr Morgan,' wrote the *Western Mail*, 'but their hostility only serves to increase his popularity. His description of himself as a miner has drawn the colliers towards him, and there is a strong probability that he will become the most popular candidate.'[35]

Chapter 6

Merthyr Decides

While the miners were deciding to put forward a labour candidate, the LA was dragging its feet. It had put out feelers and approached candidates but achieved little, so when the miners announced on 22 September that they were not putting up a labour man, the LA hurriedly met two days later, a whole month after Morgan had entered the field.

At the LA meeting, Chairman Thomas Williams read a resolution stating that the association would not support anyone who had delivered any political address or engaged in any canvassing – a statement intended to block Morgan, but one that was to come back and haunt them. There was a suggestion that only a Welshman should be selected but Williams disagreed and read out a number of names, including twelve from London, others from Dartmouth and Leicester, four Welshmen and Morgan.

Despite Williams' best efforts to exclude Morgan, the rank-and-file members insisted he should be on the ballot. After voting, just four men were left – Sir Horace Davey, 89 votes; Frank Edwards, Aberdare, 107 votes; G.W.E. Russell, 123 votes; and Richard Foulkes Griffiths, 186 votes. Morgan, to nobody's surprise, was out and Griffiths was selected. Once again, Merthyr was being told their only Liberal candidate was a man chosen by the LA: exactly the same situation that saw D.A. Thomas elected as MP.

The man the LA chose was 48-year-old Richard Foulkes Griffiths, a Welsh barrister who specialised in conveyancing (particularly opposing pub licences), who lived in London. A former Baptist minister, he was active in disestablishment and temperance, and was prominent in the Cymru Fydd movement. He was called to the bar in 1879 and in 1886, he unsuccessfully contested the South Paddington seat against Lord Randolph Churchill. Griffiths spoke Welsh but, due to many years in London, he was often reluctant to talk for long in his native language. He was a close personal friend of T.E. Ellis, MP for Merionethshire, who supported his decision to stand.

Even before Griffiths had a chance to appear before the electorate, he was surrounded by controversy. A great fuss was made of the fact that before his nomination, Griffiths had written to LA members 'begging' for support. This, some argued, clashed with the LA's resolution that no candidate who had been engaged in canvassing would be selected. Others argued that writing letters did not count. The *Western Mail* joined the attack, finding the situation 'irresistibly funny' with the 'official organ of Radicalism' being attacked by its own members.[1]

Nevertheless, Griffiths was allowed to stand. Now the campaign had truly started, the Welsh media began to pay more attention to the rivalry between the two men, although the wider British media did not.

The *Western Mail* and *Cambrian Daily Leader* were open minded about Morgan; but the *South Wales Daily News* rarely mentioned him. *Tyst* hesitated to give an opinion, other than saying that Morgan was the 'dark horse' and Griffiths, despite their support of him, was a 'weak' candidate. The Welsh-language press were Morgan's greatest critics; *Golenad* opposed everything about the Gold King; *Tarian* attempted to damage him by suggesting he registered as a Tory at Abergavenny;[2] and *Golewad* condemned Morgan for not following the lead of T.E. Ellis and support Griffiths. They wrote contemptuously of the Merthyr people for cheering Morgan.[3]

Despite accepting Griffiths, the Welsh press was not particularly enamoured with him and rarely covered his candidature before reverting to criticisms of Morgan. While *Y Celt* supported Griffiths, it ridiculed Morgan stating that 'he has only been known to express one Welsh word in his addresses, and that is cwrw [beer], which probably accounts why so many persons under its influence are found following him.' Much of the blame was attributed to the LA. *Genedl* thought the LA powerless, and recommended the withdrawal of both candidates and the selection of another; and *Seren* thought the LA ought to have found a better candidate than Griffiths, that the LA were self-appointed, and cautiously supported Morgan. *Gwalia* was surprised that a borough of the size and importance of Merthyr could not find a better candidate and thought that Morgan had been treated shabbily by the LA; while *Baner* favoured Griffiths, it felt that 'one candidate is as good as the other, and that they are much alike, politically.' Their London correspondent was more critical of the LA, claiming the candidates 'consist of the rejected of English constituencies, sinecurists, office seekers, and questionable Welshmen. This is the first time I have heard of Mr Foulkes Griffiths in connection with anything Welsh. He may know something about our wants; if he does, he has kept it to himself, or buried it in the dust of the Temple.'[4] This was somewhat unjust as Griffiths had worked on Welsh political issues but from London.

Throughout the campaign, the papers rarely changed their opinion with the exception of the *Cambrian Daily Leader* and its editor, George Hall, also a Radical. Hall had initially been cautious about Morgan but having heard him speak and then having met him, he became enormously supportive and wrote columns of glowing articles. The two men became great friends and, later, business partners.

In the end, it was only the *Western Mail* that remained relatively neutral and it saw the real crux of the contest being between the LA and the electorate. Nevertheless, Morgan relentlessly threw himself into his campaign and everywhere he went, he was cheered and mobbed. At this stage, Morgan was still being relatively fair to both the LA and Griffiths; while he criticised them for sending out only one man, he asked that nobody committed themselves to a candidate until Griffiths had a fair hearing.[5]

Griffiths duly delivered his first address on 27 September at Mountain Ash and spoke on all the main issues of the day favoured by the Liberals. He began in Welsh but claimed his constant use of English had made his Welsh somewhat stiff, so he would drop in and out of each language. He compared the Wales of twenty years ago to the current situation and argued that even if there was no Welsh national party, there was a new and more ambitious Welsh nation in existence.

Griffiths spoke of disestablishment and disendowment; the many empty seats in the Anglican Church; and tithes being collected by a regiment of soldiers – a 'very curious way', he said, of taking the collecting box around. He also mentioned familiar Liberal causes and the unfairness of Welsh not being recognised in the law courts, something that 'made his blood boil'. Griffiths argued that Welsh should be taught in schools and students should be allowed to choose Welsh, instead of French or German. It was necessary because the Welsh had to learn one more language than their English counterparts before they could be put on the same footing in exams.⁶

The *Western Mail,* the only newspaper really commenting on the speeches, kept up its campaign of undermining the LA, claiming that Griffiths was a 'bitter disappointment' and spoke too much like a preacher (he had a lecturing style of oratory previously used by Welsh preachers that had fallen out of favour). The *Western Mail* complained Griffiths' main supporters were also Merthyr preachers, who were turning out in 'exceptionally strong force' to support the ex-minister, and added that his addresses were too broad and generalised⁷ – a reproach which must have brought some satisfaction to Morgan who had been subjected to the same criticism.

Meanwhile, Morgan went back to his independent campaigning. He took offices in Merthyr and appointed D.J. Rowlands as his committee secretary, ironically a member of the LA. Morgan also went off to Mountain Ash the day after Griffiths and told the audience that he had stayed his hand until the working men could find a labour candidate but now that option was no longer viable, he would place his services 'unreservedly at your disposal.' Even in this speech, he skirted around matters where his knowledge was wanting; instead, he attributed his support for certain issues because they were 'approved of by the Liberal' party or those 'adopted by the Liberation Society', which did not endear him to the press.

Morgan did support one man, one vote for all and that the franchise should, as far as possible, be extended to women. Both he and Griffiths wanted MPs to be paid, so making labour candidates possible. He continued, 'Labour representation having for the moment been abandoned, I claim to be nearer in touch and sympathy with the working classes than any other candidate before you. I have worked myself with my own hands, and, therefore know what it is to obtain a livelihood by manual labour.' In his speeches, he would often tell his audience that he had broken two legs and an arm while working as a labourer and he was not ashamed of it. 'The mere fact of my having been, to some extent, a successful man,' he continued, 'does not make me forget the class with which I have been so long associated'. In conclusion, he pledged that if a labour man was found and supported by the majority, then he would resign his seat.⁸ Nobody, it seemed, knew about Morgan's criticism of Deane when he did exactly the same for Macrossan.

Some members of the press would accuse him of being an adventurer, and for not speaking Welsh in an area where it was the dominant language – he flippantly replied that would not be necessary in the House of Commons. Morgan told *Y Celt*⁹ that he regretted not having been taught Welsh, his grandfather could not speak English, but added that he and his children were learning and he had hired Welsh-speaking servants to assist the process.

Morgan was also accused of being a political apostate so, in response, he would take some letters with him to meetings and would read them out, one from Arnold Morley, a prominent member of the LA and the Liberal whip, who declared Morgan a 'thorough Liberal'; the other from Alderman Whitehead, the Lord Mayor elect of London, in which he said 'you are a good Liberal, and on some points even more Radical than myself.'[10]

Meanwhile, Griffiths and the LA were pushing ahead with their own meetings. At Dowlais on 30 September, the proceedings were lively, with loud groans greeting Thomas Williams, the LA chairman, while Griffiths was assailed with booing and shouts of 'six and eightpence' (the fee for a solicitor's letter, in reference to his letter-writing campaign). Williams attempted to speak but was continually interrupted; shouts of 'Baptist clique' were so persistent that he quickly resumed his seat. Griffiths also tried to speak but the pandemonium continued. Almost all his remarks were greeted with ironic comments and laughter with cheers frequently being raised for Morgan. 'I cannot see why you should cheer that particular name,' Griffiths complained, to which someone shouted, 'Because he is a man.' Struggling on, Griffiths turned to Irish Home Rule and, in answer to a question as to what the cause of the 'troubles' were, unwisely replied, 'It's all the fault of the lawyers.' At this point, the uproar became so great that he was forced to sit down while Williams and others struggled to regain control. Renewed cheers for Morgan brought Griffiths jumping to his feet, arguing that no employer, like Morgan, could be a friend to the working man, unlike himself, which sent the audience into raucous laughter with loud cries of 'no lawyers wanted'. He unwisely tried to point out that he was the representative chosen by 500 politically astute men of the LA, but that just brought screams of laughter with shouts of 'five hundred fiddle sticks' and the rowdy meeting was broken up.

The LA was now so worried that they called another meeting on 2 October, to which they invited a number of reporters. Williams said the eyes of the country were upon them (which was not true as most of the nation's press were not commenting on the Merthyr election). Many of the members wanted to start again with a new candidate, but this was vetoed on the grounds that it would give Morgan an advantage. A round of attacks on Morgan ensued including complaints that the Gold King was bent on destroying the association,[11] although this seems slightly unfair as Morgan's criticism of the LA had been mild compared to the criticism levelled at it by the press.

Just as Morgan was enjoying his dominant position in the campaign, the LA and Griffiths received a huge boost. Charles Kenshole, the secretary to the Aberdare Liberal Association, received a letter from the Irish Press Agency that confirmed Griffiths would receive the support of the Irish members.[12] As Merthyr had a large Irish population, this was a blow to Morgan.

Throughout the row, the one man who had remained silent was the sitting MP for Merthyr, D.A. Thomas. However, on 6 October, he broke his silence when he spoke at a Troedyrhiw meeting to a small audience – small because according to the LA, Saturday nights were awkward for gatherings, which raises the question why they held Saturday night meetings?

Griffiths rose and began speaking in Welsh but soon dropped into English, spending most of his time criticising Morgan. He was followed by the man the meeting was really about, D.A. Thomas – a man not popular with the entire electorate as his policies contained little for the working man. Thomas began by telling the audience that he had withheld from commenting and held no preferences, simply abiding by what the LA decided. However, he felt it was now his duty to enter the fray stating, 'I do not intend fighting with gloved hands'[13] and the remainder of his speech was a rant against Morgan. Had Morgan obtained the majority of votes from the association, he assured the audience, he would have supported him, although he also confessed it would have gone against the grain as he did not believe in the man and had no faith in his Liberalism. Thomas believed the Tories were supporting Morgan for the express purpose of breaking up the LA, something they had tried to do with him in March and were now trying to address their failure. He continued:

I have heard it hinted that one of the candidates may be a political adventurer, that he is possible a golden bubble, a gilded weathercock, or a brazen hwriegicgan [Chwyrligwgan – a whirligig]. Now, gentlemen, however much noise he may have made, or however rapidly he may have changed his political convictions, I think the appreciation of these epitaphs is much deprecated. But we cannot avoid a certain amount of personal examination into the antecedents and present attitude of the contestants, and I propose in the first place, to draw your attention to Mr Pritchard Morgan's conduct towards the association.[14]

It is interesting that Thomas was more concerned about Morgan's attitude towards the LA than his politics, but he, too, had noticed and quoted Morgan's remarks from the Newport election about not being Conservative, a Liberal, nor a Liberal Unionist, and yet now he was claiming to be a Liberal to the backbone. Thomas referred to Morgan's comment about the many 'features in the programme of the Conservative party with which I sympathise, and which may receive my support' and wanted to know what features of the Conservative Party Morgan still endorsed. He also referred to a growing rumour that Morgan was known as a Conservative in Abergavenny where his mother lived. Thomas' intentions were to leave the audience or, more importantly, newspaper readers with the impression that the Tories were supporting Morgan in order to smash the LA.

Thomas finished by saying that if Morgan was elected, he would do his best to work with him despite it being a difficult task and, in a very telling comment, told friends who were assisting Morgan that he would wage war with Morgan but not with them.

The persistent question of Morgan being a Tory caused the LA to write to the chief whip of the House asking if Morgan had any known Conservative affiliations. The whip wrote back saying that despite exhaustive inquiries, he could find none. The LA threw the whip's reply into the bin where it later found its way to the Cwmbach Road refuse tip and was accidentally found by James Hek who passed it to Morgan's team – who made good use of it to quash all rumours of Morgan being a Tory.[15]

A pattern was emerging, with both candidates doing three or four meetings a day. Morgan's gatherings were rowdy but generally supportive while Griffiths' were usually quiet and orderly but lacked the numbers Morgan was enjoying. It was also Thomas who received far more press attention than Griffiths and it was he who was doing research. Morgan's letter from Arnold Morley, which he liked to flourish at his meetings, was queried by Thomas who wrote to Morley to confirm his authorship. 'The letter,' Morley wrote back, was 'written by me in reply to a communication from Merthyr, and which was, I believed marked "private".' If it was used publicly, he continued, it certainly was not intended for that purpose, and 'as I should be most adverse to doing anything which might even have the appearance of influencing the decision of the party in the constituency in the matter of the selection of a candidate, and especially so where, as in the case of Merthyr, there is a representative organisation formed for the purpose.'[16] The *Merthyr Express* claimed it had seen the letter from Morley and it had not been marked private.[17]

As the contest heated up, Thomas realised he was overshadowing Griffiths. Thomas' friends cautioned he would lose popularity if he continued, but Thomas argued that duty came first and popularity second. In his own mind, he must have been convinced that Griffiths could not hold his own against Morgan or he would not have spoken so regularly in place of Griffiths. This was a point that was not lost on the electorate and the press – how could Thomas expect others to have confidence in Griffiths if he did not share that confidence? And if elected, would he be nothing more than Thomas' puppet?

Meanwhile, letters were piling up in the correspondence section of the newspapers. Some were querying why Thomas had supported Conservative Sir William Thomas Lewis at the last election. Some queried why churches and chapels allowed Griffiths to hold meetings, but not Morgan.[18] The general consensus was that the area was a laughing stock, with two Liberals promoting almost identical policies fighting against each other. Correspondents agreed that the sooner polling day arrived, the better, as friends and colleagues across Merthyr were falling out – with so much hostility that guards were being posted at the doors of meetings.

Thomas Williams, the LA chairman, was also carrying out research. He travelled to Dolgelly to make enquiries about Morgan, speaking to several people and hearing 'not one good word'. Morgan responded that the area he had visited was 150 miles from Gwynfynydd and that the chairman had only stayed a few hours. He issued a public challenge to

Williams to go back to the right place and find someone who spoke ill of him. Williams claimed Morgan had done nothing for good causes in Wales, which was untrue as Morgan regularly contributed towards disaster funds, as well as to the eisteddfodau, and he was extremely good to his employees and to local people. However, Williams was correct when he pointed out that Morgan had been in Merionethshire for nearly five years and if he was the ardent Radical he claimed to be, he would have supported MP T.E. Ellis, but he had never given him a helping hand nor even subscribed to the local Liberal Association.

Morgan ignored these criticisms and continued to hold very popular meetings. What was becoming evident was that he was a skilled public speaker, constantly praised for his eloquence, and continually compared to the preaching Griffiths. As Morgan's popularity grew, so animosity towards Griffiths also grew. Griffiths was nearly attacked by a crowd on one occasion. Missiles were thrown and he was cornered in a grocer's shop where three constables had to come to his rescue. Both Williams and the police complained that nothing like this had happened before in Merthyr, and Morgan's supporters were blamed.[19]

The *Western Mail* was tiring of the mudslinging, 'We never remember a political election more free from politics than this one at Merthyr.'[20] They had, they said, examined the speeches of Morgan and Griffiths, and that all they had been doing was speaking 'at' each other with no significant difference in their policies. With little to choose from, the *Western Mail* argued, one could therefore only go on personality. They denied calling Morgan a 'bad egg' (what they had actually written, about both the candidates, was that 'one bad egg is as good as another'), but did consider Griffiths' patriotism 'to have laid dormant' until he was pulled out of obscurity by the LA. Even *Seren*, which usually supported the LA, said that they should have found a better candidate.

As Morgan had been refused use of most of the chapels, he resorted to appearing in pubs to chat with the working men, and visiting workplaces and pitheads, something Thomas, Griffiths and the LA rarely did. At Aberdare, Morgan stood up in his carriage to address about 1,200 railway employees but it was little in terms of an address and more a continued attack on Thomas' campaign against him. Nevertheless, when he had finished, the men took the horses out of the carriage and pulled it back to the hotel.

He would also meet workers as they arrived home, such as at Caeharris where he stood on a mound near the train station talking to the arrivals. As he spoke, a second train arrived so altogether there were about 3,000 people. It was dark when the trains got in, and as the workers left the station, they lit up an immense number of torches – 'the scene of this vast body of workmen,' wrote the *Merthyr Express*, 'all in the sooty covering fresh from the mines, and illuminated by the flaming torches, was weird and grand.' In the evening, the *Express* continued, Morgan was at the Hermon Chapel where 'cheers were raised again and again by an immense concourse, and a grand torchlight procession was formed, a great choir of male voices accompanying all the way to Merthyr. Such a magnificent demonstration has been rarely seen in the streets before.'[21]

Travelling around could present problems, however, such as on 11 October when Morgan and others were driving to a meeting at Abercanaid. The horse took fright and the carriage tumbled down the bank, but thanks to a fence they narrowly missed being squashed by an oncoming train. No one was seriously hurt although Morgan, who managed to throw himself clear, did break a tendon in his leg. Nevertheless, he continued to his meeting as if nothing untoward had taken place.

Morgan often took members of his family on the campaign trail such as his mother, who lived in Abergavenny, two Newport sisters, and his son, Herbert; however, his wife Harriet was often absent due to poor health.[22]

Meanwhile, Griffiths appeared at carefully controlled meetings, often filled with supposedly supportive Irishmen, but even these could be fraught with difficulties. On one occasion, he withdrew, supposedly on important business, but the general opinion was he had been persuaded to leave after a group of Welshmen declared they would fill the gallery. Griffiths blamed the press, accusing them of being 'rotten to a great extent'.[23]

A meeting of Griffiths that was well attended was one where the LA invited the popular MP, T.E. Ellis from North Wales. Ellis regretted that there should be so much ill-feeling in the district and hoped that both sides would be allowed a fair hearing. He was, he said, opposed to a man who was endeavouring to break up the Liberal organisation, for the reason that liberal issues were so important to Wales, and he wanted to maintain the grand successes achieved in 1880, 1885 and 1886. If it was the wish of the constituency that a Welsh party should be formed in the

House of Commons, he said, they ought to be loyal to the association and support them.

Despite his speech being interspersed with hisses and shouts of 'Go back to the North', Ellis told the audience that it had been his work of the past few years to do all he could to organise the Liberals of Wales for all purposes – election and otherwise – for without combination, they were helpless. The Welsh Parliamentary Party would never be felt unless the whole of the members were faithful and loyal. To cheers and hisses from the audience, Ellis advised them to treat Morgan with contempt, as a man who had not pondered over the problems of Welsh requirements and did not understand the wants of the people. Ellis also implied that Morgan's motives over royalties was to promote the interests of landowners and the rich rather than the working men, particularly as the president of Morgan's organisation was Lord Harlech (1885–1964), a Conservative politician and banker.

After Ellis had spoken, Griffiths rose, but this was the signal for some in the gallery to start a fight and when order was finally restored, his speech consisted of little to interest the press.[24]

The LA was gloating about getting Ellis on its side, believing him to be of political weight but the reaction of the audience demonstrates that Ellis' name carried little influence in South Wales. In Merthyr, thirty polls were undertaken with Griffiths only topping eight[25] and, just eight days before the election, Griffiths' lack of enthusiasm left many asking why he was bothering to fight an election at all.

As polling day loomed, the police, worried about the fighting that had been taking place, drafted in a large force. Morgan and Griffiths signed the nomination forms and paid their £250 deposits. The number of voters registered were: Merthyr, 7,858 in nineteen polling districts; Aberdare, 5977 in fourteen districts; Vaynor, 376 in one district; and Llanwonno, 1203 in three districts. There was a total of 15,414 votes in thirty-seven districts[26] – although it was estimated only 10,000 people would vote. Counting would take place at Merthyr's Police Court with the result declared from the Magistrate's Room.

Prime Minister William Gladstone was then pulled into the contest when an unnamed correspondent wrote to him asking who they should vote for. His reply, supporting the LA, was published just three days before polling:

In the absence of strong and conducive objections, I should think it my duty, as a rule, to vote for the association candidate, and I have often strongly and painfully expressed my sense of the ridicule, as well as the mischief brought upon us by contents between two Liberals.[27]

Gladstone's letter had little impact and the day before polling, Morgan was in no doubt the most popular candidate.

On Friday 26 October at 8.00 am, the polls opened but given the scattered nature of the constituency and voters' abilities to reach Merthyr, results were not expected until late on Saturday. During Friday morning, people quietly came and went and most of the police stayed in the station. By the afternoon, the streets were filling up and most of the tradesmen had boarded their windows. Many working people had taken half a day's holiday and several of the collieries had closed. A choir sang on street corners with portraits of Morgan stuck in their hats, and he was out everywhere chatting to people on their way to the polling station – Griffiths was nowhere to be seen.

By 10.00 pm, the poll was closed and the boxes were brought in and placed in the prisoner's dock at the police station.

Morgan returned to the Castle Hotel followed by a large crowd of people. Unfortunately, Thomas and friends were also there and when a cry from the crowd was interpreted by the hotel owner that they were calling for Thomas, the MP went to the hotel steps to address the crowd. He was not well received and quickly withdrew, with the mob demanding Thomas be chucked out of the hotel and not be under the same roof as Morgan. To avoid further trouble, Thomas hid in the parlour until the poll was declared.[28]

About 11.00 pm, the counting clerks took up their position as Morgan, Thomas and others watched – Griffiths stayed away. The room was illuminated with wax candles and the comparative stillness contrasted with the growing excitement outside. The press sat at the foot of the staircase that led from the cells to the court.

The result was expected at around 3.00 am and a crowd had remained outside the police station in the wind and rain. When the returning officer appeared, it was with some difficulty that order could be restored as the crowd went 'mad with enthusiasm' but as he started to speak, a breathless silence fell upon the crowd, 'I have to announce to you the result of yesterday's polling. It is as follows: Mr Morgan …'

At the mention of the Gold King's name, the crowd erupted and it was some time before the returning officer could again make himself heard. Parties of men went off shouting the news down the streets at the top of their voices and many who had gone to bed got up and joined the crowd.[29] The multitude was wild with excitement and did not wait for the official numbers.

Morgan was escorted to his hotel by a band and a vast concourse of people who shouted themselves hoarse. At the Castle Hotel, Morgan appeared at one of the windows and told the crowd he was the happiest and proudest man in Wales. He said the 'great victory had taught a great many gentlemen a lesson – such gentlemen as Mr Thomas,' to which there was much hooting, 'Mr Ellis,' a repeat of the hooting and, 'Mabon' who was also hooted. The electors of Merthyr, he continued, had taught the LA a great lesson, which it was hoped, the latter would profit by. Now that the fight was over, they should bury all differences. He pledged himself again to get a labour representative for that constituency and that he would never be satisfied until he walked into the House of Commons with a working man on his arm as his fellow member for Merthyr.

The official numbers, which nobody seemed to care about, were published the next day. Out of 15,414 votes, 12,296 went to poll despite a controversy over missing registrations and counting errors. Morgan polled 7,149 votes and Griffiths, 4,956.

Later that Saturday, Morgan returned to give another speech and the hall was decked with bunting and posters. A gigantic cartoon, representing Morgan in the garb of a Roman gladiator triumphing over all his foes, including the faces of the main LA members, was posted on the wall facing the audience. Morgan was delighted with the cartoon and so impressed by the artist, Thomas Protheroe, the son of a workman at Dowlais, that he paid for Protheroe to go to London's Slade School of Fine Art.[30]

On the platform, Morgan was accompanied by his mother, son, two daughters, and various friends. He told the crowd that his magnificent majority would be written down in the history of Wales and that the election was absolutely without parallel. It was not his election, he said, but theirs. For twenty years, they had been 'ruled by a rod of iron – ruled unconscionably, perhaps – but the day had come when they demanded a voice in the selection of a candidate for their suffrage.' He promised to represent them well and appealed to them to bury their differences and sink all desires for retaliation or revenge.

Griffiths left Merthyr alone on Monday morning and Morgan, at a meeting at the Drill Hall, deplored the shabby manner in which Griffiths was abandoned to cries of 'shame' from the audience. Morgan said had he known, he would have gone to the railway station and seen him off himself.[31]

Morgan's victory was treated with caution by many. 'It was evident,' wrote the *Echo*, 'during his canvass that he knew very little of politics, and was ready to promise almost anything so long as the seat could be secured.'[32] The *Birmingham Daily Post* wrote that the LA 'bungled the business'[33] and the *Liverpool Mercury* was equally critical, questioning the wisdom of selecting Griffiths. 'A blow,' it wrote, 'has been struck at its authority' and put the figures into perspective. Rather than Morgan's 'magnificent majority', he obtained nearly as many votes as a Liberal candidate might be expected against a Tory. By deducting the Tory vote, estimated at 1,885, they calculated that nearly five-sevenths of the Liberal electors were faithful to the choice of the association. The *Liverpool Mercury* warned that the Tories 'have possibly sown seeds of disunion of which we have not seen the last.'[34]

Writing in London, the *Pall Mall Gazette* thought the Liberal caucus had been badly beaten. 'The blow will do it good. It does not come out of the affair with anything like credit. The method of selection was stupid and wrong from the first. It believed itself so strong that it took no real account of the situation and was blind up to the last to the forces at work beneath the surface.'[35] *The Times* had generally ignored the contest until it was over and then commented, 'The extent of the majority secured by Mr Pritchard Morgan is a surprise to many people. Generally, it is regarded as an indication of the appreciation by the working classes of his promise to promote the candidature of a labour representative at the next general election.'[36]

The Welsh-language press was appalled. *Tyst*, 'the most bitter than any of the papers' saw it not as a political contest but as a contest between the preachers and the independence of the voters, describing it as 'the victory of ungodliness over morality.' *Baner* blamed the LA, saying 'it was evident that the association was not in touch with the people'; *Goleuad* denounced the Merthyr electors as having not learned 'the elementary principles of political honesty'; and *Y Celt* called it a 'mystery'. *Tarian* wrote they 'never before thought how easy it was to blind people with chaff' but a *Seren* journalist thought that 'the Welsh newspapers, both English and Welsh, were utterly ignorant of the state of feeling in the borough.'

There were a number of explanations as to why Morgan won the election. Many claimed the Tories carried him through; although this is partly correct, it is also true that the colliers supported him in large numbers. He was also supported by the brewers and licenced victuallers who were not going to endorse the temperance supporter, Griffiths. The LA was split, fatally so, in March at D.A. Thomas' election, and their high-handedness in Merthyr saw many of their own members turn against them. Had they chosen more carefully, they might have won the day.

The election of 1888 saw a cohort of new Liberal men entering the House, including David Lloyd George. Most were relatively young, although 44-year-old Morgan was older than most, and nearly all, with the exception of Lloyd George (born in Manchester), were born in Wales. Most were nonconformists and their entry into Parliament was seen as a new radical force.

Chapter 7

After the Election

Once the election was over, a delighted Morgan threw himself around the country, appearing in everything from local horticultural shows, eisteddfodau, and giving speeches at them all. He was followed by hordes of people, often taking the horses from his carriage and pulling him along, surrounded by raucous bands and cheering crowds.

In November, he followed Gladstone to the Midlands to join the Liberals tour but by 8 November, he was back at Dolgelly. As the evening train approached, a cannon was fired and the local Irish band struck up 'See the Conquering Hero Comes'.

As he stepped onto the platform with his mother, son Herbert, and agent Vaughan, they were greeted by Morgan's daughter Gwendoline amid a platform jammed with local dignitaries. Preceded by the band, they processed through the town that had been strung with lights – the Ship Hotel was a blaze of coloured lights, with lamps and candles in the windows and banners around the hotel pillars proclaiming 'Success to our Gold King, P.M. M.P'.

Morgan went onto the balcony where an address was presented by the Dolgelly Liberal Club and Merionethshire Liberal Association. Morgan, shouting to the vast crowd below, said he had been laughed at when he went to stand for Merthyr, in the same way he was laughed at when he wanted to look for gold in the Mawddach Valley – but the results proved they were all wrong. He told them stories from the election, about Gladstone's tour and that on meeting Mrs Gladstone, she told him, 'I must congratulate you, Mr Morgan on your grand victory, for I believe you are one with us in fighting this great battle for the people.' Mr Gladstone also congratulated him and, in the course of conversation, had said the most important thing now was Irish Home Rule and Wales was unanimous for it. 'Yes,' said Morgan, he would 'not be content until it is entirely unanimous.' He added that, of course, he had interests in North

Wales and now he had interests in South Wales; by both these means, he hoped to prove a worthy successor to Henry Richard.

Morgan told the crowd that he wanted to get involved in setting up a Welsh Parliamentary Party with the object of securing Home Rule for Wales and alluded to Dolgelly's old Parliament House of Owain Glyndŵr, which had only recently been pulled down. He hoped, he said, to one day see a building in Wales, a House that would be representative of the people for managing Welsh affairs – but it would not be until 2006 that the Welsh Senedd (parliament) was built.

Being quizzed on his future policies, Morgan dodged questions, saying he preferred to keep a reserved attitude until he found out what the details of the Liberal Party were.[1] The local Welsh newspaper *Goleuad* was, as usual, irritated with Morgan, 'We are surprised that the Liberal Association should offer him an address,' they grumbled, 'and the subject of his speech was himself.'[2]

By 12 November, Morgan was back in London to take up his seat in the House and was sworn in the following day. He was led to the table by Denbighshire East MP Osborne Morgan (1826–1897) and cheered by the opposition, but not the PM's supporters who thought him disloyal to Gladstone (who had recommended Griffiths). The Conservatives, who may have held out a hope that Morgan would remain somewhat independent, had their hopes dashed when he so openly allied himself to the Liberals during his swearing in.

Later that month, Morgan joined a deputation of Welsh MPs of all parties to meet with Charles Ritchie (1838–1906), who was responsible for the Local Government Act 1888, to ask for it to be translated into Welsh. T.E. Ellis explained that there were several precedents: the War Office, the Privy Council, the Home Office, the Post Office and the Local Government Board had all recognised the necessity for issuing their orders in a language people could understand. The Act was important because it altered the way English and Welsh systems of local government were to be run, and many leading people who would need to use the Act, such as county councillors, those serving on boards of guardians, and highway boards, were monoglot Welsh. Osborne Morgan added he would like to have parts of the Municipal Corporations Act in the Local Government Act also translated.

In reply, Ritchie said he was much surprised at the unanimity of the request, which showed how little the government considered Welsh matters, and he would consider the question very favourably. He did, however, point out that up to that time, no Act of Parliament had been translated into Welsh and he was not sure whether the government had a right to do so as actions at law could only be conducted in English. The Welsh party offered a compromise by including an introduction that no action at law would rely on the Welsh translation and Ritchie promised to give it his full consideration.[3] The Act was repealed in 1933 and never appeared in Welsh.

Once all the Welsh MPs had settled into the House, they turned their attentions to Welsh affairs. At the annual meeting of the Council of South Wales and Monmouthshire Liberal Foundation in Swansea on 18 February 1889, attended by many of the leading MPs, various issues were discussed including the Welsh language, miners' rights and housing, but it was religious equality that was placed next in importance to Irish Home Rule.[4]

The following day, three months after his election, Morgan returned to Merthyr to address his constituents for the first time. The buildings were so crowded, vast numbers were unable to obtain admission and everywhere he was received with rapturous applause. His main focus was on the government's prosecution of those imprisoned over Irish Home Rule and calling for their release, but never one to stray far from the subject of himself, Morgan said he had been subjected to the same sort of attack – an astonishing claim to make compared to men who had been imprisoned.

As a new member, he explained, there had not been much time to get involved in issues. He had voted on a few things and, because it affected so many of his constituents, he had briefly spoken on the Employers' Liability Bill which enabled workers to seek compensation for injuries resulting from the negligence of a fellow employee. He wanted a clause allowing an opt out to be removed, as he feared employers could influence their workers to do so.[5] He had voted in the minority in favour of the Sunday Closing Act in Wales and he thought that they agreed with him, to calls from hear, hear.

He then laid out his intentions, the core of which would remain true for years to come – he was going to devote as much time as possible to mining royalties which he considered more relevant to Wales than anywhere else; and work towards disestablishment. On other issues, he generally followed the Liberal crowd, adding, in his usual modest way, that if a new LA was formed, he would be happy to put forward his name as president, vice-president or anything else.[6]

He did not remain long in Merthyr and was back in the House on 22 February to hear Stuart Rendel (1834–1913), MP for Montgomeryshire, complaining about an absence of items regarding Wales in the Queen's Speech, which had included Scotland and Ireland.[7] Morgan echoed Rendel's comments, suggesting it was because the Welsh members were mostly opposition Liberals that they had been omitted. Not willing to stray too far from his main topic of mining, he noted the Queen's Speech mentioned forming a Minister for Agriculture, and argued there should also be a Minister of Mining. The question of royalties, he added, 'is a most grievous one to thousands upon thousands of the people. Various promises have been made by the government with regard to the subject, but there is not one word about it in the Address, nor do we hear of any proposed legislation upon royalties.' So far as Wales was concerned, he continued, 'endeavours to confer benefit on the general community are retarded by the present government in every possible and conceivable way.'[8]

Bowen Rowlands (1837–1906) (Cardiganshire) added his voice, 'omission of all mention of Wales in the Queen's speech ... it is only another attempt on their part to carry out the policy of ignoring Welsh nationality, and of denying the reality of Welsh grievances.' Requests for discussions on disestablishment of the Church had been ignored. 'On one occasion, when we succeeded in getting a small discussion on Welsh affairs, by far the greater number of hon. Members opposite left the House' and he accused the government of trying to mould the Welsh into an English image.

Arnold Morley wrote to Stuart Rendel saying he understood Welsh members wanted a discussion of Welsh grievances and that he would meet with them on 25 February and asked Rendel to ensure that there were at least five or six who would be willing to speak, including Morgan who had already made an application to raise matters.[9]

In March, Morgan put a question in the House to John Brodrick (1856–1942), the Under Secretary for Foreign Affairs, regarding the Chinese government's apparent refusal of Italian demands for a presence in China. Britain had backed Italy on an Open Door policy that all countries should be allowed access to the possibilities of trade with China without being blocked by the other Powers. Morgan wanted to know why Italy was being refused when China had pledged a large area to Britain in return for a massive payment.[10] It was a subject that was to play a huge part in Morgan's later life.

It was now seven months since Morgan had been elected and he had visited Merthyr only once. In May, D.A. Thomas was touring the area and unlike Morgan, who often spoken broadly on the subject of disestablishment, Thomas provided more details, citing the example of Glamorganshire where about £3,000 of the tithes went to the Dean and Chapter of Gloucester in England. Over £5,000 went to men unconnected with the church at all and only £20 went to the purposes of charity. He thought it could be described as 'an impious robbery'. However, his audience was just as anxious to hear about his relationship with Morgan, to which Thomas simply replied it was 'his duty' to work with him but what he really wanted was to get the Liberal Party reunited in Merthyr.[11]

If a new LA was to be formed, it would still be open to ridicule if the two MPs were not speaking, so Vaughan, Morgan's agent, thought it high time the two men settled their differences, and offered to set up a meeting.[12] Little came of it, and even trying to reform the LA proved difficult. Morgan suggested forming a Liberal-Labour Association, but that, too, fell on deaf ears.[13]

They did do some work together in May when the two co-presented a deputation at the House, lobbying to improve the Merthyr County Court. Morgan, who introduced the delegate, pointed out that the Court had jurisdiction over three parishes but no accommodation. While cases could be heard anywhere, including people's houses and pubs, there was no public building in Merthyr and the inhabitants could hardly be expected to provide accommodation for the benefit of other districts, therefore the Crown should have a dedicated building. Walter Smyth J.P. blamed the Privy Council, saying that years ago the inhabitants had petitioned the town be made a municipality and if this request had been accepted, they would now have a town hall. Morgan added there was a vacant site in the burned-out portion of the marketplace and a plan could be prepared for a new building which the government promised to look into.[14] It took another nine years before the town hall was built.

Throughout the rest of that year, Morgan's life was relatively quiet but he had become involved in a project begun in previous October. A number of people floated the idea of a Welsh Exhibition in London which Morgan heartily endorsed. Speaking at the first meeting to discuss the idea, he moved a resolution that 'this meeting is of the opinion that the enterprise is one which deserves the support of every friend of the Principality, and pledges itself to further the same, as by doing so a wholesome impetus will be given to the arts, productions, and manufacturers of Wales.' An Executive Committee was formed, with Morgan on board, who believed that 'Wales just now seems to be having a revival of the national sentiment, and it is thought an opportune moment to take the occasion by hand, and indulge that sentiment in a profitable, entertaining, and, at the same time, non-political way.' Scotland and Ireland had done similar. The Glasgow International Exhibition had been opened on 8 May 1888 by the Prince and Princess of Wales, saw five million visitors and earned £165,000 – the £40,000 profit was used for promoting arts and science in Glasgow.

Suggestions for the Welsh Exhibition were to include: a summer garden with a grand spectacle of Snowdon painted on a colossal scale; scientific novelties; and popular amusements including Welsh choirs. Models of noted Welsh houses were proposed, including the well-known Llangollen cottage of Jenny Jones and Owain Glyndŵr's last Parliament House. Various districts and historical towns would be represented and old hostelries so well known to tourists would be faithfully reproduced, as well as castles. There would be statuary carved out of coal; an art collection featuring paintings and statuary that had appeared at Eisteddfods; druidical ceremonies; and imitation cromlechs with battle scenes between Romans and Britons. Welsh minerals and other raw products would be on display, quartz from Morgan's mine would be crushed and the gold extracted in front of the visitors; slate from the Carnarvon quarries would be split and prepared for the roof; and a miniature coal mine was planned which people could go down in a suspended cage. The profits would be devoted to education in Wales, or to a school of mines.

Morgan announced, 'that an exhibition may be regarded as a big advertisement. Since this is pre-eminently an advertising age, it may be asserted that the nation which does not advertise... is certainly handicapped in competition with others who do.'[15]

Much depended on where the exhibition would be located and they were looking at Olympia, Earl's Court. Exhibitions were the great rage since the Great Exhibition of 1851 and the Americans and Italians were also planning them in London.[16] The exhibition would run from June to October and numerous leading Welsh people had already promised subscriptions and grants.

Before the planning had started in earnest, the press was pointing out that the Irish, Danish and Italian exhibitions staged in London last year were held at a loss. The reason the Glasgow exhibition had made a profit was because it was held in Glasgow. The London Eisteddfod and bardic festival of 1887 failed 'so dismally that after the whole of the guarantee fund had been exhausted there still remained a considerable balance to be paid.' In the end, Olympia could not be acquired[17] and the whole event was doomed never to happen.

At the beginning of 1890, bad blood was still rumbling between Morgan and Thomas. Vaughan, Morgan's election agent, was still of the opinion that a newly formed LA could not be on solid ground until the two members came together. But Thomas had repeatedly intimated that he would not shake Morgan's hand because the leaders of the LA were averse to it.[18] Morgan said he had gone to the extreme to bury the hatchet and would travel no further, although he admitted that he did not blame Thomas but that there 'were other powers at work'.[19]

Morgan, noted the *Merthyr Express*, was 'ventilating' a great deal on the differences between him and Thomas. Indeed, all the newspapers in South Wales and many in the north were writing about it and it was, Morgan believed, taking the attention of every Welsh member in the House. While Morgan was willing to accept Thomas, he would never accept the LA, saying it was not a representative body but a self-constituted caucus. He would never, as long as he was member for Merthyr, owe any allegiance to that caucus, or the remains of it. He had done with it. It was dead and buried. But he would say that if a representative association was formed, he would be pleased to work in harmony with it.

As Morgan was the victor in the fight, it was suggested that he should make the first move and he did so through MPs and personal friends, but Thomas still refused to engage. Indeed, there was a growing irritation over Thomas who seemed to be annoying many, including the liberal press who were even refusing to write about him. Mabon, who did not get on with Thomas, was aligning himself more alongside Morgan and Randel.

The *Western Mail* wrote that Thomas 'dare not speak to his colleague lest he should offend the Caucus.'[20] *Baner* similarly wrote, 'the split in the Liberal party at Merthyr has not been repaired yet, and the two members continue the attitude of *'ci a'r hwch'* [the dog and the sow] towards each other.'[21]

Meanwhile, Morgan was working in harmony with most of the other Welsh MPs, including Alfred Thomas (1840–1927), MP for East Glamorganshire, and he seconded Thomas' motion, to a poorly attended House, an amendment to the Queen's Speech, that an Independent Department of State should be created for the conduct of distinctly Welsh affairs, presided over by a Minister acquainted with the national characteristics. Alfred Thomas stressed the difficulties in administration when English was the official language. Ireland and Scotland were provided with a Minister but Wales could only make her needs known through private members.[22] Morgan claimed Wales was 'the Cinderella among the kingdoms, but was determined to gain a foremost place in the Empire … whereat hon. members most ungallantly but audibly smiled.'[23] Osborne Morgan and the Home Secretary advised Alfred Thomas to withdraw the amendment rather than divide the Welsh members, arguing that it was a matter of policy, not administration and that the Home Office had only received 209 letters from Welsh officials and therefore could not justify the creation of a Welsh Minister. Alfred Thomas withdrew his amendment in August but made another attempt, seconded by Morgan, to show the House the necessity of creating a Welsh department – but this, too, fell on deaf ears and it was not to be realised until 1964.

Throughout the year, Morgan did not abandon his gold-mining interests. At some point in 1888, he must have had a share in the Clogau Mine because in February, the Clogau Gold Mines Limited was 'subject to an unregistered agreement' between various men, including Morgan.[24] Rothschild also still had shares, albeit overdue. On 6 March, Clogau wrote to N.M. Rothschild and Son with a due note for them to pay Clogau Mine £600.[25]

By January 1889, Morgan was looking to extend his mining operations and believing that the Welsh reefs extended across the Irish Sea, he obtained Crown authority to mine over 50 square miles in Ireland.

Morgan had sold his interest in Gwynfynydd to the Morgan Gold Mining Company the previous year, but he was still a major shareholder and had a seat on the board. However, little was happening in the area and this was being noticed by the press. 'If I am not very much mistaken,' wrote the *Western Mail*, 'a good deal of money is being fooled away in gold-mining in Wales. Twelve companies have been registered for this purpose, and the capital they ask for is £815,000. One of them is modest enough to be ludicrous. Its nominal capital is £125, divided into 10,000 shares of 3d each. Its name and object are, however ambitions enough. Its title is "The Goldfields of Great Britain (Limited),"... Verily, there must be a lot of simple folk in this world.'[26]

The Welsh correspondent of the *Liverpool Mercury* asked if the gold industry in Wales had begun to dwindle, 'The owners of the mines are now quieting and references to the National Debt are less frequent. Morgan seems to have retired from public gaze after his election and it would be well if he could spare a moment or two to reassure those who have an interest in Welsh gold.'[27]

The *Cambrian News* urged 'the inhabitants of Wales' not to take out shares in Welsh gold mines and noted the lack of information coming forth since Morgan's big find, and predicted within a year 'the Welsh gold craze will be almost forgotten.' They blamed the national papers, 'It was those wicked London and provincial daily papers who did all the mischief. They came down into Wales in gangs and vied with each other in telling lies about the gold discoveries. Where are they now? Why this silence about the gold?'[28]

In March, Morgan opened a motion in the House to amend laws relating to Mining on Crown Lands in Wales and Ireland. He was backed by Henniker Heaton (1848–1914), MP for Canterbury, who spent many years in Australia as a journalist, and Welsh MP David Randell. As part of Morgan's motion, he wanted a report on various aspects of royalties on metalliferous mines.[29]

George Goschen (1831–1907), Chancellor of the Exchequer, replied,

> I cannot state the particulars asked for in the first paragraph of the hon. Member's question without a Return; and a Return distinguishing the royalties received for each mineral for 28 years would be a long and costly business. As the total amount derived

from these royalties has been less than £8,000 a year on the average for the last eight years, I do not think I should be justified in authorizing the expenditure of time and money necessary to obtain such a Return. As to royalties received by the Treasury from 'mines Royal' on freehold lands during the same period, they were quite insignificant till the present financial year, when they amounted to £832. The cost of administering the Crown mineral property in Wales cannot be separately stated. The cost of collection and local supervision somewhat exceeds 8 per cent … I think the hon. Member can call to mind the case of a mine being sold to a company for, in shares and cash, £190,000, not so long ago. If the company in question were, in consequence of paying such a price, to make no profit, I should not consider that a reason for remitting the royalty due to the Crown. Until a few years ago, the Crown would have received one-fourth of the profits of the sale in question, and I am sorry that the Exchequer does not get such a share now.

His last remark was met with cries of 'hear, hear' and laughter from the House.

By April, there were mutterings in the colonial press (that do not appear in the British press) about Morgan's mine running into difficulties. Why, wrote the New Zealand paper *Grey River Argus*, had Lord Winchilsea severed his connections with the board and why had his brother Harold Finch-Hatton been so 'desperately anxious' to sell his shares? Why did the Stock Exchange Committee refuse to list the shares and how many shares did Morgan hold? Why had the paying ore suddenly ceased?[30]

However, these criticisms and rumours were refuted when a report on the first year's results was published:

In spite of the wide-spread distrust it inspired at the time, [it] has certainly not turned out a delusion and snare. We allude to the Morgan gold mine which has just taken stock of its first year's operations. When Morgan first announced that gold could be produced in Wales in paying quantities he was received with general incredulity, not unmixed with ridicule, but he must be held to have already proved his case up to the hilt, and refuted the sceptics, by the production for his little mine in twelve months of no less than

£36,000 worth of pure gold. Only 5,290 were crushed giving an average of 1 oz 18dwt per ton and the working cost was reduced to 6dwt per ton leaving a net profit 1oz 12dwt or £3 10s per ounce, £5 12s per ton.[31]

There was more talk of the average yield exceeding the richest goldfields in Australia owing to cheaper costs. Miners' wages were comparable to the UK average of £46 a year – 18s a week, labourers 15s and boys 5s'. The haulage was done by gravitation and the crushing by water power which saved money as well as offering greater facilities of transport. The company's first dividend was approximately 10% but that dropped in the second half of the year to 5% – partially owing to the water supply failing. The mill only ran intermittently during the last quarter of the financial year. Water power may be free but it was subject to the vagaries of weather.

In addition, the lack of profit was being blamed on the heavy royalties inflicted by landowners and the Crown, and people were waiting with interest to see what the government came up with in answer to Morgan's request for more details of royalties paid. The report concluded that while they acknowledged Morgan's enthusiastic venture, it had not progressed very far and that 'although the existence of gold in Wales in paying quantities has been amply proved, we have no proof yet that it is of sufficient extent, or so widely diffused as to warrant us looking at the Principality as a permanent source of supply or that it is a goldfield that can be ranked with those of the Transvaal and Australia.'[32]

The *Aberystwyth Observer* had put it succinctly that £140,000 had been spent to get out £50,000 in gold, justifying their advice to their readers not to invest in gold mine companies.[33]

As the talk of Welsh gold rumbled on, T.A. Readwin, the man who had devoted 45 years to the study of gold in Wales, died. His funeral took place on 11 February 1889 in a heavy snow storm at Llanelltyd Cemetery, Dolgelly. Morgan attended saying, 'had it not been for him there would have been no gold-mining going on there to-day.' Local tradesmen and the mining community were aiming to raise a subscription for a tomb.[34]

A few months later, Queen Victoria was planning to visit North Wales. Morgan sent a letter to the organising committee that was drawing up her itinerary, suggesting she should be taken on a ride from Dolgelly to Barmouth as the scenes were 'probably unsurpassed in the United

Kingdom.' Although she had asked to visit the gold mine, he said it would be impracticable as the journey was 'too fatiguing'. However, he would bring down two or three dray-loads of golden ore to Bryntirion – he even thought of constructing a triumphal arch of golden ore to be built across the road, but the idea was abandoned. Morgan was part of the reception committee and brought with him 'a very interesting gift in the shape of the first bar of gold he produced from a Welsh mine'[35] but as the proceedings were running late, he was not able to present it.[36]

In the end, the route was from Llangollen to Corwen, and at Market Square, a magnificent album containing views of Corwen and mounted with Welsh gold was presented with the Mayor handing Her Majesty, among other things, a medal of Welsh gold struck in commemoration of the visit. Enquiries at the Royal Collection have revealed that these items cannot be located; they may have been lodged elsewhere or even given away.

Morgan had been trying to present the gold bar to the Queen four months after his big find; he was even bragging about his hope of going to Windsor in January[37] but despite a great deal of press coverage, the meeting never took place, probably because Morgan had no official arrangement with the Crown Estate about his mining rights. Undeterred, for the Prince of Wales' silver wedding anniversary in March, Morgan sent a paperweight made from a solid piece of polished Gwynfynydd ore, embedded in dark green stone nearly a pound in weight, which sparkled 'brilliantly'.[38] Again, this item cannot be traced by the Royal Collection.

As the Queen was leaving North Wales, Morgan was putting Bryntirion up for rent. The mansion was beautifully furnished with fine reception rooms, a billiard room, and ample bedroom accommodation with hot and cold baths. There was stabling for a number of horses and even a pleasure boat. Included in the price were a carriage and pair of horses along with a coachman, gardeners, a market horse, garden produce and the right to fish in the Afon (River) Eden on the Eden estate. Morgan was offering his estate for 120 guineas per month for four months or 180 guineas per month for two months.[39] 'He is too restless a man to spend a great deal of time there,' wrote the *Brisbane Courier*, 'the main schemes in which he is involved are always dragging him back to London.'[40] However, in August, the family was still there, as Harriet attended a local bazaar at Barmouth.

On 4 September, a local gift was to set off a trend that was destined to play an important role in the marriages of the royals. That day, Matilda Eleanor Pudge, of Cotterell House, Towyn, married J. Chidlaw Roberts, Gwynfynydd's owner from whom Morgan leased the mine. Several presents were made of gold from the Morgan Gold Mine[41] but it was the wedding ring that was most notable as it is the first wedding ring made from pure Welsh gold that is publicly known about.

In November, Morgan was laid up in London, ill with pleurisy; by December, he had recovered but was still so weak that his doctor has banned him from travelling or exerting himself in any way. At the end of December, he was well enough to go to Dolgelly to a meeting attended by a large and influential group of tradespeople and gold miners at the town hall to congratulate him on his return after a long and serious illness. He told them he had just returned from the extraordinary general meeting of the Morgan Gold Mining Company and was glad to report since the opening of the mine, they had continual success. They were now declaring a dividend of 5%; had forty stamps with a crushing power of 100 tons; and employed about 200 men at the mine. He mentioned difficulties in having to build barracks for the men to prevent them from walking miles to and from work, and the need to make roads, residences for the managers, stores and other utilitarian work.

Morgan was happy to tell them that the directors had decided to enlarge the mines and had secured the whole of the gold-bearing reefs lying between the two mountain streams at Gwynfynydd and the water rights, particularly the use of Pystyll-y-Cain Fall and the Mawddach. The waterfalls would be used to create compressed air to run the rock-drills. They had also arranged an electricity supply and while some thought it an extravagance, Morgan had made a gift of the machinery so it had cost nothing and would be a great saving as it prevented fires and would save money on coal. He felt perfectly satisfied of the permanency of the industry or he would certainly not have entered into this contract. With the new machinery, they would expect to deal with 500 to 600 tons of quartz per day. After the meeting, accompanied by his wife Harriet and daughter Catherine, he drove to Bryntirion; although in good spirits, he was still unwell.[42]

Things elsewhere were also not going well. At some unknown time, Morgan had agreed to purchase a further 90,000 shares in the Morgan

Gold Mining Company for £25,000 but, by May 1890, the agreement had fallen through because he was unable to come up with the capital. He blamed the Crown and their delays in sorting out royalties which had cost him money – but as he had not paid the royalties, it is difficult to see how they could have been responsible. As the company was now sorely in need of cash, Morgan agreed to transfer his remaining 70,000 shares back so they could release 160,000 shares for 5s each. The Morgan Gold Mining Company would also move out of Morgan's London offices.[43]

A meeting was called and feelings were expected to run high with a number of shareholders bitter towards Morgan. Others argued it was not his fault, that it was they who had paid too much for the property and believed Morgan had done his best. The company could have sued him for damages under the terms of his contract but, on giving the matter full consideration, they felt it was not in the interests of shareholders to take that route. Some did regret that Morgan had been allowed to walk off with so much and that he should play no further part in the management. As to the company's finances, their total liabilities were £3,500 and they had got £1,500 to meet them.[44]

Several days later, it was all over. Without Morgan's £25,000, the company could not meet its obligations and had no alternative but to close. Almost immediately, the 'I told you so' brigade was out in force. 'There was no other conclusion possible from the first' wrote the *Cambrian News*, but they did not blame Morgan, 'Poor Mr Pritchard Morgan! ... Did he not warn speculators to be cautious, and did not we repeat his warning until he himself almost got angry. The people to be blamed are those wicked newspaper editors in England who sent down special reporters into Merionethshire and insisted upon writing up these gold mines.'[45]

In October, the company re-opened as the New Morgan Gold Mining Company and were in the process of resurrecting Gwynfynydd with a new set of machinery and 100 men. Morgan took out numerous shares in family names, even including a servant, and his friend George Hall was made company director; he, too, took out shares in family names.

Chapter 8

The Dead Hand of Antiquity

With the collapse and reformation of his mining company, the press was attempting to interview Morgan – but he was refusing to talk. When in Merthyr, visiting his constituents, the *Western Mail* sent a journalist who succeeded in drawing Morgan into conversation.

Morgan produced a map to show off his mining area but the *Western Mail* journalist was more interested in the growing row over Crown royalties and Morgan's unhappiness in paying them. Surely, asked the journalist, they were too small to make much of a difference in profit? Morgan replied, 'the landlords of Wales, and, indeed of this country generally, have an exaggerated opinion as to the amount of royalty on a product that should be paid them. I have had to modify and reduce these royalties three times already.' Once again, he tried to explain how even the smallest tax would affect an industry. 'Take for example,' he said,

> if it cost 5 shillings to remove a ton of stone to get at a better class of stone but you treat the poorer stone for another 5 shillings and recover 7s 6d worth of gold. Not treating the poorer stone would mean a loss of 5s but treating it the loss is reduced to 2s 6d. The Government however, would still insist on taxing the 5 shillings.

At a standard royalty rate of one-thirtieth, this would increase the loss to 3s 2d a ton. That loss was amplified because it was charged on product, not profit, so it did not take into account production costs such as making roads, police protection, payment of the postman, the building of a powder house to protect the dynamite, building barracks, even the red tape of the government in not allowing the gold to be weighed or removed except at their connivance. 'Is the list long enough?' he complained. There were so many more grievances he could have added. Nevertheless, he told the journalist, he still had great confidence in the industry being viable in the future.¹

Morgan was not a lone voice and other specialists were taking to the press complaining about the high costs of all mining in the UK. Bernard Charles Molloy (1842–1916), MP for Birr, Ireland, tried to unravel the confusion caused by variable Crown royalties in November 1888 when he worked out that a royalty of one-fifteenth on gross product, not taking into account production and set up costs, would probably amount to about 50% of the profits,² which would be destructive to any industry. Not only did Morgan and others want royalties charged on net revenue, they wanted an equality with other Crown possession countries where no royalties were charged and then imported into the UK; and they wanted to curb the landlords. Morgan had bitterly condemned the right of landlords to charge what royalties they wanted, but mining companies were in a difficult situation. While he had a good relationship with Chidlaw Roberts, from whom he leased Gwynfynydd, he leased other mines and the landlords claimed high royalties but complaining about them could sour relations and see royalties rise even further. By targeting the Crown to abolish or change their royalty, landlords could be forced into something similar.

Not everyone was convinced. The *Economist* was scathing:

> No doubt this (abolition of royalties) would suit promoters like Mr Morgan, who have successfully sold to the public, at high prices, mining properties for which they have given relatively small sums. It is, however, absurd to contend that the small profits so far obtained by the Morgan Gold Mining Company, and many other similar undertakings, are due to the moderate royalties paid to the Crown, for, as a matter of fact, they are adequately explained by the large profits which have been obtained by the promoters of the companies. And this being the case, it certainly appears rather cool of Mr Morgan to assume the role of the disinterested advocate, who seeks to relieve a promising industry from the crushing weight of the Crown's demands.³

With the vast amount of publicity being generated by Morgan, it was only a matter of time before questions were being asked in the House of

Commons about how the goldfields were being managed. W.H. Smith (1825–1891), of bookshop family fame and the First Lord of the Treasury, bowed to pressure and agreed to commission a report.[4]

One of the reasons Morgan wanted matters to move quickly was that in April the previous year, the Commissioners for the Crown had slapped an injunction on him, banning him from mining. He appealed and was allowed to continue but not to remove any gold without the Crown agent being present to check it.[5] Morgan ignored them and did not reply to their letters, so they warned him that unless he agreed to their conditions, a *rule absolute* would be applied which would ban all his mining operations.

There was public fury over the actions of the Commissioners and the following month, an open meeting, attended by a large crowd, was held at the Assembly Rooms, Dolgelly where leading men of the area took to the stage to voice their concerns. The resolution was unanimously passed and a deputation was appointed to visit G.J. Goschen, the Chancellor of the Exchequer, to present the resolution to him.[6]

Very little happened so Morgan renewed his attack in the House on 14 May:

> I think the Woods and Forests Office is conducted in a manner which shows a great want of knowledge on the subjects which it has to handle, and more especially the subject of Royalties. In no other country in the world do such charges exist as these which are imposed upon those desirous of opening up industries in Wales. Take, for instance, my own position. I am at the present moment defending an action which has been brought by the Woods and Forests Department against me to prevent me digging a hole in my own freehold land. The Office practically says, 'We are entitled to all the gold you obtain from your land, and unless you give us an exorbitant amount of the gold and silver you obtain, you shall not work there at all.' It is well known to men interested in mining that the slightest possible charge will stifle the energy of the enterprise. Take, for instance, the colony of Victoria. There they found 3s. an ounce shut up about 50 per cent of the mines in that colony. The tax was entirely abolished in deference to public opinion. In America, Australia, and in every part of the world, men are entitled to work the mines by paying a nominal amount to the authorities. But it

is not so here. The fact is the amount received by the Treasury as Royalties on gold and silver was infinitesimal until this industry was opened up by me. I believe the British Government received 11d. by way of Royalties on gold obtained on private land in the United Kingdom. But I have paid in one year – including duty on the transfer of a property, the rent of which was £70 a year – I have, I say, paid for working one adit a sum amounting to nearly £2,300. I say this is an unjust and unfair tax on what promises to be an important industry.

He added, 'I firmly believe there is not one man in this Woods and Forests Office who has ever seen a gold or silver mine in his life,' and announced that in protest of their action against him, he had 'surrendered all my Crown leases to the Crown, declining to work for so unjust and unfair a landlord.' He finished by requesting a royalty amnesty for three years in order for the industry to get established, but the Chancellor had already consented to a Royal Commission to inquire into the question of royalties generally so matters could not be reconsidered until after that report was finalised.[7] At the end of the debate, Morgan's motion to abolish royalties on gold was rejected by a majority of 45.

Morgan turned back to the press to reassert his claims. He told the *Cardiff Times*, 'When I first came to England, the Crown claimed to be entitled to one-twentieth of the gold obtained from private lands … When I brought pressure to bear on the Woods and Forests Office, the royalties on private lands were reduced to one-thirtieth, or 3½ per cent of the gold produced. Upon Crown Lands they still claim 5 per cent on the product and 25 per cent of the purchase money.' He added, 'It is quite true that sometimes we were perfectly able to pay this impost of one-thirtieth on the ton, but there were other times, as in all such mines, when the tax pressed most heavily on the value of the product.'

'Did royalties kill the mine?' the *Cardiff Times* journalist asked. 'By no means,' replied Morgan, 'but I contend they have temporarily ruined the industry.' When asked about the Crown's legal proceedings against him, Morgan, 'twitching at the thick gold bangle which he wears firmly welded around his wrist', admitted there was a suit in Chancery in which he was the defendant. The Attorney General was trying to restrain him from working for gold on private freehold lands that he had purchased and they stopped him from working for twelve months because he had not paid the royalties.

Turning to the difficulties of the old Morgan Mine Company, he explained, 'I worked the mine for three months and then handed it over to a company.' But why, asked the journalist, when things seemed to be going so well, did the share value fall? It was due to the stoppage by the Crown, replied Morgan 'as well as the media claiming the Crown royalty was 30% instead of 1–30th.'

On other mines working in the area, Morgan said, 'There is the Clogau, a mine owned by the Exploration Company of London, consisting of the Rothschilds, the Barings, and the greatest living financiers; the Gogova mine [Dolaucothi] in Carmarthenshire is in full working order; the Tynllwyn mine, situated about four miles, as the crow flies, from the Mount Morgan mine, with its machinery set in motion a fortnight ago – all these are either in full swing, or nearly so. Only a few days ago a man obtained for £5 a "take note" from Sir Watkin Wynn for some land near my own, and sold it immediately afterwards to a mining engineer in London, largely associated with South African mines, for £1,000 in cash.'[8] This was an admission that lent support to the Chancellor's argument that lowering Crown costs would allow individuals to make greater profits.

On 20 June, John Kelly (1844–1922), MP for Camberwell North, asked in the House the reason for the long delay in the Crown bringing the case against Morgan as his mining operations upon several properties had ceased, putting a lot of people out of work. Sir R. Webster (1842–1915), the Attorney General, claimed there had been no delay on the part of the Crown. Morgan had been asked to file an affidavit of documents so they could be inspected but he had claimed the time allowed was not sufficient. On 22 May, the Crown had sent another letter, allowing Morgan an extension until 19 June. Morgan failed to reply.[9]

July 1890 was a busy month for Morgan as on the 28th, the International Exhibition of Mining and Metallurgy opened at the Crystal Palace. Morgan, as chairman of the executive council, had played a leading role and he included specimens from his gold mines which attracted considerable interest. The exhibition ran until October and was deemed a great success. It was also the month that the inquiry into royalties finally began and while Morgan was pleased, he complained that the projected time for completion would be at least two years.[10]

Sir Warington Smyth (1817–1890), controller of mineral properties for the government, who had fixed the system of royalties, was one of the first to give evidence to the Select Committee of the House of Commons in the Woods and Forests Department (part of the Crown Estate). Smyth told the Committee that out of the 500 projected gold mines, not more than three or four were actually doing anything, including Mount Morgan. He believed the way public companies ran mines made it impossible for them to succeed, irrespective of what the Crown charged in taxes.[11]

George Culley, one of the Commissioners of Woods and Forests, was also called to give evidence as all applications for licences came to him. Since the revival of North Wales gold, more than 200 licences had been granted, at a cost of 5 shillings each and a uniform royalty of one-fifteenth on areas that varied from 100 to 300 acres. The licensee had the right to explore for gold in a certain area for one year and were bound to do a certain amount of work; if that work was not done, their licence was not renewed – which had seen a reduction in licences by about half. About 1,000 shillings had been received in royalties.[12]

As the Select Committee began its work, Morgan's case in the Court of Chancery, that had been pending since April 1888, finally came before Justice Ford North (1830–1913) with Morgan representing himself. The case began with a summary that on 7 May 1887, the Morgan Gold Mining Company (Limited) was registered, of which Morgan took the lead and in which he was a very large shareholder. On 8 June, the Crown granted a licence to Chidlaw Roberts, authorising him to work the gold at a royalty of one-thirtieth which was then assigned to Morgan and his company, and they paid royalties on all gold produced. Shortly afterwards, Morgan assigned all his personal interest in the Gwynfynydd mine to the company.

The Crown permitted work to continue on the mines while negotiations over the royalty took place, but Morgan was expressly told not to remove any gold or auriferous quartz without the representative of the Crown being present to check the weighing. In March 1888, a considerable quantity of gold was taken to London without complying with those conditions. In consequence, a letter was sent to him in April to the effect that, until agreements had been reached on royalties, he was to undertake not to remove any more material. The undertaking was not given and

Morgan continued working, so the Crown stopped all Morgan's mining activities.

There had been a considerable amount of correspondence between Morgan and the Woods and Forests Department, which offered to grant a licence on payment of a royalty of one-thirtieth (Morgan's mining area exceeded the 300 acres that was charged at one-fifteenth) on the value of the gold won, but they wanted an account of all gold and silver extracted from the mine since 31 December 1887 and back payments made for that amount. Morgan asserted that he had a right to mine without paying any royalty, without any licence, and did not provide the information asked for. The Crown was therefore suing him for failure to carry out their orders.

When Morgan opened his case, which was to last for five hours, he repeated much of his old arguments. He admitted the mines were being worked for gold but other metals were also being recovered. By concentrating solely on gold, he claimed the Crown had failed to make its case. Judge North dismissed his claim.

In his summing up, Judge North said he had no difficulty in coming to the conclusion that Gwynfynydd was a gold mine and Morgan's suggestion it was worked for other minerals was a fiction. Such mines had from the first, had always been, and still were, the exclusive property of the Crown, he said. North dismissed Morgan's arguments that Acts from Elizabeth I and William and Mary's time, which set out what royal mines were, no longer applied. He believed Morgan's intention was of

> appropriating to himself and his company, without payment, the gold and silver in their land which belongs to the Crown. The Gwynfynydd mine is not a copper, lead, iron, or tin mine; and no one has ever so described it; and its owners therefore are not protected by the Acts.

North also attacked Morgan's claim that the royal prerogative was against the interest of the public in that the Crown itself did not work the mine but made it difficult for others to do so, thereby stifling an industry that would create jobs and taxes. This, said North, was not a legal argument and he believed that Morgan had used it for his own purposes. He was not impressed either with Morgan or his claims and his language was highly critical:

> The Morgan Gold Mining Company, of which the defendant is the principal member and moving spirit, is not a body existing for charitable or philanthropic purposes, or even for the object of providing work for the poor inhabitants of the principality. But it is a commercial body, formed to carry on the work of mining on commercial principles with the view to the profit of its members, and nothing else.

While there is truth in North's opinion that Morgan and his board were capitalists, it does not reflect the entire picture. Morgan's concerns about the inconsistencies in royalties between the UK and those countries it possessed, and the payment of royalties on gross not net, reflected concerns throughout the mining industries as they impacted not just on profit, but on employment and the sustainability of private companies. These matters, however, were policy not law, and Morgan was in court because he had refused to obey the law.

What angered many was Morgan's portrayal of himself as a victim of the Crown when they believed he should have upheld the law and fought in other ways, particularly given he was an MP and had opportunities in the House. But Morgan, probably aided by George Hall, both experienced press men, knew that the media would soon lose interest in staid stories of policy and more sensational stories were much more likely to be printed.

Justice North was left in a difficult position; Morgan had sold Gwynfynydd and the company had paid the royalties up to date and supplied the required information, so that the only thing left to do was to decide who paid the court costs. As Morgan had insisted on his day in court and 'as I hold that he has been wrong throughout,' concluded North, 'I must judge that he pay the plaintiff's costs of the action.'[13]

The press responded in different ways. *The Times* was critical and predicted 'the public will not agree with him'[14] but the case had been confused with the issues and few journalists made the distinction. Consequently, many continued to support Morgan, believing it was unfair for the Crown to tax on product, not profit, and Morgan, replying to *The Times* fostered this confusion. He reiterated the claims of unfair competition from Imperial countries that had no royalties and the belief that laws based on those from Elizabethan times bore the 'dead hand of antiquity' and were out of touch with modern business.[15]

Despite losing the case, Morgan's reputation did not suffer and many noted how exceedingly clever his defence was. He 'did the work remarkably well and was greatly complimented by those who heard him conduct the case,'[16] or that he 'fought his case with his usual cleverness.'[17]

No sooner was it over than Morgan was back on his feet in the House, pressing for changes in royalty laws. Richard Webster (1842–1915), the Attorney General, said it was impossible for the government to make any changes until the inquiry was complete and, in the meantime, he would not deprive the country of the taxes. He did, however, invite Morgan to submit a plan of suggested changes and Morgan took up the offer. By the end of August, a report had been forwarded to the Chancellor of the Exchequer signed by 73 MPs from both sides of the House calling for mining royalties on profits, not produce. During the same period, the interim report of the Royal Commission on Mining Royalties was published, showing that during the year twenty-two witnesses had been examined, eleven of whom were connected with coal, seven with the iron trade, one witness (Sir A. West) represented the Inland Revenue and one (A. Porter) the Ecclesiastical Commissioners, while three were connected with colonial countries. The report simply presented the evidence with no commentary as they intended to take further evidence over the coming year from proprietors of mineral mines.

As well as his court case, Morgan still had to carry out his duties as an MP. When Morgan appeared at Dowlais on 3 November 1890, Albert Thomas was there supporting 'his friend' and 'very able representative'. He was glad to appear with his Welsh colleagues, Albert Thomas said, but in the case of Morgan, the pleasure was 'exceptional' for he was under a 'deeper debt of gratitude to him than to any other member of the House of Commons.' This was a reference to Morgan's support for his motion in February for an Independent Department of State for Wales, the first Welsh amendment ever moved in Parliament, but it was poorly supported by the other MPs. This was an opportunity, said Albert Thomas, of seeing how shamefully the needs of Wales had been neglected, not only by this, but by all other governments. On Home Rule, he said there was 'no more faithful follower of Mr Gladstone on that question' than Morgan.

When Morgan rose to speak, he, in turn, poured praise on Albert Thomas: there 'was no man whom he was more proud to be supported' than by his friend and that he was 'one of the most sincere, painstaking, and deserving representatives' in the House. They both agreed on the need for a Minister for Wales, which Morgan believed was more necessary than for Ireland because they used their own language whereas the Irish did not. He deplored the fact that whenever a question was asked in the House with regard to Wales, 'there was always a sneer' and comments of 'where is that place' to laughter from members.[18]

It was inevitable that Morgan would not let the court decision rest. He had lodged an appeal and on 1 November, he was back in court. Morgan claimed there was a circumstance in the Act of William and Mary which had a most material bearing upon the case, so the appeal had been granted. Morgan's argument concentrated on the fact that the royalty rate was governed on the use of gold in coinage, and as gold was no longer in general use for this purpose, the royalties should be adjusted. The judges examined his argument, dismissed it, and he was ordered to pay yet more costs.

Morgan appealed. This time, he applied to be relieved of the court costs on the grounds that a million pounds of silver had been produced since 1875, and not one pennyworth had been claimed by the Crown. He threw in a few more spurious reasons, none of which were connected to the point that he had broken the law. Unsurprisingly, he lost and now had three lots of costs to pay.

Once again, those watching the case were highly complimentary of Morgan's skill in court and his wide-ranging ability to utilise diverse arguments. Even Lord Justice Lindley noted that Morgan had most ably argued his case, but still dismissed his appeal.

Morgan spent Christmas 1890 at Bryntirion with Harriet and son Herbert, his two daughters being at school in Brussels, but as 1891 dawned, Morgan was again ill, suffering from severe chills. He had sufficiently recovered by 5 February as he was back in the House joining other MPs in their condemnation of the new Tithe Rent-Charge Recovery Bill, which gave county courts unlimited powers to deal with various cases including non-payment of tithes.

Morgan complained, 'The sentiment of feelings of the Welsh people are outraged by the collection of tithes for the benefit and maintenance of a Church in which they never worship ... Every man who expresses an opinion adverse to a learned County Court Judge will be liable to be tried for contempt.'[19] He wanted a clause added that nobody should receive a penalty or punishment, except for obstructing a bailiff, and the Attorney General replied if a clause was framed, he would consider it.

The Liberation Society issued a 'whip' urging all Liberal MPs to be in the House on 20 February when Morgan presented a motion 'that, as the Church of England in Wales has failed to fulfil its professed object as a means of promoting the religious interests of the Welsh people, and ministers only to a small minority of the population, its continuance as an established church in the Principality is an anomaly and an injustice which ought no longer to exist.' Church bodies used their publications to urge readers to write to their MPs encouraging them to be in the House to vote against Morgan's motion.

Morgan was then prevented from attending the House due to acute rheumatism which he hoped to shake off before his 'mighty effort to pull down, Samson-like, the pillars of the Welsh church.'[20] Also suffering from ill health was Gladstone, who was supposed to support Morgan's motion.

Lewis Llewelyn Dillwyn, the great champion of disestablishment, had, since the 1860s, done much of the ground work and it was mainly his arguments that had brought about a change in Gladstone's attitudes. Dillwyn argued it was the Church of the rich against the Church of the poor; an instrument of the powerful and privileged class; and raised awareness of issues such as magistrate courts being dominated by Church members with few nonconformists. But the argument was divided on party lines with the dominant Conservatives wanting to keep the status quo while the Liberals wished for change.

During the tabled debate in the House for 20 February, it was the experienced Dillwyn who was expected to lead the discussion with others, such as Morgan, following with similar motions, but by an accident of the ballot, Morgan was called to speak first. As he was not a particularly well-known MP, attendance was poor (only about a third of members were present), and as Morgan's knowledge was nowhere near Dillwyn's, this was seen as a disaster.

As Morgan rose to speak, he acknowledged his lack of experience:

> I ask the indulgence of the House in regard to the observations I have to make. Though I lack experience, I trust I shall not lack earnestness in advocating the claims of the Principality to Disestablishment, and in calling attention to the anomaly of maintaining an Established Church in Nonconformist Wales. Some hon. Gentlemen on the other side of the House may not have any great respect for the Welsh nation, nor for the national instincts of Wales, and perhaps the people of Wales have instinctively but little respect for them; but if gentlemen opposite would only listen to the arguments which can be adduced in favour of Disestablishment in Wales, and, instead of looking at this matter through the spectacles of Party, would endeavour to regard it with eyes undimmed by bigotry and with minds unbiassed by prejudice, they would speedily respect the cause we are advocating.[21]

He used statistics others had used so they had lost their freshness and 'occasionally adopted a tone which a more experienced advocate would have considered to be indiscreet' and was 'attentively, if not enthusiastically listened to.'[22]

When Dillwyn rose to address the thinly-attended House, he tried to repair the damage but Morgan had used many of his arguments and there was little left to say.

Normally in the House, after the mover and seconder had spoken, the opposition had their opportunity but everyone was shocked when suddenly, Gladstone stood. As word spread throughout the lobbies that the Grand Old Man was speaking, members rushed back into the Chamber which became so crowded many could not find a seat.

Gladstone did not 'adopt wholesale all the statements' made by Morgan, such as his claim that bishops were living in palaces for doing very little, and in a thinly veiled admonishment, added he would continue 'in my own tone and manner, my views on the question, and in dealing with the subject in a way less likely to sharpen the opposition than my hon. Friend found it necessary for himself to adopt.' In contrast, Gladstone praised Dillwyn with whom he agreed 'with almost everything that was said by my hon. Friend the Seconder of this Motion, who spoke with a weight that belongs to his high character and his long devotion to this cause.' Having given a brief history of the English Church in Wales, Gladstone confessed, 'I am bound to say that in this matter I regard myself as having no title whatever to praise on the part of the Welsh Nonconformists. I have done nothing to press their cause forward.' He admitted he opposed disestablishment and that untangling Wales from the Church would not be easy, but it had become a 'church of the few against the church of the many; and, in the second place, it is the church of the rich as against the church of the comparatively poor'. He asked, 'Wales having thus spoken, is it right, is it desirable, can it long continue, that by English opinion such a declaration proceeding from Wales should be disregarded, contravened, and overruled?' He acknowledged the overwhelming numbers of English members, and Church members at that, and warned them, 'I do not see the expediency or advantage of prolonging the controversy' and appealed to them, saying 'the people of England, who are eminently a just people, will give, and will insist on giving, to Wales in respect of her reasonable demands the same just, considerate, equitable, and conclusive settlement which, in the like circumstances, I believe they would claim for themselves.'

The Grand Old Man had spoken and for the first time, had overwhelmingly and publicly supported disestablishment but his appeal to the English MPs failed and Morgan's motion was defeated 203 to 235.

Despite the defeat, there was a great sense of accomplishment. Gladstone's reversal of his previous position was seen as a great victory and the fact the majority had been reduced to just 32 gave hope to those supporting disestablishment. Since 1870 when Watkins Williams had been the first to submit the motion before the House, the majority had been steadily falling. Then, 47 voted for with 209 against, the majority being 164 and only 7 Welshmen voted in favour. In 1889, Dillwyn submitted a motion that saw 233 for and 287 against, the majority being 53. Morgan's motion was lost on a majority of 32 and of the 34 Welsh members, 27 voted in favour.[23] Gladstone noted that only four members took part in the debate: Morgan, Dillwyn, Bryn Roberts and Rendall. He would have liked some of the younger Welsh members to speak, such as Lloyd George, particularly as he was a Nonconformist.

Although Morgan was not fully knowledgeable about the subject, a Welsh journalist in the *Liverpool Mercury* wrote that 'it would have been difficult to place the resolution in more competent hands. Mr Pritchard Morgan's speech was an important contribution to the debate and will do much to enhance his reputation both as a speaker and as a serious politician.' The *Llangollen Advertiser* called his speech 'animation and earnestness' with a 'very skilful appeal'[24] although some did criticise the hour-long length. Others, like Gladstone, took offence at some of Morgan's remarks, the *Primrose League Gazette* describing it as a 'series of disconnected and offensive statements.'[25]

When Welsh members shouted 'Clywch! Clywch!' [hear, hear] in approval of Morgan and Dillwyn, this was mangled in the English-language papers which varied from 'Clyc' to 'Clwe, Clyne' even 'Glue' and 'Clone.' (In fact, the Welsh members were not averse to using Welsh, such as 'Cau dy geg' (shut your mouth) much to the annoyance of the Speaker.)

Morgan was now on a new high of popularity but controversy was just around the corner. In March, the *Western Mail* published some leaked letters between D.A. Thomas and Morgan. The letters concerned a meeting between a deputation of the Aberdare Liberal Club and John Morley MP (1838–1923), asking him to preside over a local eisteddfod alongside Thomas and Morgan. Thomas forwarded the invite to Morgan on 3 March which seemed to offend Morgan. 'So far as my memory serves me,' he wrote back, 'this is the first time I have been honoured with a letter from you in reference to our conjoint duties as members for Merthyr.' Morgan seemed to think there was a deliberate attempt by Thomas to leave him out as Thomas' letter was postmarked the 3rd for a meeting on the 4th but he had not received it until the 5th. Given the two men had met face to face in the House, why, given the short time, had Thomas not handed him the letter? Morgan was annoyed because he had been left apologising to the Aberdare Liberal Club for his failure to attend and said he would tell them why. Thomas replied saying he was sorry the letter had not arrived, claimed it had been posted on the 3rd and to tell Aberdare what he wished. Morgan, while 'readily' accepting Thomas' explanation, added it must be the post office's fault then.[26]

The *Western Mail* described it as a 'very amusing correspondence' and blamed local preachers and deacons who had been 'thrashed' by Morgan during the election, but who still would not allow Thomas to 'shake hands' with Morgan. Even his support for disestablishment had not endeared him to them.

The *Liverpool Mercury* found the lack of cordiality between a senior and junior member for a constituency 'most regrettable' and was the cause of further division in the party: 'Though a greater unanimity now prevails in the Welsh party, they do not yet constitute a supremely happy family.'[27] The concerns were that the rift would prove decisive at the next general election, possibly letting in a non-Welsh candidate… or even worse, a Tory.

Chapter 9

The Bryntirion Injustice

The disharmony between Morgan and Thomas became increasingly important as the general election loomed and the Liberal Party wanted unison in presenting policies on issues such as the eight hours working day, and one man one vote. For the Welsh Liberal MPs, their priorities included Irish Home Rule, and Welsh Disestablishment. This was particularly important as the Welsh members were gaining a new confidence and were becoming more aggressive in their demands, as the *Aberystwyth Observer* noted

> for the first time in its history, Wales looks like possessing a true National Party, necessarily small in numbers, but by no means devoid of power, and able when the time comes to give effective expression … in each case they have sent up to Westminster men who are unmistakably Welsh in character, training, aspiration, and conviction. And they are all more or less young in years … the day of the silent Welsh member, who was content to be a mere amorphous drop in the sea of Liberalism, who meekly followed and obeyed the authority of the existing Liberal Leader on all matters, thankful for the smallest crumbs of attention in return, is over for ever.[1]

At the North Wales Liberal Foundation annual conference in April 1891, Osborn Morgan wrote the coming election would 'not only be Liberalism versus Conservatism, but Welsh Nationalism versus English Philistinism.'[2] Lloyd George urged the 'vital importance' of returning candidates pledged to immediate disestablishment and disendowment of the Church.

Morgan was willingly backing all the Liberal and Welsh issues but before his campaign really began, he suffered a personal loss. On 22 April 1891 at Glasgow Villa, Newport, where he was staying with his aunts, Morgan's son Herbert Pritchard Morgan died aged just 23. This was a year to the month after Morgan lost his mother Catherine, who died aged 71 at the Laurels, Abergavenny where she lived with her two daughters and where Morgan remained sitting by her bedside during the last week of her life.

Herbert had been a popular young man and had often joined his father on the campaign trail during the previous election, but he suffered from poor health. He had been sent to Australia to benefit from the warmer weather and to take care of his father's businesses, but his health deteriorated further so he decided to come home, thinking the voyage would brace his constitution. He arrived in March during a blizzard and was snowed in at Plymouth for several days; but the cold and rigours of the journey proved too much for him and instead of his health improving, it gradually grew worse. He died from a sudden haemorrhaging of the lungs and was buried at New Cemetery in the family vault next to his grandmother Catherine, with only a handful of mourners, including Morgan and a cousin, Archdeacon Bruce, who officiated.

Two months later, Morgan was back on the election trail promoting the unification of the Parliamentary Welsh Party – well, except himself and Thomas, he added, which brought laughter from one of his audience. However, a thaw in the Thomas-Morgan disunity started to appear in July, when 400 Aberdare tradesmen went on their annual trip. Starting at Tintern Abbey, they were joined by Morgan and surprisingly, Thomas, when 'amidst loud applause' the two men finally shook hands. It does have the air of something planned, possibly by Morgan's agent Vaughan who was determined to bring the pair together, particularly with a general election only a year away. As they stood posing for photographs, Morgan said that although they had not been on personal terms, he was sure the electors had not suffered because politically they had always worked together, which Thomas 'heartily assented'.[3] In all, the trip was considered a success with the exception of an unfortunate incident at Raglan Castle when a young man fell nearly 50ft from a wall. Morgan 'set about restoring consciousness, with the result that by the time the medical gentlemen appeared the young fellow was in a position to be removed.'[4]

In the meantime, the *North Wales Chronicle* was analysing the annual MP voting record for the 141 sittings and 416 votes. Several men scored in the 300–400s and of the Welsh MPs, Lloyd George was the most prolific, voting 319 times and the only one in the 300s. Of the thirty-four Welsh

copy of William Pritchard Morgan's birth, dated 1844. (*Her Majesty's General Register Office. Author's collection*)

stcard view of Commercial Street, Newport where the family was living when Morgan's father died. *uthor's collection*)

Cribb & Foote department store in Ipswich, Queensland, undated. (*Pinterest*)

St Paul's Anglican Church, Maryborough (1891) where Morgan and Harriet were married in 187. (*Public domain*)

'Morgan was a small man with big, black flashing eyes' from Stirling, A.W., *The never never land: a ride in North Queensland* (London: Sampson Low, Marston, Searle & Rivington, 1884). (*Public domain*)

John Murtagh Macrossan. (*Public domain*)

William Jamieson Allom's painting of Charters Towers (1895). (*Public domain*)

'Gold mining at Charters Towers' from Stirling, A. W. *The never never land: a ride in North Queensland* (London: Sampson Low, Marston, Searle & Rivington, 1884). (*Public domain*)

Thadeus O'Kane. By kind permission of the ©Charters Towers Archives Group and Charters Towers Regional Council. (*Charters Towers Archives Group and Charters Towers Regional Council*)

Lady Maria Gold Mining Co., Limited.

THE undermentioned SHARES having been FORFEITED through Non-Payment of Calls, notice is hereby given that they will be SOLD by public auction on March 15th, 1884, by Messrs. Wilson and Ayton, at their Rooms, Gill-street, Charters Towers, unless all calls due and expenses incurred on the said shares are paid previous to sale :—

Name.	No. of Shares.	Pro. No. of Shares.
William Pritchard Morgan	500	601 to 1100
Do.	250	1601 to 1850
Do.	250	5701 to 5950
Charles Kerr	250	6951 to 7200
Mary Ellen Kerr	250	6451 to 6700
William Wright	100	9901 to 10000
Do.	100	10101 to 10200
Do.	200	9701 to 9900

A. W. WILSON, Secretary.

A report mentioning Morgan's forfeiture of shares, something he was prone to do. (*Trove newspapers, National Library of Australia*)

Day Dawn Mine, Charters Towers, c.1890. (*Public domain*)

1 Queen Victoria Street, London, where Morgan had his office. (*Public domain*)

The Royal Ship Hotel, Dollgellau, where Morgan had an office. (*Public domain*)

Rhaiadr y Mawddach, the waterfall that fed the Gwynfynydd mine. (*Public domain*)

A gold miner at Gwynfynydd. An illustration from *Cardiff Times*, 24 December 1887. (*Public domain*)

Entrance to Mount Morgan Mine. An illustration from *Cardiff Times*, 24 December 1887. (*Public domain*)

Postcard view of the Gwyn Gold Mine and Rhaiadr Mawddach Falls. (*Author's collection*)

Portrait of D.A. Thomas, Morgan's arch rival. (*Public domain*)

One of Morgan's election posters, undated. (*Public domain*)

PRITCHARD MORGAN Will be PROUD to have the **VOTES** of the Men the Liberal Association call the SCUM of the place, and the ROUGHS of the Borough.

JOHN P. LEWIS, PRINTER, 46, HIGH STREET, MERTHYR TYDFIL.

PRITCHARD MORGAN IN AUSTRALIA.

An election poster emphasising Morgan as a labouring man in Australia. (*Public domain*)

The Grand Old Man, Prime Minister William Gladstone. (*Public domain*)

Bryntirion, Morgan's house in Dollgellau. (*Public domain*)

Catherine (Kate) Pritchard Morgan, who travelled extensively as Morgan's aide. (*Trove Newspapers, National Library of Australia*)

avid Lloyd George. (*Public domain*)

Morgan, from *Welsh Members of Parliament* (1894). (*Public domain*)

Postcard view of Gwyn Gold Mine and Rhaiadr Mawddach Falls, 1910. (*Author's collection*)

Li Hongzhang, Morgan's friend in China. (*Public domain*)

An election advertisement for Keir Hardie, undated. (*Public domain*)

Morgan and his Korean secretary. (*Welsh Newspapers Online*)

A 1kg gold bar from Gwynfynydd Gold Mine. (*Public domain*)

MPs, nine voted more than 200 times including G.O. Morgan, Randell, D.A. Thomas, and Dillwyn. Voting more than one hundred times were thirteen, including Mabon, Ellis, and Morgan on 193. The rest voted under 100 times.[5] This makes Morgan's voting record fairly average.

In December 1891, Morgan was at a Cardiff meeting supporting Alfred Thomas on his National Institutes (Wales) Bill. The Bill was primarily supported by Ellis, who could not attend due to ill health, and Mabon, who was supposed to be chairing but was absent giving evidence to the Royalty Commission, so only four Welsh MPs appeared at the poorly-attended meeting in the afternoon.

Alfred Thomas outlined the Bill, which included proposals for a Welsh National University and a National Museum of Wales, but he concentrated on two parts: the appointment of a Secretary of State or Minister for Wales, and the creation of a National Assembly or Welsh Parliament.

Thomas Phillips Price (1844–1932), MP for Monmouthshire, gave a brief speech in which he approved of Monmouthshire being included in the Bill. The county had, since 1542, traditionally been considered part of England, despite being in geographically located Wales, leading to the official designation as 'Wales and Monmouthshire'. It was not until 1972 that it was finally confirmed as part of Wales. Price quoted the late Cecil Raikes (1838–1891), a Conservative MP who had said there was 'no such thing as a Welsh nation' and that 'Wales was a small and obscure population', to which Price added there were many nations that were numerically small but 'yet they were nations.'

Before the evening session, there was entertainment by Clara Novello (in 1900, Morgan would present her with a conductor's baton made of Welsh gold[6]) followed by Morgan's speech. The later meeting was much better attended and Morgan was well received, the *South Wales Star* describing his speech as the best of the evening, despite the fact it was primarily on royalties. When he did get around to Alfred Thomas' Bill, he said that while supporting Irish Home Rule, he did not wholeheartedly support anything that would see a separation of the UK as he believed in building up and strengthening the Empire. With regard to Welsh matters, he thought the people were 'better educated, more intelligent, and numerous than they ever had been, and they were entitled – and if they were not, they never would be – to rule in their own particular way.'

Pointing out that there were twenty-seven parliaments under the British flag of Empire, he could not see the danger in giving Wales a Minister. He believed in an Imperial British Parliament under which each country had control of their own affairs.

Alfred Thomas concluded by pointing out that the English, Irish and Scots each had a Secretary of State and separate education and judiciary systems, and it was time Wales had the same. Wales, he said, was treated like an English county and ever since Edward I, the English had done all they could in 'perfectly unscrupulous' ways to 'absorb them as a people, to limit their language', and 'annihilate their nationality.' Alfred Thomas accepted that many Welsh MPs, including D.A. Thomas, opposed his Bill as they considered a Minister a watered-down administrative role rather than the Home Rule, however, he thought it would attract those who thought Home Rule a step too far and act as a first step towards a Welsh Parliament.

Referring to the charter for a Welsh museum, he said there was a large collection of Welsh antiquities in the British Museum quite buried away and for all practical purposes 'might be as well stored up in China.'

Both the *Western Mail* and *South Wales Star* were disappointed in the meeting, the *South Wales Star* hoping it would 'unite together the Nationalists of Wales; but the Conference has shown how disorganised and disunited we still are.' With so many of the leading Welsh MPs absent, it concluded that although 'many excellent things were said … they were not said by the right people.'[7]

Although the Bill ultimately proved unsuccessful, it did set out a number of Welsh ambitions that would be built on by Ellis and others.

As 1892 dawned, MPs were on the campaign trial but in early February, Morgan was laid up with a bad cold and missed several meetings. The same month, *The Times* was predicting a Liberal win in the general election with the Tories having no chance. Disestablishment, they predicted, would be the real fight and that Lloyd George, who won in 1890 by a narrow majority of 18, would lose his seat to the popular local journalist Sir J.H. Puleston (1830–1908). *The Times* believed Ellis, Dillwyn and Randell would win – indeed, they thought of the thirty Welsh MPs, the twenty-two Gladstonian Liberals were safe with three Conservatives and five doubtful.[8]

By March, Morgan had recovered to join Thomas at a meeting in Pontypridd that also included Lloyd George. Mabon was meant to attend but was detained elsewhere. Thomas began by drawing attention to Alfred Thomas' National Institutions Bill, arguing that 'the Welsh knew their time was coming for administering their own affairs' but he still favoured Home Rule, not a Minister. Lloyd George, alternating in Welsh and English, said generally he supported Alfred Thomas' Bill because the Imperial Parliament had no time to look after the purely local affairs of Wales, Scotland and Ireland, and because Wales was so small the government were apt to overlook it. An example, he said, was Morgan's fight over the Crown Lands in Wales. On the subject of disestablishment, Lloyd George accused the English clergy of arrogance, apathy and greed in a more vitriolic manner than Morgan had used in the House when he had been chastised by Gladstone.

When Morgan rose to speak, he admitted Alfred Thomas' Bill was not perfect and would need to be changed to get through the House, but he supported it wholeheartedly. He had little time for the arguments of breaking up the Empire and knew the benefits of Home Rule from living in Australia. Parliament, he argued, had more things to worry about than whether the building of two miles of local railway was better than a canal. He praised Alfred Thomas for pushing the Bill through, called Lloyd George's speech 'fiery' and 'excellent' but criticised the slow engagement of other Welsh members. He then expounded at length about his fight over royalties.[9]

The *South Wales Star's* explanation for the lack of engagement by Welsh members was that Alfred Thomas had not consulted them before launching his Bill,[10] but given it was the only Bill on Welsh Home Rule before the House, the *South Wales Star* believed they should all work together to make it an effective proposal.

Just as the election campaign was gathering pace, Morgan was embroiled yet again in a row with the Crown over royalties. He was refusing to pay the £500 court costs so, in March, two bailiffs took possession of Bryntirion, with Morgan allowing the seizure as a form of protest.[11]

The Crown, by not taking into account Morgan's popularity and the public sympathy for him, had made a serious error.

Morgan used the confiscation of his home to portray himself as a victim, which bolstered his public support. Even Lloyd George considered the seizure of Bryntirion as a 'rather harsh action' and requested the Chancellor not to 'enforce the execution'. He also wanted the Chancellor to stop referencing the fight over royalties as a 'personal' matter for Morgan because it was 'a matter of general public interest' as it affected mining in general.[12]

There were those who were not convinced, the *Birmingham Daily Post* voicing what many thought:

> we are at a loss to understand what Mr Morgan hopes to gain by his action in suffering the Crown to levy execution on his estates instead of paying the costs in a business-like manner. Such tactics seem puerile and wasteful, and they tend to shake one's faith in the judgement and business capacity of the discoverer of the Morgan gold mine.[13]

Building on the controversy, Morgan was back in the House on 22 March, urging the government to provide a consistent set of royalty charges. 'I object strongly,' he said, 'that one man is to pay a thirtieth part of his product, and another is to pay a twentieth' and he accused the Chancellor, Goschen, of personally being 'the sole cause this week of the discharge of 60 men in North Wales from their employment, and the wives and families of these men will probably bless the right hon. Gentleman in the end.' Lloyd George added his voice, complaining that workers from the Morgan Mine had been put out of work by the Chancellor.

Goschen repeated his worn phrase of the 'Treasury representing the taxpayers of the country' and that despite someone owning a piece of land, of the 'minerals beneath, the taxpayers have an interest, and it is that interest the Treasury are bound to defend.' Goschen returned the personal attack, saying Morgan understood 'what the share of the taxpayers would be; and notwithstanding that knowledge, and his estimate of what his share would be, the hon. Member was able to sell his rights for a very large sum.'

Morgan was stung; 'this is scarcely fair,' he protested, 'I have sent to the right hon. Gentleman a financial statement showing him that I am £50,000 out of pocket by my operations, and I have offered to submit him proof of this.'

'That is not the point,' said a weary Goschen.

'It is the point,' Morgan snapped back causing the Speaker to call, 'Order, order!'

Many people had suffered from gold-mining, Goschen stated, adding that Morgan spoke 'as if he only had been maltreated, but the taxpayers have also suffered.'

'How?' asked Morgan, but Goschen dodged the question. Instead, he referred back to the court case to continue his attack on Morgan, saying 'the law was so entirely against him' that the judge did not even call on counsel to defend the Treasury. He added, 'the Court gave costs to the Crown because the Judge thought the taxpayer should not be called upon to pay costs incurred in an action which was brought to deprive the taxpayer of a portion of his rights.' He urged everyone to wait for the Royal Commission report before discussing the matter further. In the meantime, Goschen said, if the government could take any steps to prevent cessation of work, they had the 'greatest desire to do so', the hon. Member having made an appeal with regard to the Morgan Mine.

Morgan, still on edge, snapped back that he had made no such appeal – to which Goschen smugly pointed out that actually he was replying to Lloyd George's comment about the Morgan Mine workers being laid off as Morgan was 'no longer connected with the mine which bears his name.'

The fiery Morgan was quickly back on his feet correcting the Chancellor, 'I am the largest shareholder by far. I object to be told that I, having started the mine in North Wales, am no longer connected with it. As a matter of fact I own nearly half the mine.'

Goschen seemed surprised, 'I was informed that the hon. Member had nothing to do with it,' but swiftly moved on, telling Lloyd George 'I do not see that the action of the Executive can interfere with the working of the mine, and I hope the mine will not be closed. I can only repeat that it is our duty to look to the interest of the taxpayer in these matters.'

T.E. Ellis then joined the argument, pointing out that Morgan had been mining for three years without any interference from the Crown until he started making money. This image of Morgan heroically struggling alone and then being penalised when he found gold was a persistent one, and one that generated great public support for him. The law, however, was unmistakable – he should have applied for a licence prior to starting work and ignorance of the law is never a defence. Given the extensive amount of mining Readwin, and others, had done in the area, it seems unlikely Morgan was ignorant of the fact.

Back in the House, Ellis referred to the 'dead hand of antiquity' laws, challenging the Chancellor to confirm that no prosecution had ever been recorded since the passing of the 1688 Act of William and Mary. He thought Morgan had done a public service in getting a 'declaration on a law made 200 years ago, on which there had been no decision whatever.' He hoped the government would listen to the appeal made by Lloyd George that proceedings against Morgan should be stayed until the Royal Commission on Mining Royalties had made its report.[14]

In addition, Ellis wanted to know how many tons of gold ore had been treated at the Clogau Gold Mine, from 1 November 1891 up to the present time, and all the costs involved. In February he had stated that for every £100 worth of gold, won at a cost of £80, the Crown took £15 as royalty, leaving £5 to the adventurers for taking all the risk of mining.[15] The *Cambrian News* was critical of Ellis' statement, 'We know,' they wrote, 'something about the Clogau Mine and Mr T.E. Ellis will excuse us if we do not believe that the present owners of the mine have won their gold at a cost of £80 for every £100. It may be simple and stupid on our part, but we believe that Welsh interests would be best served in Parliament and everywhere else by the simple truth, and where truth is not possible, by silence.'[16] The *Cambrian News* later published their figures showing for the past year, Clogau had realised £5,700, the royalty being around £380. They also noted that shareholders had made for their wives' massive keeper rings out of Clogau gold with monograms and the word 'Clogau'; unfortunately, the 'Saxon engraver' had written 'Clogan'. Two of the rings had been exhibited in the window of Griffith Ellis Owen, a local jeweller.[17]

Despite Goschen dismissing Ellis, Lloyd George, and Morgan's opinions on gold-mining and royalties, the public and the press were largely siding with Morgan. The cruel landlords crippling the poor workman trying to make a living was a David and Goliath story which was captivating, but had important ramifications for land owners who could be deprived of a vast income if the law was changed. Given that many of the land owners were Conservatives, the fight was being watched very closely.

The *Leeds Mercury* wrote that the feud between Morgan and the Crown 'is becoming a decidedly bitter one. Mr Morgan is one of the most determined and resolute of men, and it is not his intention to suffer quietly the action of the Commissioners ... The hon. gentleman maintains that he is making a stand on the question quite as much in the public interest as in his own, and declares that he will open the eyes of the country to a system which is inimical to – not to say prohibitive of – an important industrial development. Mr Morgan has the sympathy of a considerable section of the House, and he is going to take such opportunities as offer of ventilating his grievances in the House.'[18]

The Echo, despite questioning Morgan's logic in sinking so much money in his mines before ascertaining the law, excused him because he had spent so much time in Australia and confessed, 'we are glad that Mr Pritchard Morgan has stubbornly refused to pay the costs of the Crown in this stupid and iniquitous action, and thus has brought the question to the front. Mr Goschen's explanations are somewhat confusing. He first of all declares that the Woods and Forests had no choice in the matter, and then he says that they made concessions. If they have made concessions, they are manifestly insufficient, for a man who has sunk £60,000 in a new venture will not lightly abandon it.'[19] The *Freeman's Journal* also criticised Goschen, who they thought was 'palpably miserable and uncomfortable' in the House and the talk of throwing men out of work did not sit well with a general election so close.[20]

The *Western Mail* disapproved of Morgan bringing up the subject in the House on personal grounds as it meant Goschen could avoid getting into details, 'Unfortunately, Mr Morgan adopts the methods of the anti-tither in protesting against existing Acts of Parliament. Breaking or evading a law is scarcely the most perfect mode of illustrating its injustice. An unjust law is more likely to be repealed if honestly and squarely attacked and its unwisdom proved. It must be admitted that Mr Morgan's case is one for sympathy, and this, according to his statement to our London correspondent on Monday, he seems to be getting in the substantial form.'[21]

Two days after their spat in the House, Goschen tried to clarify that the Crown did not make concessions in reducing royalties, and that the reduction to one-hundredth had always been applicable on poor-grade ore. He then confused matters by saying this was only applicable to Gwynfynydd and would not serve as a precedent for other mines.

Throwing out an olive branch, he said if this still impeded the working at Gwynfynydd, he was willing to consider other suggestions but could not resist censuring Morgan for courting 'the martyrdom of an execution in his house' but agreed to postponing the bailiffs.[22]

There may have been more to this decision – as 'great excitement had prevailed at Barmouth and Dolgelly' following town criers broadcasting the seizure of Bryntirion. Large crowds assembled, 'exciting scenes were witnessed' and there was a feeling that any attempt to seize the house could lead to 'disturbances'.[23] Such was the anger that the government bailiffs had been boycotted by the villagers and were under police protection.[24]

The *Western Mail* wrote from its 'well-informed quarters' that the government was now considering meeting Morgan halfway due to the fact that a large number of Conservatives, along with Morgan's own political friends, considered he had been 'rather shabbily treated by the Treasury and the Commissioners of Woods and Forests.' Many in 'a perfectly outspoken manner' had expressed their sympathy for Morgan. 'There is no question,' continued the *Western Mail*, that 'if the member for Merthyr had an opportunity of dividing the House on the matter he would go very near getting an actual majority.'[25]

Morgan had, wrote the *Evening Express*, 'enlisted quite a regiment of supporters in this matter – Conservatives, Liberals, Radicals, Parnellites, and anti-Parnellites. He keeps them well drilled, and sends them into action against the Chancellor of the Exchequer with much persistency. Messrs John O'Connor, Arthur O'Connor, Bryon Reed, Barry, Kenyon, and Ellis – a strange medley – together with Lord Henry Bruce and several others on both sides, are all among his regulars.'[26]

Morgan was admired for having stuck his ground and comparisons had been made between those individuals, particularly in the Little Gold Rush, who had made money out of 'pockets' of gold and then ran, leaving shareholders and workers in the lurch. Morgan deeply believed in the industry and refused to relinquish his belief that the Welsh goldfields could be made to pay. It was costing him a lot of money and damage to his reputation as many saw him as a one-trick pony, but nevertheless he persisted. The difficulty, as the *Cambrian News* pointed out, was that Morgan 'believes in Welsh gold-mining, but he will never be able to make other people believe in it as he does.'[27]

Despite the fact that Lloyd George, Morgan, Ellis and others were complaining about men being thrown out of work at Gwynfynydd, George T. Kenyon, Chairman of the New Morgan Gold Mining

Company, wrote to *The Times* that their decision to let the fifty men go had nothing to do with the 'collision between Mr Morgan and the Woods and Forests Commissions, or by the levy of the Crown royalty, though they are distinctly of opinion that some concession on this point should be made.' It was, Kenyon said, a business decision.[28]

On 28 March, Goschen admitted that he had 'at the request of several Members of the House, consented to postpone the execution' on Morgan's property, in return for an agreement from Morgan that he would allow the Sheriff back in if required.[29]

The *Western Mail* rushed to interview Morgan. The journalist asked, given the royalty had been reduced from one-thirteenth to one-hundredth, if he was going to try and claim back money to which Morgan said yes, waving about reams of House of Commons papers, on which were written questions he still intended to put to the Chancellor. 'Had it not been for the excessive royalties, do you think the Morgan Gold Mining Company would have been able to pay more dividends?' asked the journalist.

Morgan, 'growing quite wrathful as he proceeded', claimed the government 'have had a dividend every month, and the shareholders have only had one dividend of a shilling from the time the company was stated.'

The journalist, trying to be positive, noted that 'the men have returned to work, and you have obtained a wonderful concession of 70 per cent on the product?' But Morgan was not in a 'melting mood' although he fully recognised the kind assistance of a number of Conservatives, and Ministerial Front Benchers, he was evidently 'still sore at Mr Goschen seizing his Bryntirion property, and he fully intended, he declared, to tackle the Woods and Forests people on Monday upon a motion that the Crown Lands Bill be read a second time.'

Would there have been a disturbance if the house had been seized, the journalist asked. 'I think it quite likely there would have been,' answered Mr Morgan, 'it would have been very difficult, at any rate, to avert one. One night, I believe, the miners actually did try and break into the house to get at the bailiffs. Fortunately, the housekeeper sent them away.'[30]

By May, Morgan was still working his way through his list of questions for Goschen and the Chancellor was still returning the same answers.

'Morgan,' wrote the *Northern Echo*, 'is a little gentleman, with a red face and bristly hair. He is prone to excitement, and seems to have a brisk spirit within'[31] so when he was not allowed to speak, he grew quite agitated. Morgan had asked the Speaker to let him protest against alleged inequality of treatment but the Speaker, seeing that another member had put forward a motion on royalties, refused him the floor. Morgan, deeply agitated, introduced a motion protesting against the discourtesy with which he had been treated by ministers, namely that Goschen had called him a martyr, 'I submit,' he raged, 'that the language used by the right hon. Gentleman towards me was not such as was right,' and he moved for an Adjournment of the House for a personal explanation. The Speaker was not impressed and declared Morgan out of, leaving it to Goschen to provide an explanation as to why he had used a term that caused Morgan such offence.[32]

Goschen simply replied, 'I should be sorry to wound the feelings of any hon. Gentleman. I spoke of martyrdom, and I presume he does not object to the use of the word.'

Morgan did object, 'You have always been insolent to me ever since I have been a Member of this House.'

'Order, order!' demanded the Speaker.

Goschen responded, 'I spoke of martyrdom' to cries of 'sordid' from the House. 'Does the hon. Member object to that word? I presume, then, that the word he objects to is "sordid." While I did not apply that term to the hon. Member personally, I thought that the whole proceedings connected with an execution, the selling of an hon. Gentleman's goods, had a kind of sordid aspect. As, however, I do not wish even to seem to apply the expression to the hon. Member I readily withdraw it.'[33]

What was also withdrawn, probably under pressure from the government, was the interim Mining Royalties Commission report. It would not, announced the Commission, be published until after the general election.

While Morgan had been battling with Goschen, the usual rumours that he would stand down for a labour candidate in the election, or retire, were swirling around – and a meeting at Dowlais seemed to confirm this.

Alfred Davies (1848–1907) from London declared himself a candidate with, as his election agent, John Vaughan, Morgan's previous agent. Morgan, they explained had asked D.A. Thomas for campaign money from the LA which had been refused. Unable to afford the campaign fees, he had withdrawn, urging Vaughan to represent Davies instead. Morgan later confirmed this.

The story then becomes somewhat suspicious because Vaughan apparently then called some friends, who 'laid certain facts before them', and told Morgan he was not justified in resigning as he owed it to the men who had voted for him. Persuaded, Morgan reversed his decision, decided to stand, and as soon as he did 'colliers had come to him and told him they had £2 in their pocket and another £1 or so at home to help him through his difficulties', but at the eleventh hour, relief had come and Morgan had found some funding.[34]

Once again, Morgan had managed to play the gallant victim and sympathy for him flourished. It is unlikely he was that poor but, as the *Cardiff Times* argued, most of his income was tied up in property and he was short of ready cash.[35] Morgan did put Bryntirion, valued at £40,000, up for sale, but the bidding closed at £13,400 and the auctioneer would not think of selling it at such a ridiculously low price.[36]

In the meantime, Davies refused to step aside and at the Dowlais meeting, the audience booed, blared cow horns, shouted 'Pritchard Morgan for ever' and sang 'Pritchard Morgan efe yw'r goreu' [he is the best] – making it impossible for Davies to speak. Things became more confused when Morgan ascended the stage to ask why Davies persisted with his candidature when he knew both Thomas and he were running.[37] As the stage was then invaded by youths and a barking terrier, the proceedings abruptly ended in chaos.

The unfortunate Davies agreed to step down and support Thomas and Morgan (he was elected by the Carmarthen Boroughs in 1899 and served until 1906).

D.A. Thomas was now 'greatly helping' Morgan in 'agitating the Bryntirion injustice' and the *Western Mail* wrote, 'we are to believe that birds in their little political nests at Merthyr now sweetly chirrup and agree.'[38] They asked what Morgan thought his chances of winning were, to which he replied, 'there is every probability – although I do not wish to boast – that I shall be returned at the head of the poll. But, mark you,' he added, referring to talk of Thomas' drop in popularity, 'there is going to be a stiff fight for the second seat.' Nevertheless, Morgan continued to back Thomas and, on 27 June, appeared alongside him, generating great interest in their double act. The meeting was crowded to capacity with Thomas urging the audience to put their crosses next to his and Morgan's names. Morgan, appearing late and accompanied by a brass band, was cheered onto the platform and when he spoke, enormous cheers rang around the room. He could not resist pointing out that he had come to the meeting at the express invitation of Thomas.[39]

The two men were now presenting a uniform face and appearing together regularly to great approval. Everywhere the halls were crowded with even more cramped together in the streets and whenever the two shook hands, the audience would roar its approval. The press delighted in reporting that their difficulties had been ironed out. Wherever they went, the joint message was to vote for both of them.

Not everyone was convinced by the new-found harmony and rumours abounded that Thomas was saying one thing in public and another in private. The new Liberal Association was still determined to oust Morgan, and Thomas was seen as a member of the caucus, despite his protestations to the opposite. While most of the Welsh press were even-handed in discussing both men, the *Western Mail* had taken against Thomas and wasted no opportunity to criticise him and praise Morgan. Thomas, a significant land and business owner, was not seen by the *Western Mail* and others, as someone who understood the working class in the way that Morgan, who had worked as a labourer, could. Thomas styled himself the 'working man's friend' while Morgan called himself 'the working man'.

However, that 'working man' was being seen as something of a one-trick golden pony so Morgan tried to involve himself in a broader range of politics. He threw his support behind a number of Welsh issues such as Lloyd George's Bill to ensure Welsh judges were bilingual. Despite all the Welsh MPs voting in favour, it lost, the government refusing to apologise for sending English-speaking judges to monoglot Welsh areas.

On other matters, Morgan commented on the rights of Polynesian labour in Queensland which corresponded with his attitudes towards Chinese workers while he was living there. He believed that non-white workers should be restricted as it imposed on white working-class employment, but they could be brought in to work on the sugar plantations.

Sir William Randal Cremer (1828–1908), a Liberal MP and later winner of the Nobel Peace Prize (1903), was horrified by his views, which he thought echoed 'the same kind of arguments nearly thirty years ago on the question of human slavery in the United States of America. It is the old story about the slave being better fed, clothed and housed than he would be in a state of freedom. I am satisfied that scarcely anyone in this House – except the hon. Member – will be deluded by any such sentiments.'⁴⁰ Despite Cremer's criticism, throughout his life, Morgan saw non-whites as needing the guidance of white Westerners.

Meanwhile, he was continuing the campaign trail accompanied by his daughter Catherine, or Kate as she was known. At the Plymouth mine, Kate addressed a large audience and discussed temperance, saying she had been in Germany for four years and, by comparison, felt that 'English' teetotallers 'did not do things in the proper way'. In Germany, cheap entertainments were provided as somewhere for people to go instead of the public houses, whereas in the UK drunkenness was merely denounced. This seems to be the first time that Kate had become her father's aide and addressing a crowd of what was estimated to be 8,000 would be daunting for anyone, especially an 18-year-old.⁴¹ The working relationship between father and daughter was very similar to that of D.A. Thomas and his only child, Margaret, later Lady Rhondda. Perhaps because of Morgan's bouts of ill health, it was felt necessary for someone to accompany him – but Kate was destined to become so much more.

Kate's address took place the day before the UK polls opened. They were to remain open from 4–26 July, and the Merthyr boroughs were the first to vote in Wales on the 6th, with results expected around 3.00 pm on the 7th. It was feared the event would be marked by serious disturbances and extra police were brought in, with many houses and businesses boarding up their windows.

On polling day, 36-year-old Thomas and 48-year-old Morgan drove around together drumming up last-minute support, but there was little enthusiasm. The rain poured all afternoon and only a few supporters roamed the streets with the candidates' portraits pinned to their hats. One Conservative, B.F. Williams, stood but was barely noticed. Voting was very high but it all seemed a done deal and people were losing interest.

When the results were published, Thomas had beaten Morgan by a slim majority – 11,948 to Morgan's 11,756, with Williams receiving just 2,304. Overall, the general election saw a minority Liberal government formed with Gladstone as Prime Minister.

Later that year, Gladstone toured North Wales, with Morgan in the entourage, and at Barmouth, the Grand Old Man was presented with an album of photographic views commemorating his visit. Mounted in gold plate, it was engraved with the arms of Merioneth and the Welsh leek, while around the edges were the words 'Made of Welsh gold from Clogau Mines, Barmouth, North Wales. Donated by John Evans of the Clogau Gold Company.'[42] On the way back they called at Bryntirion, which Morgan had still not been able to sell.

Four months after the 1892 election, one man, who was to play a significant role in Morgan's political career and who resurrected the desire for a local Labour MP, toured South Wales talking about the newly formed Independent Labour Party (ILP). The ILP had evolved in response to the lack of movement in electing a Labour representative and Keir Hardie (1856–1915) was their first chairman. Hardie told the *South Wales Daily News* that five years previously, in his first major foray into national politics, he had attempted to organise the Labour vote on Liberal lines at the Trades Congress in Swansea but it had failed completely. In the 1892 election, Labour candidates had made only four gains but Hardie told the *Daily News* that men were deserting the Liberal cause for that of Labour.[43] It was to be a prophetic statement.

Chapter 10

A Man with a Grievance

Since the general election, Morgan had been very quiet but in the early part of 1893, he was involved, as many MPs were, in debating the second reading of the Miners' Eight Hours Bill. This Bill, restricting the hours employers could force employees to work, had gone through a series of legal regulations since 1833 when the Factory Act limited the number of hours children could work. Over the following decades, this was expanded to include adults but while it had been achieved in some industries, it was still not law in mining.

One of the difficulties with the miners' situation was whether eight hours counted from them arriving at the surface of the mine, or when they arrived at the coalface. Getting down the shaft to their place of work could take up to an hour, particularly in old mines that had much longer underground roads. If wages started when they reached the coalface, they would lose an hour's pay. It was feared men would work faster to make up the wages, causing more accidents, and younger fitter men would earn more than older men who had families to feed.

Both Thomas and Morgan supported the principles of the Bill but from the coalface, not the bank. In the House on 3 May, Thomas moved to reject the Bill saying that in meeting after meeting he had attended, the miners had rejected it. He had tried eight hours at his own colliery but the men had asked him to return to the old system. While some mining districts had voted in favour of the Bill, the majority of South Wales miners had not. Thomas continued, 'in South Wales the colliers were now down the pits about 10½ hours a day' but from that, at least three hours had to be deducted for the time occupied in getting to and from the workplace, taking meals, and doing dead-work such as tidying and checking timbers. The result was only five hours of coal-getting and any further cuts would lead to a reduction in wages and an increase in the price of coal.[1]

When it came to voting, Morgan, Thomas, Lloyd George and others were against, but it was carried with a majority of 78.

This gave Morgan greater incentive to continue his fight for a Minister of Mines who

> shall be responsible to Parliament for provision for the better protection of the lives of the many thousands of your majesty's subjects who work underground, and whose duty it should also be to inquire into the existing laws respecting royalties and wayleaves so that the only remaining industry in the United Kingdom producing to any extent raw material from the earth may be developed to the fullest extent.[2]

The *Evening Express* waylaid Morgan in the House of Common's Lobby to ask him what he was planning to say, but Morgan would not be drawn. 'Cannot do it,' he laughed, 'Surely, you would not rob me of the plums of my speech. What would the House say? ... you can say that I am determined to leave no stone unturned until a Minister of Mines has been appointed. I have facts and data which will force the position beyond all question.' But never one to miss an opportunity to talk to the press, he continued, pointing out that seven Australian colonies had a dedicated minister but the whole of the UK was controlled by three governmental departments. He reminded the journalist that the Home Secretary had a legal background, the Chancellor of the Exchequer a financial one, and the President of the Board of Trade was in post, he claimed, as a reward for past services to their party. None were qualified in mining.

When Morgan could not be drawn any further, the journalist asked about Welsh gold and received the confession that they were doing 'very badly indeed.' The Morgan Mine had stopped and men were out of work, but they were intending to start again soon. Morgan trotted out a lot of facts and figures in comparison to the much easier job of mining gold in America. When the journalist pointed out that no dividends had been paid from Gwynfynydd, Morgan agreed and said the money had been ploughed back into the mine because the company directors were disgusted with the shareholders for not responding to appeals for more money. In fact, they had agreed to lease the mine back to Morgan and others, and within a fortnight it was hoped to be back into full production.³ Morgan, it seemed, had regained full control of Gwynfynydd.

A few days later, he took a bar of gold into Sir William Harcourt's (1827–1904) room (Harcourt had replaced Goschen as Chancellor of Exchequer), not as the *Western Mail* pointed out 'with the idea of knocking Sir William over the head or of offering a big bribe' but so the Chancellor could see with his own eyes what the Welsh hills were capable of producing. Sir William was 'greatly struck' with the bar which, a few hours later, was sold to the Rothschilds for £1,100.⁴

More news was to come the following month when the Mining Royalties Commission report was published. This was the report Morgan, and others, had been pushing for since 1888 but once commissioned, it took three years to complete. The remit had been to consider amounts paid as royalties and other charges on mining for coal, ironstone, iron ore, shale, and minerals worked in the UK, as well as their economic operation, with additional information from countries controlled by the UK. In all, the Commissioners held forty-five sittings in London, three in Edinburgh, and interviewed 142 witnesses, including working miners and their representatives, mine owners and others such as Keir Hardie. Mabon, with his great knowledge of coal mining, was on the committee and they were assisted by geologist Sir Warington Smyth and mining engineer Forster Brown (1835–1907).

The report started by outlining the importance of the UK mining industries, the vast capital involved, the half a million people employed, and the 43 million pounds in wages per annum.

When it came to consider the gold industry, they were not so positive. Gold royalties received by the Crown amounted to less than £7,000 from 1836 to 1891, and did not appear to have interfered with the investment of capital in gold-mining. While they considered that the Woods and Forests Department had done its duty when dealing with the Crown rights to gold in Wales, they did recommend attention should be paid to tightening up the administration of payments by both the Crown and private landlords. Generally, they were 'of the opinion that the system of royalties has not interfered with the general development of the mineral resources of the UK or with the export trade in coal with foreign countries.'

On the subject of a Minister of Mines, while not directly advocating for one, the Commissioners did admit that 'the Department of Mines in the

Home Office might be reorganised and extended, with such additional statutory powers as may be necessary for the purpose of collecting and publishing accurate information with regard to mines and minerals.'

The report was received with 'great disappointment', wrote the *South Wales Daily Post*, by the representatives in Parliament of the mine owners and miners. It had been expected that questions that had been asked at the outset would be answered but they were not, and the Commissioners made few recommendations. MPs quickly made it clear they were planning to challenge the findings.[5]

The *Western Mail* was scathing, questioning the £7,000 from 1836 to 1893 figure as it did not tally with figures given by Morgan, nor were his complaints embodied in the report. The *Western Mail* continued, 'it is quite clear that the commissioners, as a body, do not agree with the member for Merthyr, though I must say I always understood that there was at least one amongst them, namely, Mr Abraham, M.P. [Mabon], who considered that this case was a very strong one.' They added, 'a fresh outbreak from him [Morgan] in the matter of excessive royalties on the Welsh gold-mining enterprise may be expected, I gather, before long.'[6]

Needless to say, the anti-Morgan and anti-gold-mining *Cambrian News* supported the findings.

On top of the disquiet about the report, the government announced they were planning to raise gold royalties from 1% on product to 3½%. Mabon, Randell, and others were planning to object with Morgan arming himself with evidence demonstrating a lack of uniformity as the rise in Ireland would be from 1% to 5%.[7] The Chancellor quickly u-turned and kept the royalty at 1%.

In September, a new chance came for Morgan to continue the argument that a Minister of Mines was needed. The Chief Commissioner of Woods and Forests, the Crown's agents, had died and Morgan argued his replacement should be someone with an expert knowledge of the subject he had to control. Morgan also took the opportunity to complain the Office of Woods and Forests would not fix mining royalties for the whole of the term of a mining contract. The present Chancellor had consented to fix the royalties for five years but, argued Morgan, that was not a sufficient period for opening up a mine. At the end of the five years, when a large amount of capital had been spent on setting up, it would be necessary to go back to the Woods and Forests Department, and have the royalties fixed according to whatever they decided to charge. Landowners often fixed a period of 32 years and Morgan wanted something similar.

Harcourt, the Chancellor of the Exchequer, replied in a weary tone:

> I am a little surprised and somewhat disappointed at the tone the hon. Member has adopted towards Her Majesty's Government, for if anybody has done what he could to satisfy another man, I have done that for the hon. Member. From the first I regarded with the greatest possible favour any arrangement which could be made for the purpose of encouraging gold-mining in Wales, both to increase the gold production and to give employment in a poor country; and as soon as I entered Office in the present Government I used my authority for the purpose of fixing the royalty at 1–100th instead of 1–30th, which the mine owners had previously paid. The hon. Member has enjoyed the benefit of that reduction, and has expressed his gratitude; but he has been informed that the Government could not come to a final decision until they had the Report of the Royal Commission on Mines. The conduct of the Commissioners of Woods and Forests has been impeached, but only two or three years ago a Select Committee of the House investigated the whole conduct of the Department, including its action in this matter, and a more complete vindication it would be impossible to have had than was contained in the Report of the Committee.

Harcourt, echoed the report's findings that, in their opinion, royalties had not interfered with gold-mining in Wales, particularly after they had made generous reductions to both Clogau and the Morgan Mine. 'During the last few years,' he continued, quoting from the report:

> the Commissioners have granted a large number of licences to explore for gold in Merionethshire, on a royalty of 1–15th of the ore extracted if obtained on Crown land, and of 1–30th to landowners if obtained on private lands. The results do not appear to have been encouraging, as of a large number of projected mines only three or four are doing anything, and none have so far been successful. It has been complained that the Crown royalty is too high, as a reason for this want of success. The late Sir Warington Smyth, who, until his

death, acted as Mineral Inspector and adviser to the Commissioners, gave conclusive evidence that this complaint is not well founded.

Harcourt continued that Smyth

> called the attention of the Committee to a prospectus of a Gold Mining Company with a capital of £210,000, out of which £190,000 was to be given to the promoter, who had, no doubt, spent some money upon it, but whose bonus of £190,000 rendered it next to impossible that the company should succeed as a commercial undertaking. The company referred to in this paragraph is the Morgan Gold Mining Company (Limited), and the promoter referred to is Mr Pritchard Morgan. It is, I think, quite plain that the mining royalties could not be said to have prevented the success of that undertaking, especially when you compare the £7,000 got in royalties with the £190,000 paid to a promoter.

Harcourt explained the five-year royalty on a nominal charge was a test to see if the mine was a going concern and not subject to large payments to promoters such as that paid to Morgan. If it was viable, then he argued that a longer period would be negotiated but the nominal charge would have to be increased. He said he would like to see the industry succeed but 'I cannot say that has yet been done' adding of Morgan, 'I expected gratitude; I met with abuse.'

The 'little bald headed, excitable man' was rapidly on his feet and the House sat for more than an hour after its usual time to let Morgan 'ventilate his old grievance about the royalty charges by the Government on Welsh gold.'[8] 'I wish to tell the right hon. Gentleman some facts which he does not appear to know,' fumed Morgan, 'There have been £120,000 expended on the Morgan Mine. I spent £30,000 looking for this gold before I saw a speck of it as large as a pin's head, and the Government never interfered with me for four years. The company has paid a dividend of £10,500, and the Woods and Forests Department has received royalties to the extent of £3,000 in hard cash, or 30 per cent on the amount paid in dividends.'

Lloyd George rose to defend Morgan, clearly annoyed at Harcourt's claims that he had reduced the royalty when it had been done by the previous government. He stated that he had visited the mines himself, and found that they employed 200 very poor people, who supported a population of 1,000 and he hoped that the Chancellor would see his way to give his favourable consideration to the whole matter.[9]

The *Western Mail* called it a 'brave attempt' to sweep away the obstacles[10] but others criticised Morgan for speaking off the cuff and not tabling a question. Morgan's general disregard for Parliamentary processes had always gained him both friends and enemies.

The *Cambrian News* renewed its support for the government and urged Lloyd George not to get involved. The 'smart young man,' it claimed, was in danger of being carried away by Morgan 'flogging the dead horse of Welsh gold-mining.' However, it conceded that despite many, including themselves, having little belief in Welsh gold, Morgan did believe and he believed very strongly.[11]

Before the dust could settled on the matter, the Welsh Liberal members met with the Chancellor to urge the appointment of a Woods and Forests man who would take an 'intelligent and practical interest in the resources of the country.'[12] Morgan spoke on metalliferous matters, Lloyd George on other mining interests and the Chancellor promised to lay the views of the deputation before the Prime Minister, with whom the appointment rested.

Despite Morgan's continued battle with the government over royalties, Gwynfynydd was struggling again. Rumours had surfaced in March 1893 that the Mount Morgan Gold Mining Company was about to shut, and the following month Morgan told board members they needed £10,000 to carry on but they had only raised £1,000 from the shareholders.[13]

Elsewhere, Welsh gold was making the press due to another royal wedding ring. The Welsh National Presentation Committee had visited Prince George, later King George V, to offer Welsh gold wedding rings to him and Princess Mary (May) of Teck. Prince George said he would be pleased to accept and so a half-an-ounce nugget was sent to London jewellers, Percy Edwards and Co, where it was put on display in the shop window.[14]

The *South Wales Daily Post* expressed the hope that Morgan would see a suitable Welsh inscription inserted in the ring[15] but it is unlikely the gold came from him. The origin was said to be from 'Merioneth mines' and had it come from Morgan. he would have used that fact for self-publicity. It is more likely to have come from Clogau although there is no confirmation in the press. In the end, the inscription was chosen by Princess Mary – 'In God alone we two are one. George July 6th, 1893.'[16]

When the ring was presented, it was encased in a golden casket bearing Welsh emblems, inscriptions in Welsh and English, and the Welsh dragon on the lid. An address, read by Sir David Evans, included the line, 'this ring being the visible sign of union between your Royal Highness and Princess May, is to me very significant as a symbol of the union of Welsh hearts (and very warm they are) in their loyalty and love to the Queen, the Prince and Princess of Wales, your Royal Highness, and all the Royal Family.'[17] Prince George was, he said, 'deeply touched by the esteem and loyalty of the Welsh people and spoke of an early visit to Wales.'[18] George and Mary were married on 6 July 1893 but at a May 1894 exhibition at the London Grafton Galleries, featuring jewellery and goods 'beloved by fair women', Princess May's Welsh wedding ring was included[19] – so obviously she was not wearing it.

Shortly after the royal wedding, Morgan's fortunes seemed to be improving again. A story appeared in the *Western Mail* claiming the 'Gold King' had staggered into their office weighed down with a heavy black bag, his face 'wreathed in smiles, which showed up to advantage on a face almost purple with the laborious effort of carrying a heavy burden in a scorching sun.' He had come to show them something, he said, almost breaking his back lifting the bag onto the table which dropped with a dull thud. Morgan dived into the bag pulling out four blocks of solid gold, mopped his face with a pocket-handkerchief, and told the astonished men the gold was 'recently got out of the Morgan Gold Mine at Dolgelly.' Each, he said, weighed about five pounds and each was eighteen carats to the ounce, the remainder being made up of silver and platinum.

The editor was so impressed he offered to invest in Gwynfynydd, as long as there was assurance that it was not going to be 'hampered in its operations', but Morgan put him off. 'I can say this,' he said with his usual boasting, 'that in the future the mine will be made to produce more gold than ever, for with a number of friends, I have recently acquired the mine from the old company, and we mean to put all the energy we possess into the concern.' In reply to a question about the number of men employed, Morgan 'pushing his handkerchief inside his collar, and painfully wiping up the perspiration' said there were 100 men.

'We are going to work on a more extensive plan than ever,' Morgan continued enthusiastically, 'we are going to make things hum – hum, sir, hum, hum – and the success we shall get will astound you.' Morgan gathered up his gold bars, dashed out to the front door, whistled to a detective to see him safely to the train, and staggered towards the station.[20]

What was also staggering was Morgan's poor showings in Parliament during his political career. At the end of the September Parliamentary session, the *Rhyl Record* published an analysis of MPs' voting record. There had been 310 divisions, and Ellis was the most proficient, voting on all of them. Lloyd George was on 225; H. Randell, 155; Sir George Osborn, 151; Hon G. T. Kenyon, 147; D.A. Thomas 144; Mabon, 132; Stuart Rendel, 132; and Morgan, 102.[21] Only two other Welsh MPs voted fewer times than Morgan.

In addition, in September 1893, Morgan wrote an article for the *Westminster Gazette*, a Liberal weekly paper, about Sir George Elliot's proposal for the 'formation of a gigantic coal trust, embracing all the collieries of the kingdom.' Morgan considered the scheme excellent and supported the determination not to create a monopoly for the benefit of colliery proprietors, but he worried about who would join, and why. He used the article to widen his royalty argument, illustrating how it adversely affected other industries, particularly coal. He wrote that the economic value of minerals and base metals had not been realised when laws concerning the mining of gold and silver were made. The supposedly low-value deposits of coal and iron were allocated to landowners which now meant they could charge whatever royalty they wanted, enabling them to gain great wealth while capitalists and miners suffered losses. 'The royalty owner,' he continued, 'gets his royalty in bad as well as good times, irrespective of the fact that the mine may be carried on at a loss. By the combination of interests this iniquitous system might be swept away, and royalties paid only on profits and not on product.' By combining all the colliery owners in the proposed trust, they could bring pressure on the government to change the laws but, he added, unless they created a mining department, he could not see this happening. It was the miner, argued Morgan, who should come first, the man

> who risks his life and spends his days in darkness in order to provide light and heat for his more favoured countrymen. He must be first

considered, and received a way that will provide for himself and family a due proportion of the comfort that his labours secure for others. In addition to this, he should receive an equal proportion of the profit to the royalty owner, who risks neither his money nor his life ... I feel confident that no consumer would grudge the extra fraction per ton on the price of coal which would provide for the families of men whose labours have assisted to brighten his home, and whose lives or limbs have been lost in the pursuit of their hazardous occupation.

Morgan finished by arguing that coal mines should be nationalised, 'there is no reason why the mines should not become, as they always should have been, the property of the State, and be worked, as they ought to be to-day, for the benefit of the nation.'[22]

He continued these resolutions the following month, at the London Liberals' annual conference, 'that in order to obviate in future such disastrous consequences as exist it is the opinion of this conference that the mining industry ought to be under the control of Parliament.' The Chair ruled it outside the scope of the conference[23] but in Parliament, Kier Hardie introduced a Bill for the nationalisation of mines.

Meanwhile, back at Gwynfynydd, newspaper reports seemed to confirm a new success. 173 tons of ore had recently been taken out of the mine, yielding 130 ounces of gold, an equivalent of 15dwt to the ton – 50% over the average yield[24] – but once again, it all sounded too good to be true.

Morgan and his family spent Christmas at Bryntirion as they so often did, but during the first half of 1894, there was little 'humming' about Welsh gold, Morgan or other issues until, on 23 June 1894, an avoidable tragedy shook the nation. An explosion at the Albion Colliery at Cilfynydd, Glamorgan, became one of the worst disasters to occur in the South Wales coalfield, second only to Senghenydd in 1913 – both caused by combustible airborne coal dust.

The deaths of 290 men and boys at Albion, as well as 123 horses, enraged the public and Morgan was said to be on the warpath. He called the disaster a grave dereliction of duty by the Home Office and asked the Home Secretary, Herbert Henry Asquith (1852–1928), how it was that his department had taken no steps to prevent it, especially as an existing report had shown coal dust was particularly dangerous at Albion.

Asquith replied that the report had not reached his department until 24 May, too late to effect any changes. However, the report, prepared at his request for the Coal-dust Commission, was dated 20 August 1893 but had been issued as a Blue Book on 12 February – meaning it had been in the Home Office for about ten months, not just one.

Morgan pressed his argument that had there been an experienced mining department, it would have recognised the dangers and possibly taken action quicker than a Home Office that had little mining experience. 'For years,' he said, 'I have advocated the appointment of a Minister for Mines' and that the Miners' Federation had likewise petitioned for the same but no moves had been made. 'How many more lives,' he asked, 'must be sacrificed to the Moloch [someone demanding a high sacrifice] of officialism before the prayers of the miners are heard and responded to.'

Asquith replied there was no intention at that time to create a Ministry of Mines and when Morgan asked if he was aware the Miners' Federation, representing 600,000 men, had urged the government to create one, he simply replied, 'Yes, sir.'[25]

It was not just mining matters that were frustrating Welsh MPs; they were also becoming frustrated over the issue of disestablishment. There had been an agreement that disestablishment would be prioritised after Irish Home Rule but Gladstone was moving away from the agreement. The *Western Mail* was predicting a revolt by Welsh malcontents led by Lloyd George, David Randell, Alfred Thomas, Sir G. Osborne Morgan, Major E.R. Jones, S.T. Evans, D.A. Thomas and Morgan, with Sir Edward Reed and Herbert Lewis believed to follow suit. Despite Thomas denying such a revolt,[26] in March, a meeting chaired by Stuart Rendel was attended by many MPs and other 'London Welshmen' to keep up the fight for disestablishment. Nothing came of it so, by August, Thomas and Morgan were demanding the government take action. If the motion was not on the table in the next session, they threatened to form a Welsh party and challenge the government.

On 15 August 1894, a large meeting of Welsh members met at the House, Stuart Rendel presided and Lloyd George, Thomas and Ellis were present but Morgan was not. At the close of the two-hour meeting, they addressed a letter to Gladstone pointing out that in the official charter of the Newcastle Liberal programme, the first major measure, after Home

Rule for Ireland, would be to tackle disestablishment. They believed this agreement was responsible for the Liberal victory in Wales and they wanted the pledge to be redeemed. Failure to uphold this promise would, they felt, give them a bad reputation and put re-election at risk. Thirty Welsh MPs signed.

When Gladstone replied on 5 July, he claimed the Irish question was taking precedent and he had no recollection of the agreement. Given that the Newcastle programme was covered extensively by the press, and many Liberal MPs accredited it to their re-election, it is hard to believe Gladstone. By 28 July, the Welsh members were writing again, asserting that in the Newcastle programme the agreement had been clearly stated and they urged clarification. Gladstone, replying on 8 August, was full of flattery for the Welsh members but sidelined the issue, claiming as soon they could get around to it, they would.[27] Irritated by his reply, most of the Welsh press urged the committee on, realising the government's small majority gave the Welsh members power – but only as long as they remained united, because, as the English papers were highlighting, there were still rifts among the Welsh members.

It was Lloyd George, seconded by Ellis, who pushed through the threat that unless Gladstone did something, they would take action – but Gladstone, knowing the Welsh members were not united, was willing to take his chances, particularly as several of them were personal friends of his. His gamble paid off and the revolt came to nothing.

Seven months later, Gladstone retired and was replaced by Lord Rosebery, giving the Welsh party hope because Rosebery firmly believed in disestablishment.

Possibly due to the much higher attention Welsh MPs were enjoying than ever before, Thomas Marchant Williams (1845–1914), a Welsh nationalist, lawyer and author, wrote a satirical book entitled *Welsh Members of Parliament, 1894* with illustrations by Will Morgan. The critical sketches were, wrote the *Cambrian News*, 'ill-tempered and unfair,' and 'anybody who reads them feels that they are the ill-tempered productions of a disappointed man.'[28] However, they thought Will Morgan had 'succeeded in presenting excellent likenesses of the Welsh members.'

One aspect that was unfair in Morgan's portrayal was Williams' claim that he was 'no orator', given that Morgan was frequently complimented on how well he spoke and how well he crafted his arguments, even if it was more the language of the bush than of a high education.

> He is too flippant to be impressive; too superficial to be really powerful. His vocabulary is poor and common-place. He speaks fluently and clearly. He is very ready at taking up points and very skilful in the use which he makes of them. But, we repeat, he is no orator; he is simply a passable speaker.

Nonetheless, the sketch contained elements of truth and Morgan could not hope to escape the frequent criticisms of his poor political knowledge:

> His speech on Welsh Disestablishment was unworthy of the subject. It was too flimsy for the occasion. In a word, it was the speech of an advocate who had not carefully read his brief; who was not quite sure of his facts; who felt, from first to last, that though he had the gallery with him, the jury were inattentive and the judge was dozing.

Williams concluded Morgan could never be a great power in Welsh politics but could be 'a very useful member of parliament', having served his party and Merthyr well. Morgan's temperament was well known as Williams reminded his readers

> He is said to be a man with a grievance. Grievances sit lightly on a man of his temperament. Though his speech is that of the Saxon man of the world, his temperament is essentially that of the lively Celt. If he is quick at taking offence, he is quicker at forgiving the offender. He is too easy-going to be vindictive; too generous to be revengeful; too forgetful to hear malice. The man who can sing comic songs and spin jolly yarns has few, if any, real enemies as a rule. Mr William Pritchard Morgan is not the exception which proves this rule.[29]

Morgan's grievance was to resurface in April 1894 at a Leicester Conference of the Miners' Federation of Great Britain when the royalty question was discussed, as well as the nationalisation of minerals and mines, and a resolution was carried almost unanimously in favour of the nationalisation of both. On 6 April, Samuel Woods (1846–1915), MP for Ince, Lancashire, raised the subject in the House that as far back as 1886 at a Trade Unions Congress meeting held in Hull, an important resolution dealing with this question was raised, and the opinion of the Congress was that the

> royalty rents and other charges demanded by the landlords of this country are iniquitous and injurious. Iniquitous, because they form a monopoly of our mineral resources, where they should be used for the good of all; injurious, because they place a tax upon our staple industries, interfering with, and hindering our commercial prosperity, restricting the profits of the capitalists, and limiting the already too small wages of the workman; and this Congress instructs the Parliamentary Committee to take immediate steps for instituting an inquiry into the character and amount of these royalties and charges with the object of making them national and not individual property. That resolution was carried unanimously by the Trade Unions Congress, representing directly 1,500,000 workers, and indirectly a much larger number.

Robert Burnie (1842–1908), MP for Swansea, drew attention to the fact that 710 people held a quarter of the land of England and Wales, and it was they who were getting rich.

Morgan joined the debate by repeating his request for a mining department that would not only regulate the industry but provide accurate information with regard to mines and minerals. He said it was 'admitted on all sides that ... those engaged in the mining interests scarcely knew what official Departments they had to deal with.' On the one hand, they had to deal with landowners; and on the other, they were concerned with various departments both at the Home Office and the Board of Trade. The mine owner, he said, was at the mercy of the landowner and could not pay good wages because he was handicapped through having to give a portion of his product to the owner of the land. It was clear, therefore, that 'royalties must affect wages.' He quoted a letter sent to him from the manager of a well-known slate quarry who stated that the royalties on slate production worked out about 25%.[30]

As the argument about a Minister of Mines dragged on, Morgan became embroiled in another row which again highlighted his poor political knowledge. He had been with Thomas at Aberdare in December 1893 discussing the Eight Hours Bill, but circumnavigated his ignorance by telling his audience he would vote as they wanted him to vote, that he was their mouthpiece in Parliament. When he did get drawn into talking about the Bill, he quoted 'excellent' sources for his explanation of the sliding scale of charges on coal to produce an average price, but was challenged by David Morgan, the miners' representative as to who these excellent sources were. Morgan dodged the question. When his comments caused further confusion with colliers and employers, Charles E. Parsons, Joint Auditor of the Monmouthshire and South Wales Sliding-Scale Inquiry, felt compelled to write an open letter to the *Western Mail* saying Morgan 'must have either greatly misunderstood a brief conversation he had with me … or else he must be wanting in anything like an intimate knowledge of matters appertaining to the sliding-scale audit.'[31]

Morgan withdrew from all discussion of coal mining until August 1894 when Thomas attempted to add an amendment to the Eight Hours Bill, effectively allowing a district to opt out which, some claimed, would be disadvantageous to those who opted in as they would be working on reduced hours. Morgan, when he rose to speak, said he did not take the same view as Thomas and did not hesitate to say that eight hours' work in a mine was all that could be expected from a man with regard to his health and the safety of those who worked with him. He added his surprise that Thomas had made comments the previous day which had 'somewhat misled the Committee, though not, he was sure, intentionally, by saying that a ballot had been taken in the constituency they represented, and that the men in that locality were, by a large majority, in favour of the application to the Bill of the principle of local option.' Morgan said no such ballot had taken place and the only vote had been in 1891 when Thomas advocated eight hours from bank to bank. An angry Thomas interrupted, demanding to know where he had said that but Kier Hardie, trying to end what the *South Wales Daily Post* called a 'long and wearisome' speech by Morgan, or trying to prevent a fall out between the two men, asked that the question now be voted on but he was overruled.

When Morgan finally finished, Neville Chamberlain (1869–1940) rose saying, 'the Committee will, I think, feel indebted to the hon. Gentleman who has just sat down for breaking the monotony of the Debate' because, apart from Morgan, the 'one exception, every speaker has spoken in favour of the Amendment, while the promoters of the Bill have not ventured to say a single word against it.' Chamberlain pointed out that while he sympathised with Morgan's statement that no man should work more than eight hours at the face, most reports showed that hardly any of the mines had men working more than that; besides, it was not the issue. The larger question was whether the government had the right 'to interfere with the hours of labour of adults in mines' in any district or all districts.[32]

When the vote came, Thomas' amendment had a slim majority of five – 112 to 107 – but rather than include the amendment, the government abandoned the Bill completely and it would not be for another fourteen years, in 1908, that the Liberal government limited the hours a miner could work to eight hours per day.

Chapter 11

Persistent Endeavours

Morgan was now living almost exclusively in London with occasional forays back into North Wales. He had appointed his friend George Hall to manage Gwynfynydd but his other mines were being managed by his daughter, Kate and in 1895, the *Pall Mall Gazette's* extensive series on *Golden Wales* included a short portrait:

> She is a girl fair to look upon, a colonial, bright, common-sensible, wayward, musical, a linguist, altogether talented, and something of a New Woman, yet not. She is linguist enough to attempt the Welsh language... But, as it is, day after day has found her at the mine. She is mastering or rather mistressing the science of assay, and her mining reports to her father are reliable business documents. There is romance in Golden Wales.[1]

The piece was sufficiently novel to be republished in several newspapers under the title of 'a lady miner.' Kate was living at Aber Eden, Ganllwyd, about six miles from Dolgelly, smaller than Bryntirion but still an impressive house which Morgan had bought at the same time. Bryntirion had either been sold or rented because from this time onwards, Morgan was to use the Aber Eden address as his own.

The series of *Pall Mall Gazette* articles included an interview with Morgan ensconced in his London office, glittering with specimens of Welsh gold. Described as the 'father of the modern gold industry in Wales', he was asked if Welsh gold had a future:

> I have never changed my opinion from the time I first visited North Wales in 1884. Since then I have practically devoted not only my time, but most of my money, in an endeavour to put this industry upon a firm footing.

When asked if his relationship with the Crown was still difficult, Morgan said they were not and, for the first time, praised the Woods and Forests Department saying it was 'exceedingly desirous that this industry should be in every way developed. They take an intelligent interest in it.' Morgan confirmed that over the last few years, the Crown had taken 10% of the product in an industry that had enormous administration costs. The administration of the Morgan Mine, he said, was at one time between £8,000 and £9,000 a year. 'The royalties at that time, which previously had been greater, were still 31.3 per cent of the turnover. To-day they are 1 per cent and that is as much as the industry ought to be called upon to carry.'

The journalist, like many people, was confused as to Morgan's standing in the Morgan Mine. 'Ah!' he replied,

> It bears my name. And whenever I have had control of the management the mine has always been conducted at a profit. Except during the first few months of its existence I had nothing whatever to do with the management of the Morgan Gold Mining Company Limited, the company which originally controlled the mine. I was no party to the extravagance and stupidity which wrecked the company, although I have got the credit of it. I protested against it. I left the Board shortly after I was returned to Parliament in 1888. To show you how little was thought of gold-mining in Wales even twelve months since, I had to part with 6–10ths interest in the property as a bonus for taking an assignment of a mortgage to keep me going, and that 6–10ths is today worth £12,000 … The only profit which I made out of the flotation of the mine was in shares, and these, as I say, I gave back to the company in order to ensure the provision of the additional machinery.[2]

At the time the *Pall Mall Gazette* articles appeared, Clogau was doing well as were others, leaving journalists to ask yet again if there was going to be a boom in Welsh gold. According to the *Liverpool Mercury*, 'on reliable authority', the *Pall Mall Gazette* articles, along with Morgan's 'persistent endeavours' had influenced the new Chancellor, Michael Hicks Beach (1837–1916), and the Financial Secretary to the Treasury,

Robert William Hanbury (1845–1903), to give Welsh gold 'their special personal attention.' For years, continued the *Mercury*, Morgan had

> cried aloud against the ruinous effect of heavy Government royalties on the gold-mining industry. Mr Duguid, the financial expert of the *Pall Mall* has backed him up and it appears that there is some real prospect of the impost being considerably lightened. The *Economist* last week pointed out that the mineral statistics for 1894 show that the four Welsh mines from which gold is being obtained yielded 4235 ounces of the metal last year from 6603 tons of ore, the value of the output having been £14,811. Of this quantity the Gwynfynydd Mine (Trawsfynydd) produced 3063 ounces and the Clogau Mine (Bontddu) 956 ounces, the average total output having been about 14 1/3 dwt per ton of ore dealt with. There is reason to believe that the yield for the current year is considerably larger, and if the new mine recently opened by Mr Pritchard Morgan at Moel-y-Groseau between Trawsfynydd and Bala, realises expectations, we are likely to hear of further developments at an early date.[3]

A month after the *Pall Mall Gazette* articles appeared, Sir W. J. Ingram (1847–1924), one of the directors in the Gwynfynydd mine and proprietor of the *Illustrated London News*, published sketches of gold-mining in Wales. One drawing included two women, one of whom may possibly be Kate, watching a man panning gold.

As Kate was busy looking after her father's mining interests, Morgan was once again bumping heads with Thomas over disestablishment. On 23 June 1895, he was in Merthyr asking his constituents what to do.

The meeting, despite being thrown together by Vaughan at the last minute, was well attended and Morgan's entry received an ovation. The rush, he explained, was due to Thomas putting forward a last-minute amendment to the Welsh Disestablishment Bill concerning the allocation of tithes, which the government, and Morgan, thought should be spent locally for the benefit of agriculture and stop people leaving rural areas for better-paid town jobs – but which Thomas thought would result in an unequal share between areas high and low in population, so he proposed that tithes were pooled and shared out on an equal basis. Most opposed his amendment and tried to get him to withdraw it, Lloyd

George asking him to talk to his own constituents and abide by their vote. Thomas refused.

Morgan was, he said, less interested in the details of the amendment and more in how Thomas' lone stand was proving divisive (somewhat hypocritical as Morgan had stood almost alone against Thomas' amendment to the Eight Hours Bill). He claimed that fifty men had surrounded him in the lobby telling him, 'You, Pritchard Morgan ought to be ashamed of yourself if you don't go down to your constituents and tell them that the opinion of Merthyr is no longer heard in the House of Commons. Whilst you are loyal to your party, your colleague is the only Liberal voting on the other side to wreck this bill.'

It had nothing to do with old adversities, Morgan told his audience, but he owed his loyalty to the Welsh party in the House and that despite occasionally disagreeing with them, in matters when the majority prevailed, he voted with them.

He had tried, he reassured his audience, to contact Thomas so they could appear together but had failed to find him. Later, he discovered Thomas was at the Welsh National Conference in Llandrindod so telegraphed him saying, 'Hoped to have seen you in House yesterday. Meeting in Merthyr to-night, 7.30, to discuss with electors our voting different lobbies, and what is to be done Monday. Hope you can be there.'

A furious Thomas replied, 'Of course I cannot attend meeting. Surprised you did not mention your intention before. Don't think Merthyr electors should be asked to decide until they have heard both sides.' When Morgan read out the telegram, as requested to do so by Thomas, there were shouts of 'hear, hear.'

Notwithstanding Thomas' plea that voters should hear both sides, Morgan's excuse was that the Bill had been through the committee stages and, at such a late stage, it would be impossible to amend.[4] The truth, however, was that Thomas' stand was interfering with wider political intrigues.

If the Bill passed through the Lords, then disestablishment was achieved and the spending of the tithes could be sorted out at a later date. If the Lords rejected the Bill, as was strongly predicted, it gave Welsh MPs a reason to go back to the country in the forthcoming general election, saying the Commons, the House of the people, had passed the Bill but the mainly Anglican 'House of privilege' had denied them. This could be used as a rallying cry for the Liberal cause to send them back with an even greater majority. If Thomas succeeded in delaying the Bill, neither scenario was possible before the general election.

Morgan was seen as muddying the waters and his behaviour at Merthyr was condemned by many; even the *Western Mail*, usually so supportive of him, was not impressed and drew attention to his hypocrisy in now being a team player, whereas before he had fought his own way.[5]

On the correspondence page, Shir Gar wrote, 'if you searched all the annals of political history, you could not discover a meaner or a more despicable act than that perpetrated by William Pritchard Morgan at Merthyr.' Adding that Thomas' amendment had been before the House since Tuesday but Morgan had left it to Saturday to come to Merthyr, Shir Gar accused Morgan of wanting the field to himself. Morgan gave the impression that Thomas had done nothing to consult his constituents, but he had done so and Morgan had not been there. Also, if Morgan had not known about the Welsh National Conference, then his understanding of Welsh politics was very poor – and why was he not there?

The most likely reason why Morgan went to Merthyr was to be told how to vote. He did not have a detailed grasp of disestablishment and his name rarely appears in debates in the House. Despite proudly claiming that Gladstone finally came out for disestablishment following his speech, Morgan had been criticised by both Gladstone and the press over his lack of knowledge. After the Merthyr appearance, he suddenly went silent on the matter, garnering more criticism, but he replied that it was his duty to be silent – presumably because he was following the party line. This, wrote Shir Gar, was hypocritical because the colliers had told him to vote with Thomas on the eight-hour bill and he had not done so.

Generally, Morgan's behaviour was condemned as ungentlemanly and prophesies were made that it would cost him in the next election. It also caused the press to scrutinise Morgan's attendance record at the House.

The *Merthyr Times* found Ellis had the highest record, attending all 118 sessions; Mabon, 51; Kenyon, 26; Lloyd George, 77; Randell, 81; D.A. Thomas, 79; and Morgan on a meagre 23. It was, they wrote, 'exceedingly unsatisfactory' and while they acknowledged he had not been very well, which accounted for his absence to some extent, it was still a poor showing. They went to ask Vaughan about his client's record. 'I must frankly admit that Mr Morgan's record is very unsatisfactory,' replied Vaughan, 'There is no getting out of that. Several people have complained to me about it, and I have no defence to offer.' Had he been in the constituency, the journalist asked?

'No, he had not,' said Vaughan,

> and that is another source of dissatisfaction. Some months ago, I think it was November, he addressed meetings at Merthyr and Aberdare. But he had not visited Dowlais, Mountain Ash, or Hirwain since March, 1894. That is a very lengthy period for a member to absent himself from important centres of his constituency. As regards local questions, Mr Morgan is always ready to render assistance; but his knowledge of the locality is not as extensive as that of his colleague, and he is not able, therefore, to be as generally useful as Mr Thomas. What he can do he is always most willing to undertake.

When asked about the future Vaughan replied,

> That's just what I want to know, and what I have been trying to get at for some time. People are continually asking me, 'Is Mr Morgan going to stand again, or is he not?' And I can give them no definite answer. All I know is this: three months ago Mr Morgan told me emphatically that he intended to take the field against all comers. Since then various rumours have been flying about, and I have asked Mr Morgan for information concerning them. For some reason or other, I have failed to get any reply to my letters, and consequently I am not able to answer your question. But I am writing to Mr Morgan again to-day, and I will let you know the result, if any.

Asked about the possibility of re-election, Vaughan thought it highly likely, as 'his popularity has not declined to any appreciable degree, and he is a splendid fighter.'[6] A week later, a statement from Morgan confirmed he would be standing.

Despite Vaughan's confidence, there was a growing disquiet, particularly in the correspondence page of the *Merthyr Times*. 'A Radical' noted that Morgan's attendance record was 'a painful eye-opener to the hundreds of erstwhile supporters' and that his majority would be greatly reduced, if he won at all. Morgan's election, 'A Radical' ended, 'spells ruin.'

'A Member of the Conservative Club' wrote, 'As a Conservative I look forward with a good deal of confidence at the coming election, for though we may not succeed in ousting Mr D. A. Thomas ... Morgan will be brought to his proper level.' 'A Penydarren Elector' wrote that he had voted for Morgan at every election

> On the first occasion, it was clear to all that his knowledge of English politics was not very extensive still I thought he had in him the making of a useful member ... and, being disgusted at the tactics of the effete and cliquish Liberal Association, I gave him my support. But now the question forces itself on us. Has Mr Morgan realised the expectations of his friends? Is he to-day what we hoped he would become?

The writer pointed out that Morgan's Parliamentary record amounted to one day a week and he showed no remorse. For his own part he would never vote for Morgan again and thought him 'played out.'[7]

Morgan's speech against Thomas had, wrote the *Merthyr Times*, 'done incalculable mischief, and we question if its bad effects will not be felt by the party of progress even after the contest is over'[8] because some were predicting that the behaviour of Thomas and Morgan would see neither re-elected.

The *Western Mail* was moving away from Morgan and saw the future as Thomas and Allen Upward (1863–1926), the eccentric writer and lawyer who had also decided to stand for the general election. Herbert Lewis, the son of Sir William, whom Thomas was accused of supporting in the 1888 general election, was standing too. However, most still saw the struggle as between the man of coal and the man of gold.

Thomas then appeared in Merthyr on 8 July giving what the *Merthyr Times* described as a 'brilliant speech'. He refused to criticise Morgan but did take exception to his claim that for seven years there had been great difficulty getting Thomas on the same platform as Morgan. A month before, he had been urging his Liberal colleagues to support Morgan but now, he would leave them to make their own choice. He said it would savour of dictation and presumption on his part if he told them who to vote for, ignoring the fact that is exactly what he had done at the last election.

Despite the disestablishment row, Thomas' appearances and the support from the press saw his popularity rise enormously. Upward was also gaining in popularity. In comparison, Morgan, accompanied on his election rounds by Kate, was finding it difficult to defend his actions. At a 'cool' meeting on 4 July with barely 150 people attending, he attempted to justify his House attendance saying he was never absent without pairing (if an MP is absent, they pair with an absent government MP) and had always turned out for important Liberal matters.

He read out a letter from Vaughan to Thomas's agent in which Morgan offered to run side by side but he was rejected. Was this the cause of Morgan's attack on Thomas? Their joining of forces at the previous election had been very successful and Morgan cannot have been ignorant of the growing criticism of him. Perhaps he thought tying his candidature to Thomas would better his chances. At the meeting, he claimed he had tried to bury the hatchet several times and it was Thomas' fault the difference existed between them. The audience was not impressed and when a vote was put forward to support Morgan, only a few hands went up with most remaining non-committal.[9]

He tried again on 8 July at Aberdare but a member of the audience reported to the *Merthyr Times* that Morgan had insinuated that Thomas was supporting the Conservative candidate, Lewis. The comments were seen as jealousy of Thomas' growing popularity and groundless too, as Thomas in all his meetings advocated voting for a Liberal. 'Nothing,' wrote the *Merthyr Times*, 'could be fairer than the way in which Mr Thomas treats Mr Morgan. There are not many men who would do this after the attack which Mr Morgan made upon him.'[10]

The negative press attention was apparently playing on Morgan's mind and it was said he was despondent about his chances for re-election. The press speculated on his possible retirement and whether Upward could win. Upward had stood at the previous election but retired in order not to split the vote and it was said that Morgan should now return the favour.

One of the main criticisms that dogged Morgan was his lack of time spent in the constituency, something he had warned voters would happen if they had chosen Ffoulkes Griffiths, and various letters appeared in the local press asking Morgan to step down – he ignored them.

When he came to release his manifesto, he began by bragging that his motion in the House on disestablishment had resulted in Gladstone declaring his support for the first time and, despite all the fuss, he declared himself in favour of Thomas' amendment that tithes should be distributed locally. The rest repeated mainstream Liberal matters, which did not impress many, and the *Western Mail* thought 'the only person among the supporters of the Gold King who seems to have grasped the real situation is Miss Morgan herself.' Like Thomas, Kate urged voters to give their second vote to whom they wanted to.[11]

Two days later, Morgan and Kate arrived at Mountain Ash where he, surprisingly, received a huge welcome, the equivalent of any other candidate in the area. The room was crowded to 'suffocation' and he struggled to start his speech due to the roars of approval.

The following day, he and Kate went to meet the colliers' train. Morgan read out an article from the *Merthyr Times* saying he had gone to London to get pressure put on Upward to resign, but he had not been to London. He criticised the paper for referring to Upward as a Welshman when he came from Worcester and claimed he had come into the race to split the Liberal vote. He also denied insinuating that Thomas had recommended voting for Lewis, and that the press coverage of his poorly attended meetings was invented as were the claims he was in a despondent mood and thinking of retiring. Nothing was further from the truth, he said.[12]

Voting was due to take place between 31 July and 7 August, but it was a low-key affair with none of the drama of previous years. Against all odds, Morgan won but majorities were slashed. Thomas fell from 11,948 to 9,250 – a drop of 2,698, and Morgan from 11,755 to 8,554 – a drop of 3,201. These were the largest reduced majorities in the whole of the UK. Lewis had driven the 1892 Tory total up from 2,304 to 6,525. Upward, who was never really a serious contender, was abandoned wholesale with only 659 votes. The change in Morgan's fortunes, argued the *Merthyr Express*, came about because there was a panic that the Liberal seat was in danger and it was safer to return Morgan.[13]

However, it was the Tories who were returned to government and as the Liberals lost ninety-four seats overall, it was Merthyr's adherence to the Liberal cause that saved both Thomas and Morgan.

After the announcement of the results, the two men shook hands and drove to Dowlais together in Morgan's carriage. Kate, joined by her sister

Gwendoline, said her father was hoping to take a house in the area so they could be closer to their constituents.[14]

If the election had taught the local Liberals anything, it was that they needed to be better prepared and to do so they needed (another) new local Liberal organisation. Morgan attributed Lewis' achievement to his personal popularity and blamed the lack of cohesion between himself and Thomas for their losses. He advised everyone to join the new organisation and prepare themselves for the next election.[15] However, the Conservatives were to remain in power for the next ten years and Welsh interests suffered accordingly.

In November 1895, something happened which may explain Morgan's lack of attendance at the House – he went to Australia. Obviously, it was something he had been planning for quite a while as the *Western Mail* hinted at in October 1895

> Here is Mr Morgan, a dapper little man, in the prime of life, and apparently as 'hard as nails' just starting. The butt-end of a pistol, brought up to town to be cleaned, was seen protruding from his inner breast-pocket the other day, prognosticating the mining expedition on which he was about to engage, while his sleeve-links, of polished Welsh gold quartz, seemed to symbolise his connection with the Principality of 'gallant little Wales'. A mass of varied interests is Mr Morgan, for when not discussing the royalties on his Welsh gold mines he is advocating Welsh Disestablishment or moving the second readings of Local Veto Bills.[16]

The same month he was supposed to be in Merthyr answering constituents' questions on the Eight Hours Bill, but he called this off due to ill health. He wrote to Thomas saying he would vote with whatever was decided, as long as there was a majority.[17]

The following month, taking Kate, George Hall, and a select group of Welsh miners, he left for the southern hemisphere. Morgan was going to do some prospecting during the Parliamentary recess and his name became associated with a mine which, in 2004, was valued at 120 million Australian dollars.

It started when Thomas Tobias, originally from Aberdare, and who had voted for Morgan in the 1888 election, moved to Australia. He became a Coolgardie storekeeper and, along with A. Glendinning, Jack Carlson and Frank White, discovered a rich mine. They named it Sons of Gwalia after an ancient name for Wales, in honour of Tobias, the syndicate founder.

In one version of the story, Tobias met Morgan and asked him to visit their recent discovery. A different version appeared in 1931 in the *Western Argus* that incorrectly described Morgan's visit as a health tour and that he had not been interested in visiting the mine except that Kate 'so interested herself in the fortunes of her countryman, the Welsh prospector, that she communicated some of her enthusiasm to her father.'[18]

However, it had been Hall who had heard about the mine and purchased it with his own money, but on behalf of the London and Westralian company in which Morgan was the major shareholder.[19] Hall remained to manage the mine and within eight months, he and an ex-Gwynfynydd manager, Alexander Castle, produced 11,000 ounces of gold, today worth about £3 million. The mine soon attracted the attention of big investors but Morgan, like many 'promoters' of the time, would exploit a property, 'boom' it in the press for attention then sell at a high profit. So the mine was sold to Bewick, Moreing and Company in 1897, against George Hall's advice[20] (although both Morgan and Hall retained one-third of the mine). The man who has been incorrectly credited for purchasing the mine on behalf of the firm was 23-year-old Herbert Hoover, later the 31st President of the United States.

Morgan and Kate remained in Australia for three months doing some 'hard travelling' and he could not wait to get back to sea again. The trip out had made him feel ten years younger but all the rushing around had exhausted him. While in Adelaide, he had been in talks with the South Australian government about mining rights, which were initially declined, but after further negotiations they came to an agreement where Morgan was granted mining rights on 10,000 square miles of land (Wales is 8,023 square miles) at 5% royalties on profit, not product.[21]

5,000 square miles of that land was in Kate's name.[22] She seems to have earned it because when the *Pall Mall Gazette* later asked Morgan if he had been to view the Londonderry reef, he replied no, but Kate had gone. Indeed, *The Advertiser* wrote of her, 'the eldest daughter of Mr Morgan, who takes an active part in the management of her father's gold mines in North Wales, has accompanied him right through his travels, has camped out in the far West, and has seen everything in the Australian mining world worth a visit.'[23]

Morgan and Kate returned to the UK on 17 March 1896 and a lavish London dinner was thrown in his honour. He said

> I have made fortunes and I have lost them, and I have made them again and I hope will lose them again. I do not know whether there is anything more pleasurable in this world than losing money except it be making it. Making money is exceedingly pleasant; but spending it, to my mind, is equally pleasant, provided you do it in a way which does no harm to anybody and does good to a great many people. Nothing delights me so much as to get into a district where labour is plentiful and work scarce and to leave it when work is plentiful and labour scarce.[24]

No sooner had he returned than he was off to America. The Merthyr press was not happy. But by May 1896, he was back and in the House for a change, once again chasing the Chancellor for answers on Crown Lands in Wales and comparing them unfavourably with his recent experiences in Australia, but he got no further than he usually did.

In July, Welsh gold was back in the news. Princess Maud of Wales (1869–1938), the youngest daughter of Edward, Prince of Wales (later King Edward VII), was preparing to marry Prince Carl of Denmark on 22 July 1896. To commemorate the occasion, Sir John Puleston (1830–1908), a Welsh journalist and Tory MP, suggested the National Eisteddfod Association should present a Welsh gold wedding ring for Princess Maud, particularly as she had been admitted into the Gorsedd two years previously. The offer was accepted and gold from the Trawsfynydd Mines was sent to Percy Edwards and Co., Piccadilly to be manufactured. The Princess selected the pattern of the ring herself; it was narrow and smaller than that made for Princess May. The *Penrith Observer* noted, 'Welsh gold, by the way, is very pale in tint, needing an admixture of other gold to give it the orthodox golden yellow colour. Indeed this has had to be done with the wedding ring … it will be before the Princess's eyes perhaps more than any of the expensive gifts that will be showered on her, being but a ring after all it cannot have cost more than a few humble pounds.'[25]

Morgan presented the royal couple with his own gift. While in Australia, he bought a pair of Spathopterus Alexandrae or 'Prince of Wales's parakeet', a rare bird of the interior and they were the first of their kind to be brought to the UK.[26]

For the first time, the press was beginning to notice a pattern, with comments like, 'It is becoming an established custom for English princesses to be married with rings of Welsh gold'[27] and the *Penrith Observer* noting it was 'a custom inaugurated at the marriage of the Duke of York.' While the public undoubtedly followed suit, they rarely made the press with the exception of Frances Dorothy Maurie Evans who married Harold Frederick, a carpenter, in September 1897 and her ring, it was noted, was of Welsh gold.[28] When MP Tom Ellis married in May 1898, Morgan gave a ring of Gwynfynydd gold with the names of Tom and Nancy engraved on it.[29] At Dolgelly, two prominent people, Dr John Jones and Miss Millard, were married and she had a 'massive' wedding ring made from Clogau gold.[30] The ring worn by Lady Marjory Brudenell Bruce, daughter of the Marquis of Ailesbury, was made from a nugget of gold from Morgan's Gwynfynydd.[31]

Following this, little was heard of Morgan – until he made a highly controversial move. In October, the (ever predictable) reports that he was retiring resurfaced and when a *Cardiff Times* journalist called into his London office, Morgan became indignant and in 'forcible language' complained of having to constantly contradict 'these absurd rumours', snapping at the journalist that he declined to 'discuss any such matter in the Press.'[32]

Meanwhile, Vaughan was arranging a public meeting at Merthyr for Morgan to confer with his constituents and it was felt that something was definitely going on. Something was: Morgan was going to offer his seat to Gladstone.

Letters in Glamorgan Archives show that Morgan had written to Vaughan on 9 October

> An idea struck me that it would be a good thing if I were to hold a meeting at once and announce my willingness to resign my seat so as to enable Mr Gladstone if he should desire to do so to enter the House of Commons with the greatest majority that has ever been for the most radical constituency in the kingdom and without physical

> exertion on his part to contest a seat because it goes without saying that if he was opposed there would be a majority which would astonish the world. I am serious in this because I think the people of Merthyr should have the honour of sending to the House of Commons if he should desire to go the greatest of all living statesmen.... send me a telegram and you can announce a meeting for Monday or Tuesday night <u>not</u> stating what I am to do of course.³³

He then suggested that if the meeting was in agreement, he would hand in his resignation that night on the proviso that Gladstone accepted, and that 'at some future time I may have the seat back again.'

In another letter, dated 12 October, Morgan adds that various publications were discussing Gladstone's return 'you can see,' wrote Morgan to Vaughan,

> I have only been a few days ahead of the public opinion which is now ripening. I am hourly more than ever impressed with the necessity of taking this course because in any event Gladstone will deem it a great honour to have the seat offered to him and if he accepts it Merthyr ought to consider herself honoured by being represented by Mr Gladstone. Edmonds [Alfred Edmonds] agrees with me that the feeling in the clubs and in London is growing daily in favour of Gladstone's return as the only possible means to reunite the Liberal party.³⁴

With the Conservatives firmly ensconced in government, the Liberals were seen as being at a deadlock and Morgan believed Gladstone's resumption of the leadership might give the party the boost it needed.

The press was mixed; while many like the *Leeds Mercury* admired his action as 'one which deserves all praise',³⁵ others were sceptical of his 'quixotic' offer. It was generally known that the Grand Old Man had no desire to return to politics and Morgan seemed woefully out of touch on this.

The *Liverpool Mercury* was doubtful of Morgan's intentions to ask his constituents, as 'to consult a constituency generally means to proclaim a decision already formed' and called his offer a 'mistaken but well-meaning magnanimity', urging the Liberals to dismiss from their minds that Gladstone would ever come back: 'To cherish such a delusion serves only to aggravate the state of tension and unrest.'[36]

The *Aberdeen Weekly Journal* also drew attention to 'the desperate straits to which the Liberal party had come. The plan is too foolish – and, we may add, too cruel – to be practically carried out. To drag Mr Gladstone out of his retirement, and to expect him at his great age to lead a party broken up into so many sections, would be positive injury to the veteran statesman.'[37] Elsewhere, it was referred to as another election dodge, as a self-aggrandised advertisement, or simply a joke.

On 21 October, Morgan held two meetings at Merthyr, one organised by the new Liberal Association (Thomas had an 'unavoidable absence'). He had not come with a resignation letter in his pocket, Morgan told his audience, but to ask his constituents their advice.

Like many, Morgan believed difficulties in the Liberal Party were due to the unpopularity of Archibald Primrose, 5th Earl of Rosebery (1847–1929), who had succeeded Gladstone in 1894 as Prime Minister but now led the party in opposition from the House of Lords.

Mabon, also present, refused to comment on Morgan's idea as he was elected by the Rhondda and had no right to tell Merthyr people how to vote. But both he and Morgan felt the Liberal leadership should not come from the House of Lords, particularly as Morgan was campaigning for an end to the upper House.

The audience received Morgan's suggestion without great enthusiasm. Although the resolution in favour of the Liberal Party Leader having to be in the House of Commons was passed, the meeting overall, wrote the *Merthyr Times,* was a fiasco.[38]

Gladstone had replied to Morgan's offer but he sent it to the Liberal Association who refused to make the contents public. Two years later, in November 1898, the letter was leaked to the press. Written on 5 November 1896 from Plas Mawr, Penmaenmawr, Gladstone's Welsh home, the Grand Old Man thanked Morgan for his offer but refused it. 'The conclusive reasons against my accepting it are not one only,' he wrote,

> they are many. It is by quiet and constant care that my general health is maintained at a high level, and no variation can be made. The condition of my sight and hearing is quite incompatible with the proper discharge of Parliamentary duties... I must ... sit in

an assembly of the proceedings of which I should most largely disapprove, perhaps even more largely disapprove, perhaps even more largely than you would expect ... All this does not abate the thanks which I now repeat, remaining always very faithfully yours, W.E. Gladstone.'[39]

Morgan was left with his seat, but why had he wanted to lend it out temporarily? He had scorned Deane in 1879 for giving up his to Macrossan and here he was doing the same thing. The most telling part of his 9 October letter to Vaughan is the footnote, 'It is quite on the cards that I may be leaving England in about a fortnight for China on very important business, but as to this I do not wish anything made public as I may not go.'

He did go. On 21 November 1896, Morgan was on board ship heading to China via Vancouver. He was travelling with Li Hongzhang (Anglicised as Li Hung Chang) (1823–1901), the Chinese Minister for Foreign Affairs[40] and was to be away for three months. The *Cambrian* went to interview George Hall who informed them that Morgan had first met Li on board ship when travelling to New York.[41]

Some newspapers thought he was going on a health trip to cure a severe bronchial attack but in reality, he was, like his trip to Australia, laden down with syndicate money to explore mining opportunities. There was seven in his party, including Kate and her maid; Alfred C. Edmunds of the *Merthyr Express*, who acted as Morgan's secretary; and various mining engineers.

As soon as the news broke in South Wales, there was an outcry, with accusations that Morgan's constituents were being disenfranchised by his continued absences and that he was putting his commercial interests above those he was representing. The *Merthyr Times* made the connection between his trip and the offer to resign his seat for Gladstone[42] and sniped that it was impossible to know the true purpose of his trip because he had not taken advice from his Merthyr electors.

By May 1897, Vaughan was receiving telegraphs that Morgan was on his way home and was expected to arrive in the second week of June – he had been away for seven months.

As soon as he was back in London, the *Cardiff Times* sent someone to interview him and he waxed lyrical about his trip, describing the journeys undertaken and how Kate had 'stood the fatigues of the journey very well.' He did not think his seven-month absence had affected his constituency. 'I do not think I have during that time missed any important matters in Parliament. My constituency has not suffered much politically, and I trust it will eventually be found not to have suffered in its material interests by my travels. At all events, I have never lost sight of the fact that I represent a constituency which is a large producer of steel rails.'[43] He had, he said, been promoting Cyfartha steel for the new railroads in China but there is no evidence anything ever came of this.

Chapter 12

The Red Dragon and the Red Flag

Now back in the UK, Morgan seemed more interested in justifying his absences than dealing with Welsh issues. He was a true Imperialist, he explained at a meeting in Merthyr in March 1899, 'it made one proud to feel that one belonged to a country which, commencing with such a limited area, had extended itself now to such an extent that it had become necessary to prepare new maps of the world.' He warned his audience that the 'world was now being carved up afresh, and unless we went with our plates and asked to be served with a proportion of it we should find that the day of hunger would come by-and-by, and that, although for the moment we might feel satisfied with our stomachs full, other countries would have laid up in their larders the wherewithal for to-morrow and the days to follow.'[1]

Morgan had the patronising attitude, common at the time, that the British should 'take care' of less industrialised countries and saw opportunities for 'hundreds and thousands of our children and children's children to go to that country and teach those people the arts and sciences of Western civilization.' He told his audience that the UK 'should take of the necessity of forming a great Imperial Parliament, so that all our possessions abroad might be represented, and the House of Commons might have before them all the requirements and necessities of the other parts of this great Empire.' As well as this 'proto-Commonwealth', he also advocated universal trade and a universal coinage on the decimal system – something similar to the Euro of today.[2]

Being fond of 'roving', he said, it had occurred to him two years previously that someone from the UK should go to China and 'secure something for this country' – which was not in keeping with his other statements that he had been invited to go. Finishing, he assured his constituents that he had been promoting British and local Welsh products in China.

Morgan's return to the House was also dominated by his China interests and he had an added role as 'power of attorney' for China in reference to loans. He tried to raise £9 million to fund the Peking-Hangkor railway and a £16 million-pound loan to increase trade and pay war reparations to Japan, in what *Reuters* described as a deal 'touted around on the Continent'. As no other country wanted to get involved, Morgan asked Prime Minister, Salisbury, who refused.³

What did catapult the UK into supplying the loan was that Germany had secured a 99-year lease to Qingdao, the main port open to Europeans. China was regarded as a great potential customer of the world and the UK was not happy with this new arrangement so, in order to protect British interests, the government agreed to the loan but China, not wishing to offend the Russians, pulled out.

China's relationships with the Powers (mainly powerful European countries and America) at this time was complex and, for two years, those countries had been debating how to access and explore trade opportunities. When Italy wanted to secure a naval base, China refused, fearing a growing foreign presence on its soil, but it sparked an international outcry – other countries had been granted access, so why not Italy?

Morgan disapproved of the UK's support for Italy, stating in the House, 'I have for a period of three years taken an interest in the development of this great empire' and complained if Italy was allowed a foothold, then other countries would want the same

> And where is this partitioning of this great Empire to stop? ... if we have all the Powers of Europe occupying various parts of China, and we become, as it were, next-door neighbours, irritation must necessarily be created, jealousies must necessarily exist, with the one and only result that the occupying Powers will ultimately be at war with regard to this broken-up China. I submit that it is the duty of this House to ... see that we do not allow any further Power to acquire any interest in China.

St John Brodrick (1856–1942), the Under Secretary of State for Foreign Affairs, was shocked, complaining

> He [Morgan] is never tired of urging publicly and privately that the British Government should assume as much authority as possible in China, and should create spheres of interest or influence over the

provinces in which he himself takes an interest. But now he demands from us not only that we shall safeguard our interests, but that we shall take care that no other Power safeguards hers.[4]

Such pressure was brought to bear by the Italian and British governments that China relented, but some believed an Italian-British syndicate was being formed to work the minerals, hence the British not interfering with Italy's claims.[5]

By early April 1898, Morgan was on his way back to China to negotiate mining rights in Szechuan. In November, he signed a preliminary contract, alongside local companies, which had to be included according to Chinese rules to prevent accusations of monopoly. They were to explore what was reported to be the richest mineral-bearing and industrial province in China[6] and was supposedly one of the earliest mineral enterprises there.

The Foreign Affairs Minister, Li, congratulated Morgan on his 'well-deserved success in obtaining the concessions.' Adding, 'my long personal acquaintance with you justifies my belief that you will rise to the occasion and leave nothing undone to make a great success in Sze Chuan, benefitting alike the Government, the people, and the investors,' and signed himself 'your friend.'[7]

Russia, France and Germany were also manoeuvring to gain deals but unrest was growing – some foreign powers had brought in troops and China was asking for them to be removed.

Back in Merthyr, the news of Morgan's work in China was received with some scepticism, despite him being lauded in the world's papers. 'With such glory won as this,' wrote the *Western Mail*

> the people of Merthyr must now proceed to erect his statue to grace their sombre-looking town, and let it be composed of those minerals which Mr Morgan has found in China … the Radicals at Merthyr may well look out for a new candidate for the next general election, because there is sure to be an earldom, or at least, a barony, in store for the Chinese concessionaire.[8]

Elsewhere in the same issue, they wrote Pit Chang Moh Gang, Morgan's Chinese name, was 'gradually acquiring the earth. Some time ago he leased a portion of Australia, as large as Glamorganshire and a bit of Monmouthshire, and now he seems to have got a grip on an entire province in China.' He was not a bad sort of fellow, the *Western Mail* wrote, 'but a very indifferent member. The fact is, so far as his representation is concerned, the seat might as well have been vacant since the last general election.'⁹ The *Cambrian News* also complained, 'Sze Chuan is reputed to be the richest mineral-bearing and industrial province in China. Of course. We remember the time when it was said that there was gold enough in Merionethshire to pay off the national debt. Well, the national debt is not paid off and Mr Pritchard Morgan is not in Merionethshire.'¹⁰ One journalist at the *Western Mail* congratulated Morgan as it 'represents the first combination of Chinese and foreign capital for a common object, and is at the same time of such industrial and national value and importance.'¹¹

The *Mining Journal* was, however, generally supportive and pleased to hear of his success, adding,

> this contract will probably form a precedent in connection with mining enterprise in other provinces … we think there are many energetic men in this country capable of following the example set by Mr Morgan, and of bringing home some valuable concessions for the benefit of the capitalist and investor. We feel quite assured that in the near future a vast deal of money will flow from this country into China, not for railways and industrial enterprises alone, but for the opening up of its inexhaustible mineral resources.'¹²

In February 1899, after being away for eleven months, Morgan returned. Some doubts were expressed about anyone recognising him, but he boasted to the press that, in 1896, the Chinese government telegraphed him to advise them on the opening of mineral resources. 'My first recommendation,' he said,

> that no concessions at all should be granted. I have persistently advocated the creation of an Imperial Mining Department at Pekin, such as exists in Australia and America, to control the mines of the whole empire, and I urged that provincial Departments of Mines should be organised under the direct control of the central authorities with the special object of securing uniformity of mining laws.¹³

Morgan was appointed Mining and Administrative Adviser of the government. In a way, he had got his Minister of Mines, just in a different country.

Morgan claims that he had opened Szechuan to the world 'through his own personal mission' was seen as an exaggeration. China had numerous ongoing negotiations, but most were in secret. The reason he could openly discuss matters was because he was not, at the time, a government representative. Despite the concession being covered by all the major international papers, it was considered just another Chinese contract but as always with Morgan, he had to spin it as the biggest and the best.

He was proud of his achievement and declared that in his China mission, he had 'discovered his life-work',[14] something that did not sit well in Wales. The *Times* was scathing, pointing out that Morgan's appointment was only that of an administrator and deplored his Imperialistic portrayal of the inhabitants as backwards, given the general opinion of Szechuan was that it was one of 'the richest, most prosperous, and most peaceful of the provinces of China, the inhabitants being, it is said, highly intelligent, and, from a Chinese point of view, in the van of progress.'[15]

The *Western Mail* sprung to his defence pointing out that he had been asked to go by Li who was 'singularly impressed with his abilities' and that

> his friends claim for him the credit of being the pioneer of Chinese development. Certain it is that at a time when the opening up of China was but a bare possibility he went out there, and, with all the stubbornness of his race, fought for British interests against all comers. Since that time he has pursued his objects with unflinching courage. He has not hesitated to spend his money lavishly and live among the people to carry his plans into effect. The Chinese now regard him, not as a bird of passage, but as one who is interested in the better government of their country and anxious to promote its welfare … until recently the Chinese were not allowed to become partners in business with foreigners, but owing to Mr Morgan's efforts this edict has now been withdrawn, and one of the barriers which existed against trade development has, therefore, been removed.[16]

Of course, all the news of his appointment meant speculation about where he was going to live, and whether he would resign his seat. Morgan said his Chinese post only required him to visit occasionally and that would be during Parliamentary recess.[17] However, few could understand how he could administer the mineral workings of an area the size of Britain and France combined and still continue with ministerial duties.

The *Western Mail* wrote that Morgan had 'probably, a greater knowledge of China and of its government than any member,' adding, 'he is also an attractive personality and a man of singular courage and versatility. Add to this that he is a man without either fads or crotchets and has never yet attempted to bore the House, and we find good reason for his general popularity and assured position.'[18]

Other journalists took the opportunity to describe Morgan and his boundless energy. 'A.K.' in *The Echo*, wrote that Morgan, 'dresses with tasteful tact, and carries a certain femininity to the extreme of wearing a single gold cable-bracelet.' Others had also commented on this 'huge' bracelet he always wore. 'Perhaps if a curious acquaintance inquired about the history of that bracelet,' continued A.K, 'he might learn that it began somewhere in the depths of the Welsh mountains and came of gold which the hon. gentleman dug for and found there.' He noted Morgan's 'deep faith in the gold deposits of Wales, that it only needed the Principality to be called Coolgardie to have the world go mad about it. Wales was simply in the wrong place,' before concluding, 'we all confess to a fondness for this dapper, easy-going gentleman, and his constituents share the prevalent interest in their Member. They are all delighted when he visits them, and good naturedly don't worry about him when he does not.'[19]

This was perhaps a shade too forgiving as Morgan's popularity in Merthyr was waning, particularly as, in September 1899, he was summoned to visit China again. Morgan had received a telegram from the Empress of China, Dowager Cixi (1835–1908), requesting he return at once to begin mining in Szechuan as, according to the rules, he should have started work within six months and he had failed to do so. Morgan replied that he was leaving Genoa on the 19th and expected to reach Pekin (Beijing) at the end of October.[20] This time, Harriet and Gwendoline accompanied him. As was to be expected, this obedience raised eyebrows and it was felt he was once again deserting his constituents.

Not content with China, Morgan hopped over to Korea, obtaining a concession of about 260 square miles to work all minerals for seventy-five years for the Pritchard Morgan Syndicate. On net profits, they were to pay 25% to the Korean government – Morgan had learned from his UK fight over royalties and in all his foreign dealings, he insisted on net royalties.

However, nothing Morgan did was ever easy. A British man called Chance was working Morgan's spot, the 'Pearl of Korea' mine. Infuriated, Morgan telegraphed Prime Minister Salisbury, who advised him to insist on his rights, and Chance backed down but the Korean government refused to surrender the mine. Not to be daunted, Morgan sent in his staff with 150 armed Japanese, a force he had gathered in Seoul with the assistance of the Japanese Consul, and took possession. This concerned the Koreans as Morgan essentially had a small army on their soil.

John Jordan (1852–1925), the British Chargé d'affaires in Korea, met with the Emperor but used such 'violent and threatening language' for two hours that the Emperor was made quite ill, but still refused to grant the mine.

Eventually, William Franklin Sands (1874–1946), American Adviser to the Household Department of Korea, became involved and secured a cash payment in settlement, but suddenly the matter was taken out of his hands. Morgan, apparently with the aid of heavy bribes, was granted his mine on the condition he removed his Japanese force, on the promise of protection from the Koreans.[21]

Morgan promptly renamed the mine, regarded as one of the richest in Korea,[22] the 'Gwendoline', presumably after his daughter, but a few years later, as he was apt to do, he sold his interests. However, before then, in return for his 'investments', the Emperor appointed Morgan the London Consul General for Korea.[23]

The Aberdare Liberal Club, concerned about the appointment, wrote to Morgan asking if this necessitated his resignation from Parliament. He replied,

> When the Emperor of Corea [sic] expressed his strong desire that I should act as his Consul-General in England I agreed to act in that capacity, and, of course, in an honorary and unpaid manner. Before accepting the appointment I telegraphed to Lord Salisbury, who consented to my accepting the post. It does not in any way affect my seat in Parliament.[24]

However, he now had to fight for his seat in Parliament in the 1900 general election – in a country divided over the Second Boer War (1899–1903). The British Empire and two independent Boer states were fighting, broadly speaking, over Britain's influence in South Africa, as well as the discovery of diamonds and gold, and who was entitled to them.

Thomas was anti-war while the Imperialist Morgan supported the government and went so far as to accuse Thomas of being disloyal for his opposition, stinging Thomas into replying in the *Western Mail* on 9 June in an article entitled *Members for Merthyr Squabbling*. Thomas wrote of his regret that the discharge of his duties had not met with the approval of the junior member and that he had not consulted him upon 'questions of urgency' that arose in Parliament during Morgan's 'prolonged absence' in Australia, China, and Korea.' He could not have known, he added, that Morgan would take a course 'adopted by no other Liberal member' in supporting the war. Was it not natural for him to assume that Morgan would have voted with his leaders? After all, that was Morgan's last message to his constituents, that he would vote with the party.[25]

Morgan did not reply, possibly because he was organising a lavish wedding. Kate was getting married. She had travelled the globe, made political speeches, ran gold mines in Wales and Australia, taken part in several elections and was extremely popular in North Wales. Now she was marrying the 'blue-eyed, flaxen and rosy' Count Erik Piper of Snogeholm, Sweden, a nephew of a former Swedish Minister to Britain.

They married on 1 June 1899 at St. Martin's-in-the-Fields Church, London, with Morgan walking Kate down the aisle in a ceremony conducted by the Lord Bishop of North Queensland. Kate's bridesmaids were her sister Gwendoline and Piper's sister, Countess Ebba Piper, and a couple of friends. Morgan gave her a string of pearls and a massive pendant as wedding presents (no Welsh gold wedding ring is mentioned), the Chinese Ambassador gave Chinese silks and 'Welsh music' was played throughout. Despite the antipathy between the two men, Thomas and his wife sent a silver bowl, but given their wives were working together on female suffrage, it may have been sent by Mrs Thomas. The couple honeymooned in the south of England;[26] their first child was born on 24 January at Finnhult, Skine, Sweden and Kate no longer played a leading role in her father's business affairs.

Once the wedding was over, Morgan concentrated on the election, one which changed UK history … because of him. The desire for labour representation in Merthyr had never really gone away. The Welsh coal strike of 1898 had played a definitive role in changing attitudes, as had the formation of the South Wales Miners' Federation. The two Liberal MPs were seen as out of touch, Thomas for being a capitalist and Morgan for rarely being in the constituency. The *Western Mail* reported that among the labour supporters of Morgan, there was 'considerable dissatisfaction' and the Merthyr and Dowlais Trades and Labour Council was soliciting support from the Miners' Federation for a labour candidate.[27]

A candidate did appear, from a completely different direction. Scotsman Keir Hardie had been MP for West Ham South, then in Essex, from 1892–1895. In 1894, he created controversy after the Albion colliery disaster in Cilfynydd (that Morgan had complained about over the report on coal dust). Hardie asked for a message of condolence for the victims' families be included in an address on the birth of the royal heir, but the request was refused so he verbally attacked the monarchy, to the disapproval of many, and consequently lost his seat.

Having spent the intervening years helping to build up the Independent Labour Party (ILP), Hardie announced in late September 1900 he would be standing in the election for both Preston in Lancashire and Merthyr – standing in two places was not uncommon as voting was often held over several weeks, in this case from 26 September to 24 October. Hardie thought his best chances lay with Preston so he stood there first but lost, so the 'rough-looking candidate in the large soft hat and suit of homespun'[28] sped to Merthyr to try his chances.

This was not his first appearance in the area. On 5 June, he had held a 'well-attended' meeting when he was introduced as 'the well-known Labour leader' and gave a lecture on 'Democracy and War'. His opening remarks would have hit a chord with locals when he said that the cause of the troubles in China and South Africa was due to the fact that 'certain people' had more money to invest than they could find opportunity at home. What, he asked, if Morgan's attempt to get gold in Wales had succeeded? What if all the adventurers of the earth came here and overwhelmed the Welsh population and wanted to have a say in what the Welsh were to do?[29]

From this and other appearances, where he had often spoken on anti-war issues, Hardie did not come to Merthyr as an unknown but from the moment he arrived, he made it clear he was targeting Morgan's seat. This was a job made easier as Morgan had left himself wide open for criticism with his poor attendance record in the House, his constant absences and his lack of time spent in the constituency. Morgan's international investments in gold and coal seemed unpatriotic and his talk of cheap Chinese coal was seen as a threat to Welsh production. These were things that did not go down well in a coal-producing area and were something Hardie took advantage of: producing handbills quoting Morgan saying he was going to flood the world's markets with cheap Chinese coal.

When Thomas and Morgan released their manifestos, both adhering to the same Liberal issues that had dominated Welsh politics for so long, they also explained their views about the war. Public attitude played a pivotal role in the general election, afterwards referred to as the 'Khaki Election 1900' (there were other, later, khaki elections) and the country was divided. Morgan was proud of Britain's role and felt those who opposed the war were being disloyal. He produced posters announcing 'Vote for Keir Hardie and D.A. Thomas, both pro-Boers', a serious error as it linked in voters' minds the two men as a viable alternative to Thomas and Morgan.

Anxious to address his critics, Morgan gave a number of talks. At Merthyr, he told constituents that he felt it to be his duty as soon as he had arrived back in 'England' to come to Merthyr and give them an account of what he had been doing. He assured them he had paired with Colonel Ward, a Conservative, so in no way had his vote as their representative been lost. He disagreed with Thomas' anti-war stance and believed that having gone to war they had to see it through, and while he did not defend the government nor the war, he reminded his audience that the Boers declared war on Britain, not the other way around and therefore he could not fault the government.

He did not like Hardie's policies and warned his audiences that socialism was the opposition of everyone except socialist. A dislike not unique, there was a long-held belief throughout the UK that socialism wanted to reduce everything to one level and that it was associated with anarchy and violence.

As for China, he said that for years he had seen trade competition rise and felt Britain was falling behind so he had taken it upon himself to find new markets for UK products, particularly as he believed China was going to be one of the greatest countries in the world and they needed to seize the opportunities there. He had worked with others on the expansion of Chinese railways and hoped local steel could be used. He denied China would compete for coal because it was largely an interior supply and the railways had not been built to ship it to ports; when it did become available, it would still be more expensive than Welsh coal and therefore was not a danger to home trade.

He assured his audiences that his international duties were now finished, so he could dedicate himself to them again.[30]

Scepticism was rife, how could he dedicate himself 'again' when there had not been much dedication in the first place? His previous election wins were now being examined and his first success was attributed to a wave of rebellion against the Liberal Association, with the second a means to stop a Tory gaining a seat. His victories were now seen not as his, but as reactions to other events. He did retain significant support, however, there were those who disapproved of a non-local being brought in again and thought Morgan better than a Scotsman. There were also those against socialism and the continued determination to keep the Tories out (medical reasons had prevented Herbert Lewis standing again). Many saw Morgan as the best of three bad candidates and if the sceptics were right, it would see him win again.

In September, Morgan launched another attack on Thomas. Ignoring calls for unity, he wrote that Thomas' publicly-expressed intention of supporting a labour candidate was proof of his wish to oust Morgan from his seat. He wrote, 'I join with you in a desire to have at least one labour representative for this borough, and, if you are as sincere as I am, which I very much doubt, I make the following suggestions.' He proposed Trade Unions and other associations be approached to nominate a labour man and empower Mabon to oversee the selection. He added that whoever was elected, for as long as they represented Merthyr, should pay £100 annually towards the support of the labour representative, 'which suggestion,' he added, 'I should not make if I did not know that such a contribution would be immaterial to you.'[31]

Thomas was appalled, 'I fail to see,' he began, 'that any expression of mine should lead you to the conclusion that in my opinion you no longer enjoy the confidence of the electors,' adding a telling dig, 'I made no reference whatever to yourself at Merthyr.' As to the labour candidate, if one was to be brought forward with the general approval of the workmen, then he would honour the pledge he made when he was first selected as a candidate and, with another dig, 'before you were in any way associated with the boroughs' he would adhere to that pledge. Of Morgan's accusation of supporting a Tory candidate (despite the fact no Tory stood in the area), Thomas wrote, 'You are in error in stating that I expressed regret that a Tory candidate was not forthcoming, but I did say that I regretted the circumstances which prevented Mr Herbert Lewis taking the field, intending thereby to convey my sympathy with him in his illness.' Returning to the matter of the labour candidate, it was 'entirely a matter for the workmen of the boroughs and not one for nomination by either you or myself, or our friend Mabon. In regard to providing the election expenses, the labour candidate, I cannot but think that the workmen themselves will be prepared to make provision for their direct representative and would prefer that in that respect their representative should be entirely independent of and not beholden to you or myself.'[32]

Morgan's reply was short. 'I regret I can only construe your letter as evasive and a refusal also put to the only possible test your sincerity with regard to a labour representative. I am quite willing to leave to the calm judgment of the working men of the electorate the effect of your having declined to accede to my suggestions.'[33]

The press merely sighed with frustration that they were at it again. Four days later, on 3 October, the Merthyr boroughs voted. The *Western Mail* called it the 'quietest ever known in the history of the constituency' with absolutely no excitement and 'little to indicate that a big Parliament battle was being fought.'[34] It rained all day as the three candidates did their last-minute rounds: Thomas and Morgan in carriages and Hardie 'the great Socialist champion ... adopting a newer form of conveyance,' a motor-car.[35]

The poll closed at 8.00 pm and the ballot-boxes were sealed and taken to Merthyr police station for the votes to be counted the following day. Morgan lost. D.A. Thomas polled 8,598; Hardie, 5,645; and Morgan,

4,004; and Merthyr became the first industrial town in Wales to return a Labour MP.

The plumping figures showed 77% of Hardie's votes were those in association with Thomas; only 867 used one vote for Hardie[36] and his victory, it was said, was thanks to Thomas' support.

There are a number of reasons for Hardie's victory: progressive dissatisfaction with the dominance of the Tory and Liberal parties, the fight for workers' rights, the desire for a labour representative, the growth of trade unions, and a new generation of workers no longer willing to accept the conditions under which they had been forced to work. Hardie himself wrote in 1914 that he won the seat 'though only with the aid of some principled members of the Anti-Morgan party.'[37]

Nevertheless, the country was shocked. J. Bruce Glasier, in his biography on Hardie, wrote it was 'one of the "providential occurrences" lying outside the region of ordinary political probability.'[38] The *South Wales Daily Post* called it 'the greatest possible surprise' and 'an astonishing result'. *The Times* reported that it was 'a result for which few people outside the district were prepared'[39] and the *Glasgow Herald* wrote about the 'shock of surprise', adding, that the

> House of Commons will certainly miss Mr Pritchard Morgan, who was remarkable not only for his keen business habits and his spirited attempts to develop gold-mining in Wales, but more than all for the exhaustive knowledge of current affairs in the Far East. It is not too much to say that during the last session of Parliament he was the best informed man on events in China to be found in the whole House, and on more than one occasion his information proved to be more accurate than that obtained by the Government themselves through their official channels. It will, therefore, be a serious loss to Parliament generally to be without his services in the coming session, when Chinese affairs are likely to come so much to the front.[40]

However, the *New York Times* noted that the government and the public had largely 'ignored his advice on Chinese affairs.'[41]

One *Western Mail* London correspondent wrote the result was 'received with amazement, tempered by amusement' as it was not generally known of the split between Thomas and Morgan.

Hardie, who was as surprised as anyone that he had won, gave his reactions. He was delighted to see the strength of the anti-war feeling in that part of Wales and rejoiced because it endorsed his view of the war and that it threw back at Chamberlain that his 'audacious claim that the nation was behind him in his crime'. However, Merthyr's attitudes toward the war were no different from the rest of the country and was not the sole reason for his election. He would, Hardie continued, assist in selecting other labour representatives at the next election and that work must begin at once. He would see to it that an organisation was created in the Merthyr boroughs as, at present, they were open to any adventurer who came around: quite a statement from someone not local. He would not, he added, be an absent member in the House and deemed it his duty to visit his constituents often in order to consult with them and tell them what he thought of current issues.[42] This was something Morgan had been failing to do.

The *Western Mail* raced around to Morgan's office where they found him in remarkably cheerful spirits. He was not a man, they wrote, who would 'sorrow without hope' and had taken his rejection in good grace. He admitted his absences from the constituency played a part in his loss, but also the 'duplicity' of Thomas in having allied himself with the ILP and Socialist Party which, according to him, he declined to do when approached to pair with Hardie a few weeks earlier. He claimed Thomas' committee rooms, which he shared with Hardie, were covered with portraits of Hardie and posters urging electors to vote for them both. Thomas had known Hardie for years, respected him greatly, and knew him to be an 'absolutely sincere and honest man who had only the interests of the country at heart'. So Morgan hinted at a conspiracy that Thomas had brought Hardie down 'for the purposes of ousting me from the seat'. He would be back, he assured them, to ensure the constituency would be represented by two men who had honest Liberal principles and not men whose principles 'from a political view, are open to severe criticism.' And he ended in usual Morgan style that when he returned, it would be with an 'overwhelming majority'.[43] Two weeks later, when opening a bazaar at Aberdare, he referred to his loss as 'a mere accident'.[44]

There were rumours that Morgan would copy Hardie's tactics and stand for Merioneth as polling would not finish there until 24 October, but Morgan made no attempt to stand anywhere else.

One final footnote provided a bizarre end to Morgan's association with Merthyr. He offered the District Council a bust of himself. Even more odd was the sculptor was called D.A. Thomas, also of Aberdare.

> Morgan offered it because
> I naturally have much affection for the place and for the people, and I should esteem it an honour if the council would accept the bust and place it in some corner of the Town-hall, so that in years to come my friends may occasionally be reminded of me. I need scarcely say that unless the council are unanimous in accepting the bust I have no desire to foist it upon them.

Like most things Morgan was involved in, controversy immediately followed. One council member refused, saying he had yet to learn what service Morgan had ever done for the town and that the whole constituency had pronounced their opinion of him. Despite the annoyance of some and the apathy of others, the council did accept Morgan's offer.[45]

On 18 October, Aberdare Liberal Club unveiled a 'handsome' bust on a marble plinth on a mahogany pedestal and when Morgan arrived to unveil it, he was received with enthusiasm. The sculptor said Morgan had commissioned four identical busts, had materially assisted his progress, and had introduced him, and many other students, to art patrons[46] (as he had done during the 1888 elections when Morgan funded the artist Thomas Protheroe). None of the busts can be found.

Chapter 13

Standing Alone in a Strange Land

Morgan's loss of his Parliamentary seat certainly did not slow him down in any way, particularly as his Chinese concessions were in trouble and needed his attention.

When the Foreign Office Blue book (an almanack of statistics and information) was published in March 1900, it included correspondence between Morgan and the Chinese government showing the enormous difficulties he had overcome to secure his contract. It showed that promises made were broken but, recognising that Morgan had spent considerable money at Li's request, the Chinese felt obligated to give him some contracts. The French government had objected, claiming a monopoly was being formed, and two months later were awarded six districts in the Szechuan region. Morgan objected in return and so the Chinese ratified his contract on the proviso that if he had not started work in six months, the contract was void.[1]

As Morgan's staff began work, rumours began surfacing that the area was suffering 'riotous demonstrations' and the Chinese government had despatched troops.[2]

Unrest had been growing since 1899, as indigenous people began to feel overwhelmed with foreign Powers enlarging their presence in China, causing anti-Christian and anti-foreign sentiment to grow. Missionaries were seen as corrupting Chinese beliefs and the government seemed unable to stop the growth of leading groups such as the 50–100,000 strong 'Militia United in Righteousness', referred to as 'Boxers' by Westerners because many members practised martial arts.

As tension increased and the world's press was reporting heavily on what was being referred to as the Boxer Rebellion, the *Western Mail* sought Morgan's views. While he wanted an end to the 'spheres of interest' by the Powers and China allowed to govern herself, he felt it was the responsibility of the Powers to keep order, as 'distinguished from absolute control.'

'It would be a hopeless task for any of the Powers to attempt to govern China,' he added, 'in the same manner as we govern India' because the people had become so used to their methods of government that any 'violent alterations would create no end of complications.' Morgan's Imperialist attitudes never saw other cultures as equals, but people who should be taught and taken care of.

Of the Boxers, Morgan thought them a friendly society who wanted to protect themselves against foreign religions, and naively added, 'in the excitement of the moment all foreigners are being attacked.'[3] By 20 June, Morgan's staff were locked in their area of Szechuan as the revolution had reached there.[4]

On 21 June, the Prime Minister, Salisbury, wrote to Sir Chichen Lo-Feng-Luh (1850–1903), the London Chinese Ambassador, asking if he could find information on Morgan's staff and that of another company. They were in China legally, Salisbury stressed, and needed protection. Chichen replied on the 23rd saying he had telegraphed the Viceroy of Szechuan, requesting measures be taken for their special protection and a second letter on the 26th confirmed that protection was now in place.[5] True to Chichen's word, by 7 July, Morgan's staff had received protection from the Viceroy of Szechuan with an escort of 212 men.

In July, a month before he lost his seat, Morgan had asked in the House about British residents and the Legation (diplomatic personnel and their staff) at Peking as there were the gravest fears for their safety. He hoped they could hold out until relief arrived but continued, 'we do not know who is the ruling power in China to-day; we do not know whether it is the Dowager Empress, or whether she has been removed; and we do not know whether it is Prince Tuan or his son.'

Morgan then confused matters by adding that he knew a provisional government had already been appointed, consisting of various viceroys with Li at the head – the same man who organised Morgan's visit to China and who called himself Morgan's friend. Due to poor methods of communication in China, it was difficult, Morgan said, for these Chinese officials to stay in touch so the British government should appoint a Regent, a man with extensive knowledge and experience of Chinese affairs. There was such a man, said Morgan, 'the strongest man in China', Li Hung Chang, the only one he believed could put an end to the 'disturbances'. Morgan wanted the UK government, and other

Powers in Europe and America, to 'consider the question of creating this Regency at this critical moment, and later on consider the question of whom you are going to put on the throne.'[6]

Here, in Morgan's speech, was the background of the Boxer Rebellion: foreign powers deciding what was to happen in China and who 'to put on the throne.' Morgan also overlooked the fact that there was a man who held the influence he was suggesting. Sir Robert Hart (1835–1911), a British diplomat and Inspector-General of China's Imperial Maritime Custom Service since 1859, was described as the most powerful man in China. Yet he knew of, and acknowledged, Morgan's importance in China, writing to Lady Hart, 'keep your eye on him and get acquainted.'[7]

Ignoring Hart's importance and given Morgan and other independent reports confirmed that the powerful Chinese viceroys had formed a provisional government, Morgan's suggestion of a Regent was misplaced and the prevailing attitude was the UK should not interfere. However, the UK and the Powers were sending in large numbers of troops with warships off the coast. The Under Secretary of State for Foreign Affairs, St John Brodrick (1856–1942), admitted the UK government did not know who was really in charge in China, but they had been in touch with the provisional government and informed them that as long as they used their efforts for 'preservation of law and order Her Majesty's ships and Her Majesty's forces will, to the full extent which the officers in command consider possible, co-operate with them and use their power in that respect.' For the time being, the UK's priority was the safety of the Legation and British nationals, and the 'complete accord' with the other Powers.[8]

On 17 July, Brodrick was questioned in the House on the safety of the Legation, Morgan asking if he was aware that it was still standing on the 9th of that month, and that Li had left Canton that morning for Peking with the view of taking supreme command in China?[9] Brodrick was not aware of either fact.

Morgan's assertion that the Legation were alive caused enormous confusion. The press was reporting that their massacre had taken place on 7 July, yet Morgan claimed he had received a telegram on the 9th that they were alive. He was also, according to some reports, 'the first person in this country to be advised' that Li was attempting to take supreme control.[10] Morgan told the press, 'I have sound reason to believe the good news about the British Legation, but with regard to Li Hung Chang, I see in his movement cause for much anxiety. The withdrawal of this powerful old man from the fighting province of the south may be followed by a rising against the Manchu dynasty.'[11]

On 21 July, Morgan called into the *Western Mail* offices, still pushing for his friend Li to be made Regent: 'he is Senior Grand Secretary,' he told them, 'senior guardian of the Heir-Apparent to the Throne, which means in China that he is the guardian not of any particular person, but the guardian of the dynasty, and, therefore, of the Heir Apparent to the Throne – considering all this, not only the English Government, but all the other Powers, should recognise him as the Regent of China during the present critical crisis.'[12]

Morgan's advocating for Li to be in control of China could be seen as self-interest, but as with Welsh gold, when he believed in something, he became passionate and rarely moved from his convictions. He seems to have had a great respect and liking for Li and his belief in the man's ability to restore order in China seems genuine. That belief, however, was not universally shared and many of the Powers refused to negotiate with Li. Today, he is still a controversial figure and while it is acknowledged Li did much good for China, it is believed he also failed on several fronts.

At the beginning of August, confirmation came through that the British Legation was alive but being held hostage. The *Western Mail* claimed Morgan had the right to say 'I told you so' and in the House he 'received the congratulations of members upon the accuracy of his knowledge', even though he still held fears for their ultimate safety. 'Everything,' he said,

> depends upon the action of the Powers. If the allies disregard the warning of Li Hung Chang and advance on the capital, then we may fear the worst, for it is safe to assume that the Ministers are in the hands of the 'Boxers' and the rebel Imperial soldiers, who will not hesitate to go to extremes should they believe that a campaign of vengeance is being entered upon ... If I were locked up in Peking to-day I would pray to God to prevent the allies from advancing.[13]

Meanwhile, Morgan's Peking house, filled with many Chinese curios, and of which he was 'very proud', had been totally destroyed along with its contents.[14]

On 4 August, Morgan sent a message to Li urging that allied troops be permitted to enter Peking to escort the British out and so avert war. He told a press representative in the House lobby that he wanted to save the lives of the Europeans in Peking, but also worried that their local servants could also be killed.

On 8 August, Li replied to Morgan saying it was 'absolutely impossible' to allow troops to enter the city, adding that the British Legation had left Peking on 2 August, although this had not been confirmed. Morgan forwarded the messages to Lord Salisbury, accompanied by a statement that the allies should take no steps to endanger the ministers.[15]

Morgan's communications from Li did raise curiosity as to the 'intimate relations' he had with the provisional Chinese government, but the explanation was that he was not an official diplomat and Li was therefore more willing to communicate with him.[16] However, shortly afterwards, communications appear to have ceased, along with Morgan's intimate knowledge with it.

The Boxer Rebellion finally came to an end in 1901, and an exhausted Li died that same year.

Morgan continued his mining operations in China but like much of what he did, it was surrounded by controversy. Half of his concession, acquired in 1899, was sold off that same year to the Eastern Pioneer Company Ltd (EPCL), in which he was appointed a director. By 1904, only one mine in the vast district was being worked and shareholders were suggesting an abandonment of the project;[17] also, the company had to renegotiate a contract with the new government which was still being debated in 1905.

On 2 January 1906, Morgan requested the Foreign Office inform the Chinese government that he was about to proceed with explorers and engineers to Szechuan to carry out development of his area.[18] However, by January 1910, little progress had been made[19] due to the fact the UK government was not convinced of the validity of Morgan's claim. Sir John Jordan (1852–1925), a diplomat in China, convinced them and they agreed to support the demand of the EPCL. The matter was brought to arbitration with the Chinese government, but it changed little.[20] The EPCL did not meet again until December 1916 when shareholders were complaining about the lack of progress and information about the terms under which Morgan had financed the company. It was decided to adjourn for another month to raise the capital needed to acquire Morgan's half interest[21] but it was not until May 1917 that Morgan agreed to sell for £290,000 in shares and to retire from the board.[22]

In 1919, he was still involved, writing to Lord Curzon (1859–1925), the Foreign Secretary, pointing out that 'immense deposits of Petroleum Potash and other raw products which exist with the limits of our charter are solely needed by ourselves and our allies.' He requested an interview but Curzon's assistant replied stating that it was not possible, besides, Curzon was familiar with the situation and if Morgan had any new points to make, perhaps he could make them in writing.

Notes on the back of the letter by someone with an indecipherable signature offers to see Morgan if Curzon wished 'but it would be perfectly useless as I have nothing to add to what … has been told over and over again for the last 10 years now. I saw him [Morgan] frequently in 1912 and I saw 2 of his directors a few weeks ago. This ridiculous concession stinks in the nostrils of this Dept and the Legation in Pekin.' Underneath, Curzon had written 'a fatuous bore. Please let me escape him.'[23]

With no support from the Foreign Office, and after fighting for 22 years, the EPCL gave up and was absorbed into the Yang-tse Corporation.[24] Herbert Edwards, the EPCL's chair, praised Morgan but also criticised him

> whilst expressing the very greatest admiration for the enterprise, zeal, and foresight which resulted in the securing of such a remarkable charter, one cannot help feeling that, had the concessionaire possessed a little less masterful individuality, or had he been blessed with just a little of the leaven of compromise, we should have found ourselves in the position of controlling the destiny of what we believe will one day be a very important Anglo-Chinese commercial undertaking, for it was his determination to carry through this gigantic enterprise unaided, so far as leadership was concerned, and his intolerance of anything like cooperation, no matter how great the financial assistance that cooperation would have ensured, that resulted in his having to relinquish such Herculean efforts and to leave to others the realization of a project which in its conception possessed potentialities as great as any of the initial efforts that laid the foundation of our vast Empire overseas.[25]

As well as his Chinese interests, Morgan was also struggling with his Korean concessions. Like China, Korea had become a 'happy hunting-ground of concessionists. British, American, and German syndicates are already established on mining properties which are, at least, as promising as any in China.' The Powers were complaining about corruption and that Korean officials were selling mining rights for a fraction of their worth and charging no royalties or rents, consequently mining companies were flocking in.[26] Morgan's concession consisted of some 40 square miles in the south-west prefecture of Gunsan, which was, of course, according to him, the most valuable gold in all the world as he told the *Victoria Daily Colonist*:

> Doubled up on his stateroom couch, his long legs folded up jack-knife fashion into his chin, and the tortures of rheumatic gout frequently causing an involuntary expression of pain to be wrung from the thin close-pressed lips, he did not seem at first acquaintance the type of man imagination had pictured him, standing alone in a strange land against its government and all other meddling states for the execution of his contract to mine for gold. There is that in the eagle eye, the strong aquiline nose, and the wearing of the grizzled grey moustache, however, that indicates a man of indomitable will, and one is the better able to judge after meeting Mr Pritchard Morgan how much his own force of will has had to do in the winning of the day against Corean [sic] duplicity and Russian intrigue. The story of the fighting for the Pritchard Morgan concession is without alteration worthy of a high place in literature.[27]

Other publications sought his opinions and a number included a picture showing Morgan with a Korean secretary, causing one writer to question whether 'the intelligent young secretary is man or girl.' Morgan was frequently asked who his lady friend was, or the gender of his secretary (whose name is not known), and had caused some excitement when he took the Korean to the House as the clothes consisted of a yellow silk gown, with an over-mantel of blue, and of full white trousers that were gathered in tight at the ankle, displaying white shoes painted with strangely coloured flowers.[28] Interest was also generated by the hat and the letter-writer pondered if it was a mark of respect towards Wales, as it was similar to the Welsh black hat. It was not: the headwear was a *gat*, a hat restricted to men who had passed civil service exams. On the subject of clothes, it was rumoured Morgan had attended the funeral of Queen Victoria as the Korean representative wearing white trousers, white waistcoat and a white tie.[29]

As with the China situation, years would pass and little was done on Morgan's Korean concessions. In October 1903, the Japanese were rumoured to be moving on Korea, and Morgan, still Consul General, was interviewed expressing the view that if the Powers did not interfere to protect the interests of the Korean Empire, Japan would unquestionably fight Russia for it, because Korea was an 'overflow country for Japan's growing population'. Without it, Morgan argued, Japan would be reduced to a very small Power in the East.

In 1905, Japan annexed Korea and recalled Korean diplomats, replacing them with Japanese. Yi Han Eung (1874–1905), the Korean Chargé d'affaires in London, committed suicide as he was said to be depressed about the loss of his country. Morgan took charge of his office until other arrangements could be made[30] but seven months later, on 22 December, he handed it over to the Japanese, along with his title of Consul General. In January 1907, the Japanese embassy presented Morgan with an insignia of the Korean Order and a diploma which the Emperor of Korea had conferred on him in recognition of his services, bringing Morgan's connections with Korea to an end.

In the meantime, he had been living in Staines, Middlesex, with Harriet, daughter Gwendoline and four servants. But, in February 1901, he sold the house and contents. Chinese brasses, some over 3,000 years old, realised 650 guineas; a Louis XIV commode, 135 guineas; a Japanese cabinet, 90 guineas; and an ivory statuette of Henry VII, 60 guineas.[31] Morgan's fight for his Chinese concession had nearly bankrupted him. In a letter to Sir John Jordan, he wrote

> To keep the Chinese business alive I have had to mortgage everything I have in this world and when I tell you that I have for the past two or three months, been reduced not only to borrowing from the Jews at enormous interest, but even to parting with my wife's trinkets, you can imagine the fearful straits to which I have been subjected.[32]

All Morgan's mining operations seem to have stalled, despite retaining a number of gold-mining interests. He was receiving money from the Gwalia mines in Australia and investments in other overseas concerns but, for years, he paid rent on his Irish mines but did nothing with them. Welsh gold had sunk back into silence, despite a number of mines continuing to work. Since Readwin's death, there had been no grave marker in the St Illtyd Churchyard, Llanelltyd, so a committee was formed in 1903 to raise money. Morgan was one of the subscribers and enough money was raised to erect a marble headstone.[33]

Six years after Morgan had lost his seat, a general election was held in 1906. Morgan did not stand, instead working hard to get his local Staines Liberal candidate elected. Thomas and Hardie were returned in Merthyr: Thomas saying his relations with Hardie were 'of a most pleasant nature; indeed, even more pleasanter than they had been' with Morgan.[34]

The election was a Liberal landslide and across the UK, the defeat of the Conservatives was momentous, with Prime Minister Arthur Balfour's government being regarded as one of the most unpopular of all time. Lloyd George, who had been tipped to be Minister for Wales, instead became Chairman of the Board of Trade and was the first Welsh cabinet member for fifty years.

The Labour Party, in only its second general election and the first in its modern form, returned twenty-nine MPs whereas in 1900, there had been only two including Keir Hardie. Within a decade, the traditional Liberal Party in Wales was but a pale imitation of its former glory and Labour would come to dominate Welsh politics.

Three years later, prior to the 1910 general election, Morgan decided to return to Merthyr. D.A. Thomas had moved to Cardiff and Morgan obviously saw an opportunity. Hardie was going to stand again and his seat was considered safe but who would take Thomas'?

At first, Morgan refused to disclose his plans when he appeared at Mountain Ash on 19 November accompanied by Gwendoline, in what was described as a 'lively meeting'. Morgan claimed he was merely there having been invited to speak on Lloyd George's budget, despite not having been invited or spoken in Merthyr for six years. The *Aberdare Leader* reported that a private group of Liberals had asked him to stand[35] but they were cautious, noting, 'Labour has become a great power in our midst, and it will be interesting to know what will be the attitude of

Labour towards our erstwhile member.'[36] The following month, they were complaining that 'never in the history of this Borough were the Liberals so unprepared for a General Election … all is confusion as to who will be the official candidate.'

On 4 December, Morgan officially announced he was standing, supposedly to 'great enthusiasm'.[37] He wrote to the Liberal Association requesting their support and on 20 December, the LA met to consider his request, Morgan asking them to read out his letter. He said he would be 'much honoured in accepting an invitation' to be their candidate, would bear all the election expenses himself and, if elected, would 'join and work loyally with the Welsh party, as I did for the twelve years during which I was one of your representatives.'[38]

In an echo of his 1888 general election, the LA wanted nothing to do with him and once again, he stood as an Independent Liberal. Undaunted, Morgan appeared at Mountain Ash before a large audience – 'a poor orphan' following the LA rejection. He had done nothing wrong nine years ago, he told them, but obviously the electors thought he had. Despite accusations of putting Chinese coal above local coal, he swore blind he had no interest in coal as 'coal investments were not exciting enough for him'. But telling a mainly mining constituency he had 'no interest in coal' seems self-defeating. However, his blunders did not stop there. When Li invited Morgan to China, he went because he was 'not a busy man'. Again, telling his prospective voters they had not kept him busy enough last time, something unlikely to endear him to them.

Morgan then began a rambling story about how he had met Li. After failing to get an introduction through the Foreign Office and knowing Li was sailing to New York, he made an attempt to see him on the ship which also failed. So, he offered £50 (about £6,000 today) to any passenger who would sell his ticket, an offer quickly snapped up. Suddenly realising he was supposed to be talking on the budget, he asked the audience if he should speak of the budget or go on with the tale – 'the tale', replied the audience.

He met Li on board the ship and had a conversation about railways, giving him the opportunity to secure thousands of pounds worth of orders for Dowlais Ironworks. This is the first and only time he claimed a direct influence in acquiring orders (which never came about) and the majority of Morgan's activities in China concerned mining, not railways.

Morgan swore on his honour he went to China to open up British trade and while he admitted he was absent from Parliament, he believed he was serving his country. Besides, he added, he blamed the ineffectiveness of the Liberal Party who were 'in a helpless minority' and therefore had little impact in the government.[39]

Despite being warmly received, Morgan's policies had barely changed and he had no definitive manifesto[40] – he received little press coverage and was already looking outdated.

Four candidates stood for the two seats: Edgar Jones (1878–1962), the official Liberal; Arthur Fox-Davies (1871–1928), for the Conservatives; Morgan, an Independent Liberal; and Hardie for Labour.

As 1910 dawned, electioneering started in earnest. An election song to the tune of *Little Brown Jug* promoted Liberal Unity (Hardie and Davies objected to the depiction of themselves). The song was probably from Morgan's office as it had him as 'one in whom there is no sham' and urged voters to put a cross by his name.[41]

On 3 January, Morgan was at Cwmdare and Trecynon, accompanied by his friend and partner George Hall, but at the latter venue he was continually heckled by youths. He referred to a speech by Hardie who had said the Labour Party would have no agreement or alliance with the Liberals and when the audience applauded, a puzzled Morgan asked, 'Do you cheer that?' Later, when asked if he was still in favour of a Labour candidate, he reminded them he had offered to pay for one in 1888 and when someone asked if he was prepared to give Hardie that now, he replied, 'Certainly not'.[42]

On 8 January, he was photographed in dramatic pose, arms aloft, on the front page of the *Daily Mirror*, his hair white and sporting an impressive white handlebar moustache while the headline quoted him, 'Socialism means no government, no king, no God – Darkness.'[43] *The Times* was unconvinced, writing, 'it is unlikely that Mr Morgan will command a large following.'[44]

In Merthyr, the Liberals were afraid if Hardie came top of the polls, it would mean the end of Liberalism in the area. Hardie had been busy criticising Edgar Jones and Fox-Davies, however, it was, according to the *Aberdare Leader*, the duel between Hardie and Morgan that was causing feelings to run high.

Morgan promoted Edgar Jones for the other seat while losing no opportunity to attack Hardie and socialism. As the two swapped verbal blows, their animosity was reflected in their supporters who took every opportunity to clash. Hardie took against the *Aberdare Leader* as it appeared to criticise him and support Morgan, which the *Leader* denied and took to counting press inches as to whom they had covered the most and found it fairly even.

In the end it was the Liberal Edgar Jones who headed the poll with 15,448; Hardie, 13,841; and Fox-Davies, 4,756; with Morgan trailing on 3,639. Following his defeat, little is heard of Morgan until the 1911 Investiture of the Prince of Wales.

Prince Edward, later King Edward VIII, was 16 when on 23 June 1910, he was created Prince of Wales. Lloyd George, on the suggestion of the Bishop of St Asaph, persuaded the King to carry out an Investiture ceremony, which was duly planned for 13 July 1911 at Caernarfon, the birthplace of the first English Prince of Wales.

The National Committee of Wales commissioned an insignia, designed by distinguished Welsh artist Goscombe John (1860–1952), and made by Messrs. Garrard, the royal London jewellers.

Shortly after the insignia was made, questions were being asked about where the Welsh gold originated from and how much was used. It was not until the 1940s that light was shed on the matter when the insignia was transferred to Amgueddfa Cymru-National Museum Wales and research was undertaken. A letter from Garrards to Hugh J. Owens, Clerk of the Peace, County Merioneth County Offices, Dolgellau on 1 August 1947 explained:

> While there is some ambiguity in the question of whether or not the whole of the Regalia was made in Welsh Gold, description of the clasp, where Welsh Gold is specifically mentioned, in the other description it is not. From your receipt of June 1911 where 5.4 ounces were to be added to the rest of the gold, it would certainly appear that the whole quantity was Welsh. In such a place it would be unthinkable to mix Welsh Gold with any other.

This was confirmed by Hugh Owen in a letter of 8 August 1947 to the Secretary of the National Museum:

I think it is now clearly established that all the gold used for the Regalia was Welsh Gold. I think it is equally clear that part of the gold, if not all of it, came from a Merionethshire mine.

A private letter from George Hall, in Dolgellau to T.H. Roberts, a dealer who had sold the gold to Morgan, contained more details:

I herewith hand you for realisation the two bars of gold obtained from the two small crushings of Barlchylli ore. With reference to the larger bar you will please note that oz 5.4 [5.4 oz] were cut off by Messrs. Garrard & Co. (as per their receipt herewith) and received by them for the balance of the gold necessary for the Insignia of the Prince of Wales.
Receipt from Garrard & Co. 20th June 1911
Receive from Pritchard Morgan Esq.
Gold bar weighing oz 5.4 [5.4 oz] @ 66/-   £17.16.5
(pencil note: to be added to 25.230)

The total weight of gold then was 30.63 ounces.

Garrards' records are incomplete although in their book *The Story of Garrards*, there is a reference to the gold coming from Caernarfon. However, Hugh J. Owen in his *Treasures of the Mawddach* (1947) found that there were no mines in the Caernarfon area. An *Illustrated London News* article also states Caernarfon as the source but then names Merionethshire mines – the verge from St David's; the chaplet, Gwynfynydd; and the ring, from Prince Edward's, but does not provide a source. Given the paper's editor was a close friend of Morgan's, it may have come from him and unfamiliarity of Welsh locations created confusion as to where the mines were situated. Garrards merely cites Mines A and B for the 25.230oz and that Morgan's 5.4oz was merged. In return for his gift, Morgan was given a special seat at the Investiture.

In 1913, the regalia was put on show in *An Exhibition of Works by Artists of Welsh Birth or Extraction* at Amgueddfa Cymru-National Museum of Wales and proved to be a great success with over 16,000 people attending over four months. After the exhibition, the regalia was returned, in a first-class compartment on the Great Western Railway, to Buckingham Palace from where it was then sent to Paris for an exhibition of British

Art. It was removed to the British Embassy in Paris on the outbreak of war and later returned to Amgueddfa Cymru-National Museum of Wales, where, because of its significance to Wales, permission was granted for the insignia to be left on permanent deposit. It was not used again until the coronation of Prince Charles, the twenty-first Prince of Wales on 1 July 1969.

After the outbreak of the First World War, little is heard of Morgan. He was now seventy and his difficulties with arthritis and gout had slowed him down, but he appears not to have been involved in any war efforts. He did attempt to get involved in a miners' conference in Cardiff in 1915 but was refused permission to speak.[45]

That year, he also suffered the loss of George Hall – the man who was perhaps his best friend, and the man who had used his newspaper to provide invaluable support for Morgan in the 1888 election. Morgan had attempted to work Gwynfynydd back in 1910–11, and had bought a house, The Rock at 5 Porkington Terrace, Barmouth, overlooking the estuary amid mountain scenery and had created a job for George as manager of his mine. The two men had dined together at Dolgellau and as the 59-year-old Hall was returning home late at night, it was believed he lost his footing when walking along the Pistyll Caen Waterfall and fell over the 45-foot precipice.

The two men had been close but according to Alwyn Evans

> Morgan deserted his friend. Though he attended Hall's funeral in Llanelltyd, he did nothing subsequently for Hall's family. Pritchard Morgan denied in a letter to Herbert Edwin, George Hall's eldest son, that his father had any financial interest in his China ventures. Morgan did not even erect a headstone for Hall; the family, who all remained in Australia, were horrified to learn that their father had been buried in an unmarked grave. Hall's burial is recorded on 23rd January 1915 in the BMD for Llanelltyd churchyard, but the grave location is forgotten.

Given other remarks about Morgan's loyalty to his friends, this does seem odd and could be a reflection of his lack of finances at this time.

After the war, the first general election was in 1918, and the first in which there was only one day to cast all UK votes. Morgan decided to stand as an Imperialist for Uxbridge but quickly withdrew. He then threw his hat in for East Fife as an Independent against Asquith, the leader of the Liberal Party, who had been replaced as Prime Minister by Lloyd George in 1916. Morgan's views were poorly understood in the district and his campaign amounted to little more than attacks on Asquith, accusing him of rarely visiting his constituency – a little disingenuous given Morgan had rarely visited Merthyr. He believed Asquith should retire to the House of Lords where he could lead the miserable remains of the Liberal Party,[46] despite having previously condemned Rosebery for leading the Liberals from the Lords. Neither Morgan nor Asquith won.

That same year, 1918, Morgan, Harriet, and Gwendoline moved to a house called Byways, Barley Mow Road, Englefield Green, Egham, about 20 miles west of London. Morgan's arch-rival D.A. Thomas also died that year; Keir Hardie had already gone in 1915. In 1920, Gwendoline, now aged 44, married a soldier, George Hutchinson Ardagh, and they moved in with her parents.

Four years later, Morgan was dead. He was eighty when he died on 7 July 1924 and the funeral service was held at St Jude's, Englefield Green, Guildford. Interestingly, 1924 is seen by some as the final demise of the old-style Liberalism.[47]

Harriet died two years later in 1926; Gwendoline and George remained at the Byways until 1927 when they moved to Maida Vale, Middlesex. They had no children and when George died in 1930, he left his wife about £7,000; when Gwendoline died in 1968, she left around £17,000 but it is not known to whom. Kate had predeceased her sister in 1958; she and Eric had four children but efforts to contact the family to see if they have any archival material on Morgan have been in vain.

Historians, when they write of Morgan at all, are generally not kind, and for good reason. He was self-aggrandising, an adventurer, loyal to his friends and generous to many, but ruthless with those who did not agree with him. He had grandiose dreams and ill-conceived ideas, rarely took advice and threw himself into projects only to just as quickly forget about them. He was a shameless self-publicist and similar to Donald Trump in advocating everything he did was 'great' and the 'best ever' – claims which often came back to haunt him.

While the mining of Welsh gold existed before, and after Morgan, no other individual in the industry captured the media and the public attention as he did, and most of the press coverage during the second half of the nineteenth century was linked to him. It was the character of the man that captivated the press with his offers to pay off the national debt and claims that Wales was going to equal the goldfields of California and Australia. His David and Goliath battle against the government to have taxes paid on net, not gross, not just on gold but all mining, made him a hero to all, despite losing the battle. In that sense, he put Welsh gold on the world map and drove up the desire in many of us to own just a small piece of that elusive metal.

Chapter 14

Welsh Gold after Morgan

After Morgan's death, Welsh gold continued its traditional boom and bust existence. In 1920, a Governmental Secretary of Mines position was finally created and in June 1930, a petition by the Merioneth Mining Development Committee asked the government to look into the prospect of mining for gold and minerals in the Welsh mountains. The group consisted of 'public-spirited men in the county' (who were mainly mine owners), with the support of the county council and all other local governing bodies with an aim of possibly reviving the industry.[1] The government agreed to a public inquiry intending to provide a 'complete economic and geological survey of the field and a revision of mining laws and their administration'. It opened on 8 October 1930.

Owen Parry Hughes, the Dolgelly Local Excise Office, who acted as secretary and convener of the committee, prepared a document giving a history of various gold-mining enterprises in the district during the last 50 or 60 years. He surmised that all such enterprises had broken down through incompetence in mining, financial inflation and the greed for quick profits. The Commissioner asked, 'I have had it hinted to me that a good deal of gold was stolen from the mines.' Hughes agreed, 'I am afraid that is perfectly true however deplorable. There was no means of checking the men. Quite a lot of people went on living in comfort after the mine had closed down.' As a result, Hughes reported, 'not 30 per cent of the gold actually mined was recovered by the promoters.' Consequently, the precise value of any mine was never ascertained, and the actual returns were of doubtful value because of the inefficiency of the record.

A number of witnesses continued to believe the area could be a going concern and that failures had been due to poor practices. Several miners gave evidence to the 'slackness and inefficiency of the method of the management in the past' so that vast quantities of unrecovered gold had gone down the river, and they too admitted gold had been stolen. However, some mine owners denied the inefficiencies, such as

T. J. Ritchie, part-owner of the Prince Edward mine, near Trawsfynydd. While he had been mining fairly successfully, he believed there should be more government assistance as 'at present financial London laughs at the idea of Welsh gold, and until mistaken ideas are corrected the industry cannot make headway.'[2]

A. M. Clegg of the Mines Department said that after the inquiry he, along with Professor Henry Louis (1855–1939), President of the Iron and Steel Institute; Mr Vaughan, Assistant Inspector of Mines for North Wales and owner of the gold mines; and Mr David Williams, a farmer, who had engaged expert gold miners for the afternoon; would inspect the once-famous Gwynfynydd gold mines and after that, he would present his report to the government.[3] The 75-year-old Professor Louis and his party duly spent two hours underground at Gwynfynydd accompanied by gold miners, David Davies and David Jones, and removed several quartz samples.

On 5 December 1930, Professor Louis released his damning report. Gold-mining in Wales was not viable. 'Careful study,' he wrote, 'of all the facts which I have been able to ascertain concerning the Merionethshire gold belt has led me to exactly the same conclusion as appears to have been arrived at by all the other authorities who have studied this property; in particular I feel bound to agree with the opinions expressed by Mr Foster Brown in his report of December, 1921, to the Commissioners of Crown Lands, from which I extract the following passage:

> The gold is found in very occasional rich patches, and in this respect is totally different from the South African Rand mining, where the gold is disseminated fairly evenly through the conglomerate. This means that a large amount of development and cost has to be incurred in the hope of finding one of these rich patches. There is no indication of where these rich patches are likely to be found; they are very concentrated.

'In my view,' continued Louis, 'there is very little chance of these mines being developed in such a way as to make them of any material value in the question of giving employment, and I could not recommend the expenditure of public money on such speculative undertaking as gold-mining in Wales has proved itself to be.'[4]

The gold was all too sporadic, he wrote, and almost all of it recovered from Gwynfynydd and Clogau, adding, 'I regret that I am forced to this unfavourable conclusion, but fear greatly that no other interpretation can be placed upon the facts that I have collected.' The government, he concluded, should never invest taxpayers' money in Welsh gold.

Despite the damning report, mining did continue, although there was a significant difference between the new era and its predecessors. It no longer relied on the seeking of shareholders to obtain funds, and was financed mainly by private money. However, the excitement had gone, and the anxious and eager amateur had been replaced by the coolness of the professional investor.

Gold-mining in North Wales was far from easy and one only has to refer to the pages of the *Mining Journal* of the time to see how those who mined the area reached a point where they felt that Nature herself was conspiring to prevent the recovery of gold. The once dominant phrase 'rebellious ore' summed up the feelings of those struggling to extract gold. In the end, those 'rebellious ores' won through.

Five years after the report, a fire broke out at Gwynfynydd with the damage estimated between £20,000 and £30,000. J.H. Wright, the managing director of the Hillside Mining Company, London, which had taken over the mine, told the press that for several months workers had been constructing a building and they were almost ready to open. It had departments for a mill, laboratories, offices, a testing room, machine rooms, and just a few days earlier, the latest gold-mining plant from London had been installed. An old miner stated that he had been alarmed by a loud explosion and he and other workers tried to do what they could using buckets and water from the river, but it was of little use. Several miners risked their lives endeavouring to save some of the machinery but in the end, all that remained was thousands of tons of debris and twisted steel.[5] Gwynfynydd was worked up to 1999 and now belongs to the Clogau jewellery company.

What did continue in relation to Welsh gold was the tradition of wedding rings and the 'extra precious' value of rare Welsh gold. Princess Alexandra, Duchess of Fife, was married in 1913 with a wedding ring of Welsh gold from the Clogau Mine; Princess Mary (1897–1965), the only daughter of King George V and Queen Mary, got married in 1922 and the ring's gold was presented by Morgan. She was followed in 1923 by the

Duke of York (later King George VI) who commissioned W. Bertolle, a West End jeweller, to make a ring for Lady Elizabeth Bowes-Lyon (later Queen Elizabeth The Queen Mother). This ring came from the same nugget supplied by Morgan for Princess Mary but it had to be specially moulded due to the smallness of Elizabeth's fingers.[6]

In 1932, gold came from the Bedd-y-Coedwr Mine for Princess Marina's ring and the mine was renamed in her honour. Both Princess Marina and Elizabeth Bowes-Lyon's rings were made by Johnson, Matthey & Co., London.

Three years later, the London Mining Syndicate working the Prince Edward Mine sent one 24-carat ounce for Lady Alice Scott's ring.[7] Following the wedding, the *Western Mail* reported that 'young men and women are clamouring for rings made of Welsh gold … but, alas, there are few brides who have the satisfaction of being married with a hoop of gold mined in the hills of Wales.' At that time, there were only about thirty men employed in the mines and, according to the *Western Mail*, the whole of the output was being purchased by L.R. Crouch, a Cardiff Jeweller. 'Almost every grain is used to make wedding rings,' they continued, 'and, so far, nearly 100 have been sold. Hundreds more have been ordered, but many of the applicants will have to be disappointed.'[8] The gold was to be an amalgamation from five mines: the Marina, St David's, Gwynfynydd, Prince Edward and Dolaucothi in South Wales.[9]

When the Duke of Windsor married Mrs Simpson in 1937, the one-ounce wedding ring made by a Paris jeweller was fashioned into two rings. An eccentric priest, Thomas Michaeliones (1880–1960), owned the Graigwen Gold Fields from c.1938–1953, and when Princess Elizabeth (now Queen Elizabeth II) was to marry Prince Phillip, in 1947, Michaeliones offered to provide the gold in order to maintain the tradition of royal brides wearing rings of Welsh gold. The ore was put on show at the Industrial Wales Exhibition. G.R. Owen who had managed two small mines in Dolgellau also offered to supply the gold.[10]

An alternative story is that the jeweller Bertolle wrote to Princess Elizabeth suggesting she had a ring made from the same Clogau nugget as her mother and grandmother's, and she was 'delighted with the idea'. He then measured her finger size and gave the gold to the same craftsman who had made her mother's ring. When it was finished, Lieutenant Mountbatten gave him an inscription, written by Prince Phillip, to be engraved inside.[11] This means the current Queen wears a wedding ring from gold donated by Pritchard Morgan.

In 1960, the same nugget was used for Princess Margaret's ring, and in 1973, for Princess Anne's wedding ring. Despite fears that the nugget had been exhausted, there was sufficient remaining to supply the ring for Lady Diana when she married Prince Charles in 1981. David Vyvyan Thomas, the son of a Swansea chemist, designed the wedding rings and the Queen's goldsmiths, Collingwood of Conduit Street, made the ring. Only a sliver, about one gram, was left and it was reported to have been consigned to the Privy Purse Office.[12]

In his book, *A Dress for Diana*, David Emanuel, who designed the wedding dress, commissioned a jeweller, Douglas Buchanan, to make a tiny gold horseshoe from 18-carat Welsh gold, which was sewn into the back of the label on the dress. 'Nobody could see our private gift when the dress was being worn; it was just there as a little token, a little good luck charm, from us to Diana.'[13]

When Prince Andrew married Sarah Ferguson in 1986, the gold was taken from a new 36g of 21-carat nugget that had been presented to the Queen by the Royal British Legion in 1981 and came again from the Clogau Mine. Sarah's ring was 36 grams, made by Garrard's and inscribed with a Welsh dragon and the initials C.S.D. (Clogau St. David's).[14]

Due to media coverage claiming Welsh gold was running out, the Britannia Gold company which had taken over the Gwynfynydd mine (it closed in 1989), donated a 1kg bar to the Queen. But elsewhere, jewellers were struggling to keep up with demand.

When Prince Edward and Sophie Rhys-Jones married in 1999, they worked with the Crown Jeweller, David Vyvyan Thomas, on the design for the 22-carat ring. 'The rings took two or three days to make,' Thomas told reporters, 'which is a normal length of time for wedding rings.' 10–20 grams were donated by the Cambrian Goldfields which had been carrying out explorations at the Prince Edward mine.[15] Edward, like brothers Charles and Andrew, kept to royal tradition and wore his wedding ring on the signet finger, not the usual third finger.

Charles continued to wear his wedding ring to Diana on his signet finger until he and Camilla Parker Bowles married in 2005. There were rumours that Charles, as Duke of Cornwall, would break with tradition and choose Cornish gold to avoid links with Diana, but this proved not to be true and both rings are Welsh gold. A 1.27-ounce piece was extracted from that presented to the Queen by the Royal British Legion in 1981. Charles also wears cufflinks of Welsh gold.

Finally, Prince William and Kate Middleton married in 2011 and their wedding rings used the same Royal British Legion nugget, as did Meghan Markle's ring in 2018.

As well as royalty, numerous celebrities, particularly if they were Welsh, wanted the rare wedding rings. Former Tory Leader William Hague and his wife Ffion wanted pure Welsh gold, but had to settle for an 18-carat alloy because there was not enough available in 1997. In 2000, Hollywood film star Michael Douglas reportedly paid £3,500 for a Welsh gold ring inscribed with an ancient Celtic design and Aur Cymru (Welsh gold) for his marriage to Swansea-born actress Catherine Zeta-Jones. Douglas had bought the ring from T.J. Davies Jewellers in Aberystwyth after reading about the history of Welsh gold on the internet. Catherine's aunt Thelma Jones ran a seafront hotel in Aberystwyth and contacted the jewellers on Douglas' behalf. The gold came from Morgan's old mine, Gwynfynydd, then owned by mining engineer, Roland Phelps.

In 2004, weather presenter Sian Lloyd was engaged to MP Lembit Opik, then the MP for Montgomeryshire, and the engagement ring was a heart-shaped diamond ring of 18-carat Welsh gold, handmade by jeweller Kelvin Jenkins from Machynlleth.

Members of the public were rarely mentioned as having the rings with the exception of Morgan's friend George Hall when he married Gladys May Evans of Swansea in 1912; she wore a ring given to her by Hall from Gwynfynydd gold.[16] Throughout the late nineteenth to early twentieth centuries, reports appeared sporadically in the media noting brides who had Welsh gold wedding rings, such as Audrey Bewlex of Llandudno who married T.O. Williams in October 1937 with such a ring.[17]

It was not just rings that were being made of Welsh gold. The largest object of pure Welsh gold was made using gold from the Castell Carn Dochan mine at Llanuwchllyn, the most easterly mine within the Merioneth gold-mining area and where a gold lode was discovered in 1863. This was part of the 20,000-acre estate in Merioneth owned by Sir Watkin Williams-Wynn (1820–1885), who, at the time, was from the richest family in Wales. A dispute between the landlord and the Crown over mineral ownership delayed its exploitation, but a company, chaired by the MP John Bright (1811–1889), was formed to develop the mine. This paid the Wynnstay estate a royalty of one-twelfth, while the Crown received a licence fee of one-twenty-fourth. Initial results were encouraging, with a ton of quartz a week being crushed and the recovery of between two and six ounces of gold. In 1861, the company built a larger mill and produced 837 ounces of gold in 1865, but in 1866, the yield began to decline. The mine closed in 1873 (it was subsequently worked on a small scale from 1887 to about 1905).

Sir Watkin was rich enough not to need a financial income for the royalties so he received it in gold, some of which was used to make a large ornate 'cup' in 1867. The London jewellers R & S Garrard and Co. based the design on a drawing by Hans Holbein the younger (1497/8–1543) in the British Museum for a cup given by King Henry VIII to Queen Jane Seymour in 1536–37. Jane Seymour's cup was melted down on the orders of Charles I in 1629, but is described in a 1574 inventory of royal plate.

Sir Watkin's copy is nearly 40cm high, made of 22-carat gold and inscribed 'Made of Gold the Royalty from Castell Carndochan Mine 1867' and hallmarked by R & S Garrard and Co., Haymarket, London. The inscriptions include several family mottoes: *eryr eryrod eryri* ('the eagle of the eagles of Snowdonia'), *y cadarn ar cyfrwys* ('the strong and the sly'), *bwch yn uchaf* ('the ram is on top') and *cwrw da yw allwedd calon* ('good beer is the key to the heart'). The lid has the Williams-Wynn arms, including a young ram on top, supported by a pair of cherubs. The marks are those for 22-carat gold (91.6% pure, with the minimum of alloy required to make the metal hard enough to work, and the same standard as gold coins). It weighed 63 ounces 5 dwt 12 carats (1,978.9 grams).

The cup remained in the Williams-Wynn family until 1964, when it was bought at auction with the assistance of the Heritage Lottery Fund for a relatively modest £22,300 (about half of this being the value of the bullion). It can now be seen at Amgueddfa Cymru — National Museum Wales.

Other items include:

- Royal St David's Golf Club, Harlech St David's Gold Cross (1930) made of pure Welsh gold.[18] It is not known where the gold came from but given that Lord Winchelsea, who was President of the golf club, had been chairman of the Morgan Gold Mining Company at one time, it may have come from Gwynfynydd.

- Both Merthyr and Cardiff Mayoral chains are reputed to be of Welsh gold.
- The Glyndŵr Award, founded in 1994 by the Machynlleth Tabernacle Trust, recognises outstanding contributions to the arts in Wales. The award consists of a large silver medal with Machynlleth marked with a bead of Gwynfynydd gold.
- In 1997, Archbishop Desmond Tutu had some Welsh gold included in a clasp that holds his cope.
- In 1988, Sally Burton, widow of Richard Burton, presented a medal of Welsh gold to the National Eisteddfod of Wales in Newport to commemorate the Welsh actor's death four years previously. It was presented to winning playwright, Dafydd Jones, of Bangor, Gwynedd.
- In 1989, the Royal Mint at Llantrisant produced a limited edition of 3,000 18-carat Gwynfynydd gold dragon coins weighing 1/4oz and advertised extensively in the Sunday newspapers. The obverse shows the Welsh dragon, with the words 'Aur cymru' and in English 'Welsh gold' along with the weight and year of production. The Welsh Maiden is depicted on the reverse side and is a registered mark of authenticity for gold produced from the Gwynfynydd mine. Since 1984, this trademark has become synonymous with Welsh gold. The reverse side combines several emblems of Welsh heritage, including a harp, a daffodil, a dragon shield, a crown and branches of oak and laurel. These emblems are encircled by the words 'argraffiad cyfyngedig' meaning 'limited edition'. In the 1990s, due to the lack of availability, jewellers were offering to buy the coins, then worth about £1,000 each, so they could be melted down and made into wedding rings generating a higher income for the jewellers. The coins now retail for around £6,000 each. Unfortunately, the Royal Mint Museum has no record of where the gold originated.
- A Snowdon Lily (a rare and fragile flower that only grows on the mountain) brooch in white and yellow gold, created for the late Queen Mother, was reproduced especially for a 2002 exhibition at the Tannery Gallery, Willow Street, Llanrwst, timed to coincide with the Queen's Golden Jubilee. Colwyn Bay designer David Elson used gold from the Cambrian Gold Fields gold mine in Dolgellau, and said, 'My work offers the opportunity for people to belong to the exclusive club who choose pure Welsh gold.' New technology enabled items to be engraved

with PWG (Pure Welsh Gold). Accompanying the exhibition was a show telling the story of Welsh gold, its royal connections, heritage and natural origins. Nuggets from the rivers, and gold in its natural settings on the rock face also featured, along with historical photographs of the Welsh gold-mining industry over the centuries in the area.[19]
- The world's first Welsh Fabergé egg went on sale in 2003 for £15,999 at Cardiff jewellers, Clive Ranger. Only twenty-five of the German-designed eggs were made and were 5 inches (12.7cm) tall; when a seal was pressed, the egg opened to reveal gold daffodils. One gram of Welsh gold was used in the golden dragon which stood on top of the shell.[20]
- Opera singer Katherine Jenkins was presented with a Welsh diamond daffodil pendant and matching earrings from Welsh jeweller, Clive Ranger in 2005. The 18ct gold pendant, priced at £499, contains a small amount of rare Welsh gold and the 0.15ct diamond had the Welsh dragon laser-etched on to its surface.[21]

Probably one of the most significant inclusions of gold was in the Honours of the Principality of Wales, the regalia used at the Investiture of the Princes of Wales, made up of a ring, a rod, a sword, a girdle, a mantle, and a coronet. All had previously been used for Prince Edward's Investiture in 1911, with the exception of the coronet.

The title Prince of Wales stretches back almost 700 years. The first and only native-born prince to be fully acknowledged was Llywelyn ap Gruffudd (c.1223–1282). Following a grievance with King Edward I, Gruffyd refused to acknowledge the king and war broke out between England and Wales, resulting in Gruffyd's defeat and death in 1282. In 1301, Edward created his 17-year-old son, Edward of Caernarfon (later King Edward II), as the Prince of Wales and tradition followed that the English monarch could confer the title. It is not automatically assumed by the heir to the throne; it is the prerogative of the monarch to decide when, to whom and if it is to be granted, though by tradition it is to the eldest son. Queen Victoria made her son Prince of Wales a month after his birth. Queen Elizabeth made Charles the Prince when he was nine years and eight months old. Not every English monarch held the title in his youth and in nearly 700 years, there have been 374 years without a Prince of Wales. The longest periods were over 100 years between Henry VIII in 1490 and Prince Henry in 1609; and 300 years between Prince Charles (Charles I) in 1613 and Edward VIII in 1911 when the Investiture ceremony was not used. A poll conducted by ITV Wales in 2018 on whether the title should be abolished showed that 57% thought Prince William should inherit the title, with 22% wishing to see it removed.[22]

In 1728 a coronet had been made for Frederick, Prince of Wales, the eldest son of George II, which was later used by his son, George III, then George IV, and finally Edward VII. However, due to its age, a new coronet was made for George V and subsequently added to the insignia of Prince Edward in 1911.

However, when Edward went into exile in 1936 as the Duke of Windsor (formerly King Edward VIII) after refusing to give up his partner, Wallis Simpson, he controversially took the coronet with him. It remained in France until 1972 when it was returned to the Tower of London and put on display alongside the previous coronet.

This meant a new coronet had to be made for Prince Charles' Investiture. It was presented to the Queen by the Goldsmiths' Company and designed by Louis Osman (1914–1996), architect, silversmith, and jeweller, and his wife Dilys Osman, an enameller. It weighs about 3lb (1.36k), consists of a circlet and single arch of 24-carat gold, decorated with four pattée crosses (for protection) and four fleurs-de-lis (for purity) of Welsh gold, surmounted by an orb with a cross on top, engraved with heraldic attributes, glittering with seventy-five diamonds and twelve emeralds.[23] The design conformed to a royal warrant issued by Charles II in 1677 about how the heir apparent's coronet should appear.

Osman had hoped to make the whole crown in Welsh gold but there was not a sufficiently large quantity, nor were there any 24-carat standards so it was confined to the pattée crosses and fleur-de-lys of 22-carat gold. It has a base of ermine and a cap of purple designed to match the prince's mantle and the cost of making it was £3,600, but the labour and artistry were free so a more realistic value for the time was £6,000 – it is now priceless.

The technology was unique, being the first coronet or crown made by electro-forming by chemists rather than by craftsmen beating out sheets of gold. A wax mould of the coronet was immersed in a plating bath for two and a half days, while the gold was deposited on it. This made it thinner and half as heavy than if it had been made by traditional methods.

Just as the goldsmiths were about to hallmark the coronet, they found a problem. If by some chance it were to slip from the Prince's head and fall, it would shatter, so a second had to be made, reinforced with iridium platinum and the precious stones hastily transferred. This, however, proved too large for Prince Charles and throughout rehearsals, it would slip down over his eyes. It was altered for the Investiture but not until 1988 was it revealed that the crowning glory, the golden sphere orb on the top, was nothing more than a humble ping-pong ball. The idea was the inspiration of David Mason, who worked for the electroplating company. 'It was obvious,' he said, 'that a large lump of gold was going to be too heavy. The Prince would have been bowed down by the sheer weight. The headache was to find a light hollow structure. Ten days before the Investiture we were still scratching our heads then it suddenly came to me when I was watching a table tennis tournament on television.'[24] The ball was silver-coated to conduct a current and then placed in a vat of gold.

Nowadays, there are few items made of pure Welsh gold due to its rarity. No mines are currently working and panning for gold in the rivers is prohibited. Jewellery companies such as Clogau include a 'touch' of gold in some products, about the size of a rice grain, but really the only way to own a pure Welsh gold item is to buy one second-hand, but prices are high with the average wedding ring starting at around £1,000.

It is unlikely that mining for gold in Wales will ever be revived unless a more cost-efficient way is invented, but perhaps one day, someone like Morgan will come along again.

Notes

Introduction
1. Thatcher, Margaret. *Speech at dinner for South Korean President*. From the Thatcher Archive: speaking text. 3 May 1986.
2. Johnson, Donald Hector, 1994 "To Silence a Jackdaw Gagging the Northern Miner" *Journal of the Royal Historical Society of Queensland* Vol 6, Brisbane
3. *South Wales Star*, 4 September 1891

Chapter 1: Becoming Rich
1. *Western Mail*, 27 August 1888
2. Morien, 'The Discovery of Gold at Dolgelly' in *Weekly Mail* (17 December 1887)
3. *Y Celt*, 18 January 1889
4. *Western Mail*, 27 August 1888
5. *Carnarvon & Denbigh Herald*, 3 August 1888
6. *Western Mail*, 22 April 1887
7. *Y Celt*, 18 January 1889
8. Rowlands, John & Rowlands, Sheila, *Welsh Family History: A Guide to Research*, 2nd edition. (Baltimore: Genealogical Publishing Company, 1999)
9. Jenkin, Geraint H., *A Concise History of Wales* (Cambridge: Cambridge University Press, 2007)
10. Johnson, Donald Hector, 1994
11. *Western Champion*, 14 September 1929
12. *Western Mail*, 27 August 1888
13. *Brisbane Courier*, 2 February 1866
14. *Maryborough Chronicle*, 6 April 1866
15. *Brisbane Courier*, 1 June 1872
16. ibid
17. ibid
18. *The Telegraph*, 22 November 1873
19. *Brisbane Courier*, 5 December 1873
20. *Queenslander*, 20 December 1873
21. Vagabond, 'The Mining King of Wales' in *West Australian* (12 January 1888)
22. *Brisbane Courier*, 24 January 1874
23. *The Bulletin*, 5 April 1890

Notes 211

24. *Carnarvon & Denbigh Herald*, 3 August 1888
25. *Queenslander*, 29 December 1877
26. *Western Champion*, 14 September 1929
27. *The Capricornian*, 1 January 1876
28. *Brisbane Courier*, 1 January 1876
29. *Capricornian*, 8 January 1876
30. *Brisbane Courier*, 10 January 1876
31. *Rockhampton Bulletin*, 2 November 1877
32. Vagabond, 1888
33. Hughes, Ian, 'A State of Open Warfare: Frontier Conflict in The Cooktown Area' in *Lectures on North Queensland history*. (Second series, Chapter 3, 1975)
34. *South Australian Register*, 13 April 1876
35. *Queenslander*, 26 June 1875
36. *Brisbane Courier*, 28 September 1878
37. *Townsville Daily Bulletin*, 7 June 1921
38. Browne, Spencer, *A Journalist's Memories* (Brisbane: Read Press, 1927)
39. *Western Champion*, 14 September 1929
40. *Townsville Daily Bulletin*, 7 June 1921
41. Browne, Reginald Spencer, 1927
42. *Brisbane Courier*, 5 November 1878
43. ibid
44. *Brisbane Courier*, 23 November 1878
45. *Brisbane Courier*, 15 January 1879
46. *Brisbane Courier*, 22 February 1879
47. *Morning Bulletin*, 14 February 1879
48. *Morning Bulletin*, 17 March 1879

Chapter 2: The Turbulent Goldfield
1. *Gympie Times*, 26 July 1876
2. *Western Mail*, 27 August 1888
3. *Brisbane Courier*, 4 February 1882
4. *South Wales Daily News*, 27 August 1888
5. Patrick Perkins (1838–1901) an Irish man, a miner, brewer, and storekeeper who was elected a member of the Queensland Legislative Assembly but was accused of electoral fraud and his seat was voided. He attempted to re-stand amid controversy but reconsidered and left for the UK.
6. *West Coast Times*, 4 January 1888
7. *Townsville Daily Bulletin*, 14 October 1952
8. Vagabond, 'The Mining King of Wales' in *West Australian*, (12 January 1888)
9. Johnson, Donald Hector, 1994
10. *Northern Miner*, 31 March 1881
11. *Queenslander*, 16 April 1881

12. *Queenslander*, 24 December 1881
13. *Queenslander*, 16 April 1881
14. *Northern Miner*, 21 February 1882
15. *Northern Miner*, 11 May 1882
16. *Queenslander*, 9 September 1882
17. *Northern Miner*, 13 May 1882 p. 2
18. *The Brisbane Courier*, 31 May 1882 p. 1
19. *Northern Miner*, 9 May 1882
20. '*Queenslander*, 10 June 1882
21. '*Queenslander*, 16 April 1881
22. *Queenslander*, 9 September 1882
23. *Western Champion*, 27 October 1882
24. *Queensland Figaro*, 21 April 1883
25. Johnson, Donald Hector, 1994; *Brisbane Courier*, 3 June 1882
26. *Warwick Examiner and Times*, 15 November 1882
27. *Mercury*, 27 June 1876
28. *The Argus*, 29 June 1876
29. Vagabond, 'The Mining King of Wales' in *West Australian* (12 January, 1888)
30. *Western Champion*, 14 September 1929
31. Stirling A.W., *The Never Never Land, A Ride in Northern Queensland* Sampson, (London: Low, Marston, Searle and Riverton, 1884)
32. Sam. 'A Soliloquy' in *Queensland Figaro* (9 February 1844)
33. Sam. 'Truthful Sam Again' in *Queensland Figaro* (9 February 1844)
34. *Brisbane Courier*, 22 November 1876
35. *Brisbane Courier*, 11 May 1881
36. ibid
37. *Queenslander*, 9 April 1881
38. ibid
39. *Warwick Argus*, 17 May 1881
40. *Northern Miner*, 17 February 1883
41. *Queensland Figaro*, 10 March 1883
42. *Queenslander*, 17 March 1883
43. *Cardigan Observer*, 17 December 1887
44. Wodehouse, John; Hawkins, Angus & Powell, John, *The Journal of John Wodehouse, the first Earl of Kimberley, 1862–1902* (New York: Cambridge University Press, 1998)
45. Proceedings of the Royal Colonial Institute, 1884, *The Royal Colonial Institute*, Vol 15 (London: Sampson Low, Marston, Searle & Rivington 1833–1884)
46. *Colonies and India*, 14 March 1884
47. *Morning Bulletin*, 24 February 1885
48. ibid
49. *Brisbane Courier*, 1 March 1884

50. *The Mercury*, 26 February 1884
51. *Northern Miner*, 18 February 1884
52. ibid
53. *Leeds Mercury*, 23 February 1885
54. *Colonies and India*, 27 February 1885

Chapter 3: Finding Welsh Gold
1. *Northern Miner*, 18 May 1885
2. *West Coast Times*, 4 January 1888
3. *Brisbane Courier*, 23 July 1886
4. Shopland, Norena, 'Gifts of the Welsh Gold King' in *Amgueddfa Blog* (27 November 2019)
5. *Iron*, 18 September 1885
6. *Queenslander*, 28 November 1885
7. *Brisbane Courier*, 3 June 1886
8. Ramsay, Prof. A. C., 'On the Geology of the Gold-Bearing District of Merionethshire, North Wales' in *The Quarterly Journal of the Proceedings of the Geological Society* (18 January 1854)
9. Hall, G. W., *The Gold Mines of Merioneth*, 2nd Edition. (Kington: Griffen Publications, 1990)
10. *Chemical News*, 17 October 1860
11. *House of Commons papers*, Volume 28, 1862
12. Hall, G. W., 1990
13. *The Times*, 10 December 1887
14. *Brisbane Courier*, 24 April 1885
15. *Pembrokeshire Herald*, 9 December 1887; *Western Mail*, 8 December 1887
16. *The Times*, 19 December 1887
17. Hall, G. W., 1990
18. *Cardigan Observer*, 17 December 1887
19. Morien, 'The Dolgelly Gold Mines' in *Western Mail*, 10 December 1887
20. *Cambrian News*, 23 December 1887
21. *South Wales Daily News*, 12 December 1887
22. 'News in Brief', *West Coast Times*, 11 February 1888
23. *Pall Mall Gazette*, 9 December 1887
24. Shopland, Norena, *The Curious Case of the Eisteddfod Baton* (Cardiff: Wordcatcher Publishing, 2020)
25. *Cambrian News*, 23 December 1887
26. Hall, G. W., 1990
27. Hall, G. W., 1990
28. Edmonds, Alfred, *The El Dorado of Wales* (London, 1890)
29. Dominy, Simon C., Phelps, Roland F.G., Bussell, M. Andrew & Guard, Clare L., 'Geology and Exploitation of Complex Gold-Bearing Veins in the Gwynfynydd Mine, Dollgellau, North Wales, UK' in *British Mining*, No. 57 Northern Mine Research Society, 1996

30. *London Gazette*, 17 August 1887
31. *Western Mail*, 1 March 1888
32. *The Watchmaker, Jeweller & Silversmith*, 1 July 1887
33. *Cardiff Times*, 10 December 1887
34. Hall, G. W., 1990
35. *North Wales Chronicle*, 26 November 1887
36. *The Times*, 1 December 1887
37. *Birmingham Daily Post*, 8 December 1887
38. Edmonds, Alfred, 1890
39. *The Times*, 7 August 1890
40. Evans, Alwyn, *George W. Hall, Newspaper Man and Goldfields Entrepreneur in Wales and Australia*, M.Phil. dissertation, 2015.
41. *Glasgow Herald*, 16 December 1887
42. *The Times*, 7 December 1887
43. *Brisbane Courier*, 13 January 1888
44. Brock, William Hodson, 2008, p. 416
45. *Liverpool Mercury*, 8 December 1887
46. *Leeds Mercury*, 10 December 1887
47. *The Times*, 28 December 1887
48. *Glasgow Herald*, 16 December 1887
49. *Birmingham Daily Post*, 14 December 1887
50. *Glasgow Herald*, 16 December 1887
51. *Birmingham Daily Post*, 19 December 1887
52. *Pall Mall Gazette*, 13 December 1887
53. *Wales Daily News*, 8 December 1887
54. *Western Mail*, 9 December 1887
55. *Birmingham Daily Post*, 8 December 1887
56. ibid
57. *South Wales Daily News*, 12 December 1887
58. Morien, 'The Discovery of Gold at Dolgelly' in *Weekly Mail* (17 December, 1887)
59. *South Wales Daily News*, 12 December 1887
60. *The Times*, 13 January 1888
61. *Birmingham Daily Post*, 19 December 1887
62. Pugh, Hugh, 'Notes on the Merionethshire Gold Mining Industry', Item ZM/636/2 Meirionnydd Archives, Gwynedd Archive Service, 1888
63. *Cardiff Times*, 24 December 1887

Chapter 4: Entitled to a Seat in Parliament
1. *North Wales Chronicle*, 31 December 1887
2. ibid
3. *Colonies and India*, 24 December 1887
4. *Liverpool Mercury*, 28 December 1887
5. *Western Mail*, 27 August 1888

6. *Western Mail*, 22 April 1887
7. *Y Goleuad*, 24 December 1887
8. *Liverpool Mercury*, 28 December 1887
9. *The Times*, 1 January 1888
10. *Lloyds Weekly London Newspaper*, 1 January 1888
11. *The Era*, 24 December 1887
12. *The Times*, 3 December 1887
13. *The Times*, 22 December 1887
14. *South Wales Daily News*, 3 January 1888
15. *St. Martin's-le-grand*, Volume 3, 1893
16. *The Times*, 4 January 1888
17. *Daily News*, 6 January 1888
18. *Hawke's Bay Herald*, 12 January 1888
19. *The Times*, 7 January 1888
20. *The Times*, 10 January 1888
21. *The Times*, 13 January 1888
22. *The Times*, 17 January 1888
23. *The Times*, 13 January 1888
24. *The Echo*, 7 January 1888
25. *North Wales Chronicle*, 14 January 1888
26. *Reynolds's Newspaper*, 9 January 1888
27. *Belfast News-Letter*, 30 March 1888
28. *Freeman's Journal*, 3 April 1888
29. *North Wales Chronicle*, 28 April 1888
30. *The Times*, 1 May 1888
31. *The Times*, 28 January 1888
32. *The Mercury* (New Zealand), 26 January 1888
33. *Brisbane Courier*, 3 February 1888
34. National Archives BT 31/4140/26701, Morgan Gold Mining Company
35. Evans, Alwyn, 2015
36. *Nelson Evening Mail*, 26 October 1888

Chapter 5: The Classes and the Masses
1. *Liverpool Mercury*, 22 August 1888
2. *Western Mail*, 27 August 1888
3. *Western Mail*, 24 August 1888
4. *The Echo*, 24 August 1888
5. *Pall Mall Gazette*, 21 August 1888
6. *Western Mail*, 25 February 1888
7. *Western Mail*, 25 August 1888
8. *South Wales Daily News*, 27 August 1888
9. *Pall Mall Gazette*, 23 August 1888
10. *Western Mail*, 29 August 1888
11. *Queenslander*, 4 August 1888

12. *South Wales Daily News*, 27 August 1888
13. *Western Mail*, 27 August 1888
14. *Freeman's Journal,* 14 September 1888
15. *Western Mail*, 20 March 1888
16. *Western Mail*, 28 August 1888
17. *Western Mail*, 27 August 1888
18. *South Wales Daily News*, 27 August 1888
19. *Western Mail*, 28 August 1888
20. *Western Mail*, 29 August 1888
21. *Western Mail*, 30 August 1888
22. *Western Mail*, 1 September 1888
23. *Western Mail*, 4 September 1888
24. ibid
25. *Birmingham Daily Post*, 27 September 1888
26. *Western Mail*, 5 September 1888
27. *Western Mail*, 6 September 1888
28. ibid
29. ibid
30. *Western Mail*, 7 September 1888
31. *Western Mail*, 11 September 1888
32. *Western Mail*, 12 September 1888
33. *Western Mail*, 13 September 1888
34. *Western Mail*, 17 September 1888
35. *Western Mail*, 14 September 1888

Chapter 6: Merthyr Decides
1. *Western Mail*, 28 September 1888
2. *Western Mail*, 25 September 1888
3. *Western Mail*, 18 September 1888
4. *Western Mail*, 10 October 1888
5. *Western Mail*, 26 September 1888
6. *Western Mail*, 28 September 1888
7. *Western Mail*, 29 September 1888
8. *Western Mail*, 27 September 1888
9. *Y Celt,* 18 January 1889
10. *Western Mail*, 1 October 1888
11. *Western Mail*, 3 October 1888
12. *The Times*, 5 October 1888
13. *The Times*, 8 October 1888
14. *Western Mail*, 8 October 1888
15. *Aberdare Leader*, 7 June 1913
16. *Daily News*, 9 October 1888
17. *Merthyr Express*, 13 October 1888
18. *Western Mail*, 11 October 1888

Notes 217

19. *Daily News*, 13 October 1888
20. *Western Mail*, 11 October 1888
21. *Merthyr Express*, 21 October 1888
22. *Merthyr Express*, 3 November 1888
23. *Western Mail*, 16 October 1888
24. *Merthyr Express*, 21 October 1888
25. *Western Mail*, 19 October 1888
26. *Western Mail*, 6 October 1888
27. *Birmingham Daily Post*, 25 October 1888
28. *Merthyr Express*, 3 November 1888
29. *Merthyr Express*, 29 October 1888
30. *Western Mail*, 27 November 1888
31. *Merthyr Express*, 3 November 1888
32. *The Echo*, 27 October 1888
33. *Birmingham Daily Post*, 27 October 1888
34. *Liverpool Mercury*, 29 October 1888
35. *Pall Mall Gazette*, 29 October 1888
36. *The Times*, 29 October 1888

Chapter 7: After the Election
1. *Western Mail*, 9 November 1888; *Daily News*, 9 November 1888
2. *Western Mail*, 20 November 1888
3. *Liverpool Mercury*, 27 November 1888
4. *Aberdeen Weekly Journal*, 19 February 1889
5. *Hansard*, Orders of The Day, Volume 331: debated on Friday, 7 December 1888
6. *Western Mail*, 20 February 1889
7. *Hansard*, 22 February 1889 vol 333 cc140–212
8. Hansard, 1889 'Adjourned Debate' 22 February
9. Morley, Arnold, 1889, 'Letter to Stuart Rendel', National Library Wales, 22 February
10. *Western Mail*, 7 March 1889
11. *Aberdare Times*, 4 May 1889
12. *Cardiff Times*, 4 May 1889
13. *Western Mail*, 17 June 1889
14. *Western Mail*, 14 May 1889
15. *Western Mail*, 9 February 1889
16. *North Wales Chronicle*, 8 November 1888
17. *The Star*, 26 March 1889
18. *Western Mail*, 30 January 1890
19. *Cardiff Times*, 1 February 1890
20. *Western Mail*, 11 February 1890
21. *Western Mail*, 12 February 1890
22. *Aberdeen Weekly Journal*, 25 February 1890

23. *Pall Mall Gazette*, 21 February 1890
24. *South Wales Daily News*, 27 February 1888
25. Smith and DeCrane, 'Messrs N M Rothschild and Son', Rothschild Archive, 6 March 1889
26. *Western Mail*, 9 January 1889
27. *Western Mail*, 18 January 1889
28. *Cambrian News*, 11 January 1889
29. *Hansard*, 15 March 1889 vol 333 cc1792–4
30. *Grey River Argus*, 4 April 1889
31. *Birmingham Daily Post*, 19 April 1889
32. *Birmingham Daily Post*, 19 April 1889
33. *Aberystwyth Observer*, 29 March 1890
34. *Cambrian News*, 15 February 1889
35. *The Times*, 27 August 1889
36. *Cambrian News*, 24 May 1889
37. *Leeds Mercury*, 17 December 1887
38. *Blackburn Standard*, 24 March 1888
39. *Birmingham Post*, 25 May 1889
40. *Brisbane Courier*, 29 July 1889
41. Cambrian News, 13 September 1889
42. *Western Mail*, 23 December 1889
43. *The Times*, 6 May 1890
44. *Western Mail*, 12 May 1890
45. *Cambrian News*, 16 May 1890

Chapter 8: The Dead Hand of Antiquity
1. *Western Mail*, 28 January 1890
2. *Birmingham Daily Post*, 9 November 1888
3. *The Economist*, 16 February 1889
4. *South Wales Daily News*, 3 April 1888
5. *South Wales Daily News*, 28 April 1888
6. *North Wales Chronicle*, 2 May 1888
7. Hansard, 'Class II, Commons' 14 May 1889.
8. *Cardiff Times*, 11 May 1889
9. *Hansard*, HC Deb 20 June 1889 vol 337 cc316–7
10. *The Times*, 25 July 1889
11. *The Echo*, 13 July 1889
12. *Daily News*, 18 July 1889
13. Colt, Frederick Hoare, *Law Journal Reports, for the year 1890*. Vol 59 (London: F.E. Streeten, 1890)
14. *The Times*, 8 August 1890
15. *The Times*, 16 August 1890
16. *Cambrian News*, 15 August 1890
17. *Queenslander*, 30 August 1890

18. *Western Mail*, 4 November 1890
19. *Hansard*, HC Deb 5 February 1891 vol 350 cc51–110
20. *Western Mail*, 19 February 1891
21. *Hansard*, HC Deb 20 February 1891 vol 350 cc1241–318
22. *The Independent*, 27 February 1891
23. *Daily News*, 27 March 1891
24. *Llangollen Advertiser*, 27 February 1891
25. *The Primrose League Gazetteer*, 28 February 1891
26. *Western Mail*, 12 March 1891
27. *Liverpool Mercury*, 18 March 1891

Chapter 9: The Bryntirion Injustice
1. *Aberystwyth Observer*, 2 April 1891
2. *Daily News*, 3 April 1891
3. *Western Mail*, 10 July 1891
4. *Western Mail*, 11 July 1891
5. *North Wales Chronicle*, 22 August 1891
6. Shopland, Norena, *Gifts of the Welsh Gold King*, Amgueddfa Cymru — National Museum Wales Blog
7. *South Wales Star*, 18 December 1891
8. *The Times*, 11 February 1892
9. *Western Mail*, 11 January 1892
10. *South Wales Star*, 18 March 1892
11. *Evening Express*, 21 March 1892
12. *Hansard*, 22 March 1892 vol 2 cc1536–54
13. *Birmingham Daily Post*, 22 March 1892
14. *Hansard*, 22 March 1892 vol 2 cc1536–54
15. *Western Mail*, 18 February 1892
16. *Cambrian News*, 26 February 1892
17. *Cambrian News*, 18 March 1892
18. *Leeds Mercury*, 23 March 1892
19. *The Echo*, 23 March 1892
20. *Freeman's Journal*, 24 March 1892
21. *Western Mail*, 23 March 1892
22. *Hansard*, 24 March 1892 vol 2 cc1676–81
23. *Aberdeen Weekly Journal*, 26 March 1892
24. *Pall Mall Gazette*, 26 March 1892
25. *Western Mail*, 24 March 1892
26. *Evening Express*, 4 May 1892
27. *Cambrian News*, 1 April 1892
28. *The Times*, 26 March 1892
29. *Hansard*, 28 March 1892 vol 3 cc49–51
30. *Western Mail*, 31 March 1892
31. *Northern Echo*, 6 May 1892

32. *Hansard*, 5 May 1892 vol 4 cc168–72
33. *Hansard*, 5 May 1892 vol 4 cc189–91
34. *Aberdare Times*, 25 June 1892
35. *Cardiff Times*, 2 July 1892
36. *Western Mail*, 24 June 1891
37. *Western Mail*, 23 June 1892
38. *Western Mail*, 25 March 1892
39. *Western Mail*, 28 June 1892
40. *Hansard*, 27 May 1892 vol 5 cc79–108
41. *Western Mail*, 4 July 1892
42. *Trewman's Exeter Flying Post*, 22 October 1892
43. *South Wales Daily News*, 18 October 1892

Chapter 10: A Man with a Grievance
1. *Hansard*, 3 May 1893 vol 11 cc1841–900
2. *Western Mail*, 30 January 1893
3. *Evening Express*, 10 February 1893
4. *Western Mail*, 13 February 1893
5. *South Wales Daily Post*, 10 April 1893
6. *Western Mail*, 10 April 1893
7. *Western Mail*, 19 May 1893
8. *Birmingham Daily Post*, 14 September 1893
9. *Hansard*, 13 September 1893 vol 17 cc1117–32
10. *Western Mail*, 15 September 1893
11. *Cambrian News*, 22 September 1893
12. *Western Mail*, 15 September 1893
13. *Cambrian News*, 7 April 1893
14. *Daily News*, 15 June 1893
15. *South Wales Daily Post*, 24 June 1893
16. *Cambrian News*, 7 July 1893
17. *Montgomery County Times*, 8 July 1893
18. *Western Mail*, 1 July 1893
19. *Daily News*, 17 May 1894
20. *Western Mail*, 18 August 1893
21. *Rhyl Record*, 30 September 1893
22. Morgan, Pritchard W., *The Proposed Coal Trust*, Westminster Gazette, 29 September 1893
23. *Northern Echo*, 2 November 1893
24. *Western Mail*, 8 December 1893
25. *Western Mail*, 5 July 1894
26. *Western Mail*, 16 February 1893
27. *Birmingham Daily Post*, 16 August 1893
28. *Cambrian News*, 26 October 1894
29. Williams, T. Marchant, *Welsh Members of Parliament, 1894* (Cardiff: Daniel Owen & Co.)

30. *Hansard*, 6 April 1894 vol 22 cc1523–64
31. *Western Mail*, 11 December 1893
32. *Hansard*, 14 August 1894 vol 28 cc1001–47

Chapter 11: Persistent Endeavours
1. *Pall Mall Gazette*, 9 August 1895
2. *Pall Mall Gazette*, 20 August 1895
3. *Liverpool Mercury*, 26 September 1895
4. *Merthyr Times*, 27 June 1895
5. *Western Mail*, 25 June 1895
6. *Merthyr Times*, 6 June 1895
7. *Merthyr Times*, 20 June 1895
8. *Merthyr Times*, 4 July 1895
9. *Merthyr Times*, 11 July 1895
10. ibid
11. *Western Mail*, 12 July 1895
12. *Merthyr Express*, 13 July 1895
13. *Merthyr Express*, 18 July 1895
14. ibid
15. *Merthyr Times*, 26 September 1895
16. *Western Mail*, 22 October 1895
17. *Aberdare Times*, 12 October 1895
18. *Western Argus*, 21 July 1931
19. Evans, Alwyn, 2015
20. *Western Argus*, 21 July 1931
21. *The Mercury*, 14 March 1896
22. *Northern Territory Times*, 20 March 1896
23. *The Advertiser*, 4 Mar 1896
24. *Brisbane Courier*, 17 August 1896
25. *Penrith Observer*, 28 July 1896
26. *The Advertiser*, 4 Mar 1896
27. *Milwaukee Journal*, 12 September 1896
28. *Cambrian News*, 24 September 1897
29. *London Kelt*, 21 May 1898
30. *Cambrian News*, 11 July 1901
31. *Otago Witness*, 28 August 1907
32. *Cardiff Times*, 17 October 1896
33. Glamorgan Archives, DD Vau 16/1
34. Glamorgan Archives, DD Vau 16/2
35. *Leeds Mercury*, 21 October 1896
36. *Liverpool Mercury*, 21 October 1896
37. *Aberdeen Weekly Journal*, 22 October 1896
38. *Merthyr Times*, 22 October 1896
39. *Llandudno Advertiser*, 24 November 1898
40. *London and China Telegraph*, 28 November 1896

41. *Cambrian*, 24 March 1899
42. *Merthyr Times*, 26 November 1896
43. *Cardiff Times*, 3 July 1897

Chapter 12: The Red Dragon and the Red Flag
1. *Western Mail*, 21 March 1899
2. *Western Mail*, 8 June 1900
3. *Aberdeen Weekly Journal*, 7 January 1898
4. *Hansard*, 13 March 1899 vol 68 cc539–53
5. *San Francisco Call*, 14 March 1899
6. *Aberdeen Weekly*, 28 November 1898
7. *The Echo*, 30 November 1898
8. *Western Mail*, 1 December 1898
9. *Western Mail*, 21 November 1898
10. *Cambrian News*, 2 December 1898
11. *Western Mail*, 18 January 1899
12. *Cambrian*, 9 December 1898
13. *Aberdeen Weekly Journal*, 7 February 1899
14. *Western Mail*, 11 February 1899
15. *The Times*, 17 February 1899
16. *Western Mail*, 15 February 1899
17. *Northern Echo*, 21 February 1899
18. *Western Mail*, 14 March 1899
19. *The Echo*, 16 March 1899
20. *Western Mail*, 4 September 1899
21. Allan, Horace N., 'Foreign Interests' in McAfee McCune, George; S. Burnett, Scott; Arnold Harrison, John. *Korean-American Relations; Documents Pertaining to the Far Eastern Diplomacy* (Berkeley: University of California Press, 1989)
22. *London and China Telegraph*, 7 May 1900
23. *Brooklyn Eagle*, 17 May 1900
24. *Aberdare Times*, 4 August 1900
25. *Western Mail*, 11 June 1900
26. *Brisbane Courier*, 20 July 1899
27. *Western Mail*, 26 May 1900
28. *Cambrian*, 5 October 1900
29. *Western Mail*, 6 June 1900
30. *Western Mail*, 6 June 1900
31. *Western Mail*, 26 September 1900
32. ibid
33. *Western Mail*, 29 September 1900
34. *Western Mail*, 3 October 1900
35. ibid
36. Davies, John, *A History of Wales* (London: Penguin; Revised ed. Edition, 2007)

37. *Merthyr Pioneer*, 19 September 1914
38. Glasier, J. Bruce, *Kier Hardie: The Man and his Message* (Independent Labour Party pamphlet, 1919)
39. *The Times*, 4 October 1900
40. *Glasgow Herald*, 4 October 1900
41. *New York Times*, 4 October 1900
42. *Western Mail*, 4 October 1900
43. ibid
44. *Aberdare Times*, 20 October 1900
45. *Western Mail*, 18 October 1900
46. *Western Mail*, 20 October 1900

Chapter 13: Standing Alone in a Strange Land
1. *Western Mail*, 30 March 1900
2. *Belfast News*, 6 April 1900
3. *Western Mail*, 9 June 1900
4. *Los Angeles Times*, 20 June 1900
5. Foreign Office, *Correspondence Respecting the Insurrectionary Movement in China* (London: 1900)
6. *Hansard*, 3 July 1900 vol 85 cc416–34
7. Robert Hart and James Duncan Campbell, *The I. G. in Peking: Letters of Robert Hart, Chinese Maritime Customs, 1868–1907* (Cambridge, Mass: Belknap Press of Harvard University Press, 1975)
8. *Hansard*, 3 July 1900 vol 85 cc416–34
9. *Hansard*, 17 July 1900 vol 86 c218
10. *Glasgow Herald*, 18 July 1900
11. *Leeds Mercury*, 18 July 1900
12. *Western Mail*, 23 July 1900
13. *Western Mail*, 1 August 1900
14. *Western Mail*, 2 August 1900
15. *Freeman's Journal*, 8 August 1900
16. *Belfast News-Letter*, 11 August 1900
17. *The Times*, 16 January 1904
18. Foreign Office, Correspondence with Private Persons: China FO 881/9301
19. Foreign Office, Correspondence with Private Persons: China FO 881/9574
20. van der Putten, Frans-Paul. Corporate Behaviour and Political Risk: Dutch Companies in China 1903–1941 (Leiden: Research School of Asian, African and Amerindian Studies, 2001)
21. *The Times*, 20 December 1916
22. *London and China Telegraph*, 7 May 1917
23. National Archives, Correspondence with Private Persons: China, FO 800/150
24. *London and China Telegraph*, 8 August 1921
25. *The Times*, 18 July 1924

26. Whigham, H. J., *Manchuria and Korea* (London: Isbister and Company Limited, 1904)
27. *Victoria Daily Colonist*, 17 May 1900
28. *Daily Express*, 16 June 1900
29. *Daily Mail*, 1 December 1905
30. *Daily Express*, 13 May 1905
31. *Cambrian News*, 14 February 1901
32. Foreign Office papers, FO228/2489, Pritchard Morgan to Sir John Jordan, 3 January 1913. Quoted in Alwyn Evans.
33. *Dydd*, 17 July 1903
34. *Aberdare Leader*, 20 January 1906
35. *Aberdare Leader*, 6 November 1909
36. *Aberdare Leader*, 20 November 1909
37. *Aberdare Leader*, 11 December 1909
38. *Aberdare Leader*, 25 December 1909
39. ibid
40. *Aberdare Leader*, 20 November 1909
41. Glamorgan Archives, 1910 Election Song DX EV 6
42. *Aberdare Leader*, 8 January 1910
43. *Daily Mirror*, 8 January 1910
44. *The Times*, 10 January 1910
45. *Merthyr Pioneer*, 17 July 1915
46. *The Times*, 11 December 1918
47. John Shepherd and Keith Laybourn, *Britain's First Labour Government* (Basingstoke: Palgrave, 2006)

Chapter 14: Welsh Gold after Morgan

1. *The Times*, 9 October 1930
2. ibid
3. *The Times*, 10 October 1930
4. *The Times*, 6 December 1930
5. *The Times*, 21 February 1935
6. *Sheffield Daily Telegraph*, 26 April 1923
7. *The Times*, 28 October 1935
8. *Western Mail*, 5 January 1935
9. *Sunderland Daily Echo*, 15 October 1935
10. *Manchester Evening News*, 30 August 1947
11. *Sunday Post*, 23 November 1947
12. *Staffordshire Sentinel*, 28 June 1986
13. David and Elizabeth Emanuel, *A Dress for Diana* (Shoreham-by-Sea: Pavilion, 2006)
14. *Staffordshire Sentinel*, 28 June 1986
15. *Aberdeen Press*, 16 June 1999
16. *Lloyds Weekly News*, 1 September 1912

17. *Liverpool Echo*, 18 October 1937
18. *The Tatler*, 22 September 1937
19. *Daily Post*, 31 May 2002
20. *Western Mail*, 10 December 2003
21. *Western Mail*, 1 March 2005
22. *ITV News*, Poll: Should Charles be the last Prince of Wales? (6 July 2018)
23. *The Times*, 25 June 1969
24. Murray, Daisy, 'One Of The Royal Crowns Has An Actual Ping Pong Ball In It, No Really: Prince Charles' coronet features a gold plated ping pong ball' (*Elle*, 5 March 2019)

Bibliography

Allan, Horace N., 'Foreign Interests' in McAfee McCune, George; S. Burnett, Scott; Arnold Harrison, John, *Korean-American Relations; Documents Pertaining to the Far Eastern Diplomacy* (Berkeley: University of California Press, 1989)
Browne, Spencer, *A Journalist's Memories* (Brisbane: Read Press, 1927)
Calvert, John, *The Gold Rocks of Great Britain, Ireland and a General Outline of the Gold Regions of the World, with a Treatise on the Geology of Gold* (Chapman and Hall, London, 1853)
Dominy, Simon C., Phelps, Roland F.G., Bussell, M. Andrew & Guard, Clare L., 'Geology and Exploitation of Complex Gold-Bearing Veins in the Gwynfynydd Mine, Dollgellau, North Wales, UK' in *British Mining*, No. 57 (Northern Mine Research Society, 1996)
Evans, Alwyn, *George W. Hall, Newspaper Man and Goldfields Entrepreneur in Wales and Australia*. (M.Phil. dissertation 2015. Accessed online)
Hall, G.W., *The Gold Mines of Merioneth*, 2nd Edition (Griffen Publications, Kington, 1990)
Jenkin, Geraint H., *A Concise History of Wales* (Cambridge: Cambridge University Press, 2007)
Johnson, Donald Hector, 'To Silence a Jackdaw: Gagging the Northern Miner' in *Journal of the Royal Historical Society of Queensland*, Vol. 6 (Brisbane, 1994)
Murchison, Roderick, *The Silurian System* (John Murray, London, 1839)
Pugh, Hugh, 'Notes on the Merionethshire Gold Mining Industry', Item ZM/636/2 Meirionnydd Archives (Gwynedd Archive Service, 1888)
Ramsay, Prof. A.C., 'On the Geology of the Gold-Bearing District of Merionethshire, North Wales' in *The Quarterly Journal of the Proceedings of the Geological Society* (18 January 1854)
Readwin, T.A., 'The Gold Discoveries in Merionethshire' in *Transactions of the Manchester Geological and Mining Society*, 2 (1860)
Readwin, T.A., 'List of Gold Ores from Merionethshire, North Wales, exhibited at the International Exhibition (Examiner Office, Manchester, 1862)
Readwin, T.A., 'On the recent discovery of gold near Bala Lake, Merionethshire' in *Report of the British Association for the Advancement of Science* (1864)
Readwin, T.A., 'Gold in Wales', a paper read before the Geologists' Association, University College, London, on January 6th, 1888
Rowlands, John & Rowlands, Sheila, *Welsh Family History: A Guide to Research*, 2nd edition. (Baltimore: Genealogical Publishing Company, 1999)

Shopland, Norena, *The Curious Case of the Eisteddfod Baton* (Wordcatcher Publishing, Cardiff, 2020)
Shopland, Norena, 'Gifts of the Welsh Gold King' in *Amgueddfa Blog* (27 November 2019) Accessed online.
Stirling, A.W., *The never never land: a ride in North Queensland* (Sampson Low, Marston, Searle & Rivington, London, 1884)
Williams, T. Marchant, *Welsh Members of Parliament, 1894* (Daniel Owen & Co., Cardiff, 1894)
Wodehouse, John, Hawkins, Angus, & Powell, John, *The Journal of John Wodehouse, the first Earl of Kimberley, 1862–1902* (New York: Cambridge University Press, 1998)

Index

Abraham, William aka Mabon, 62, 87, 96, 121, 123, 137, 138, 143, 155, 165, 178, 179
Asquith, Herbert Henry, 144–45, 197
Australian gold rush, 4

Bellairs, Kenneth Ffarington, 51–2
Berdan's Gold Quartz Crushing, 32
Boer War, 175, 177
Boxer Rebellion, 183–187
Bryntirion, 34, 43, 101, 113, 119–135, 144, 151
Bushell, Thomas, 36, 53–5

Calvert, John, 39, 54–5
Castle Hotel in Merthyr Tydvil, 86–7
Chamberlain, Neville, 149–150, 181
Chidlaw Lode, 35–6
Chidlaw, Roberts, 37, 102, 105, 109
China, vii, 93–4, 166–173, 175–8, 180, 183–190, 192–93, 196
Clogau Gold Mine, 31–2, 36, 42, 52, 53, 97, 108, 126, 134, 139, 142, 152–53, 163, 201–203, 209
Crookes, William, 29, 38, 39, 58
Crown leases, 37, 107
Cymru Fydd, 63, 64, 75

Day Dawn Gold Mine, 20–26
Dean, Arthur, 30–31
Deane, John, 14, 23, 78, 166
Diana, Princess of Wales, 203
Dillwyn, Lewis Llewelyn, 71, 114–115, 116, 117, 121, 122
disendowment, 48, 60, 71, 77, 119
disestablishment, 48, 60, 64, 70, 71, 75, 77, 93, 114–16, 119, 122, 123, 145–47, 153–55, 158, 159, 160
Dodd, Theodore, vii

Dolaucothi (Ogofau) Gold Mine, 53, 108, 202

Eight Hours Bill, 70, 119, 135, 149–150, 154, 160
eisteddfodau, 34, 35, 64, 71, 83, 90, 95, 96, 117, 162, 206
Ellis, Thomas Edward, 64, 67, 76, 83, 84, 85, 87, 91, 121, 122, 125, 126, 128, 143, 145, 146, 155, 163
Empress of China, Dowager Cixi, 173, 184

Foulkes Griffiths, Richard, 75–80, 82–9, 91, 158

Gladstone, William, 48, 60, 66, 71, 73, 85–6, 90–91, 112, 114–117, 123, 133, 145–46, 155, 159, 163–66
Glover, John, painting of gold panning in the Mawddach, 31
Glyndŵr, Owain, 34, 91, 95
gold baton prize, 35
Goschen, George, 98, 106, 124–130, 137
Grant, John O., 50
Great Exhibition, 96
Griffith, Sir Samuel, 16
Gwynfynydd Gold Mine, 31–3, 35–8, 42, 44, 50–59, 82, 98, 101–103, 105, 109–111, 127–28, 136–37, 141–42, 144, 151, 153, 161, 163, 195–96, 200–206

Hall, George, 37, 59, 77, 103, 111, 151, 160–161, 166, 193, 195, 196, 204
Hall, George W., 33
Hardie, Kier, 134, 137, 144, 149, 176–77, 179–181, 191, 193–94, 197

Index 229

Home Rule, 48, 62, 63, 66, 70, 79, 90, 91, 92, 112, 119, 121–23, 145

Independent Department of State for Wales, 97
Ingram, Sir W. J., 153
Investiture of the Prince of Wales, 194–95, 207–209

Johnson, Donald Hector, vii, 1, 4

Korea, vii, 173–75, 189–190

labour candidate, 61, 69, 70, 73, 75, 78, 130, 176, 178, 179, 193
Labour Party, 62, 94, 134, 176, 180, 191–93
Liberal Association (LA), 47–8, 50, 61, 66–9, 71–3, 75–91, 93, 94, 96, 130, 132, 157, 165, 178, 192
Li Hung Chang, 166, 184, 186
Little Gold Rush of Wales, 31, 33, 44, 52, 128
Lloyd George, David, 64, 89, 116, 119, 120, 122, 123–26, 128, 132, 136, 140–41, 143, 145–46, 155, 191, 194, 197
Local Government Act 1888, 91–92

Mabon, see William Abraham
Macrossan, John Murtagh, 13–16, 23, 78, 166
Mawddach Gold Mining Company, 35
Mawddach valley and river, 31–2, 34, 53, 90, 195
Minister of Mines, 136–38, 148, 172
Morgan Gold Mine, 36, 99, 102, 124, 142
Morgan, Osborne, 91, 97, 145
Morgan, Owen aka Morien, 43
Morien, see Morgan, Owen
Mount Morgan, 42, 57–58, 108–109, 141
Murchison, Roderick, 31

Novello, Clara, 121

O'Kane, Thadeus, 16–24, 27, 40

Pistyll Cain, 36, 44, 196
Prince Charles, 196, 203–204, 207–209
Pritchard Morgan, Catherine (mother), 1–2, 81, 84, 95, 120
Pritchard Morgan, Gwendoline (daughter), 11, 87, 90, 160, 173–74, 175, 190, 191, 197
Pritchard Morgan, Harriet, née Attwood (wife), 6, 7, 20–21, 30, 35, 84, 101, 102, 113, 173, 190, 197
Pritchard Morgan, Herbert (son), 7, 35, 84, 87, 90, 113, 119, 120
Pritchard Morgan, Kate (Catherine) (daughter), 7, 87, 102, 133, 151, 153, 158–59, 160–62, 166–67, 175, 197
Pritchard Morgan, William,
  as a musician, 8, 9, 12, 27
  Australian mining interests, 24–9, 160–62, 191
  Chinese mining interests, 93–4, 168–173, 183–89, 190, 192–93
  Crown seizure of his house, 123, 128, 129, 131
  descriptions of, 8, 9, 25, 43, 65, 107, 129, 147, 160, 173
  early life, 1–3
  fights with O'Kane, 17–20
  general election of 1888, 60–89
  general election of 1892, 130–33
  general election of 1895, 156–160
  general election of 1900, 175–181
  general election of 1910, 191–94
  Gwynfynydd, see Gwynfynydd Gold Mine
  in America, 162
  in physical fights, 11, 24
  Irish gold mining interests, 97–9, 191
  Korean mining interests, 189–190
  leaving Australia, 30
  legal career in Australia, 5–6, 9–11, 19, 26
  marriage to Harriet, 6
  Morgan v the Crown court case, 109–112, 113
  motion for disestablishment, 114–117
  moving to Australia, 3
  nationality, 29, 63, 66, 69–70
  newspaper owner, 11

offering his parliamentary seat to Gladstone, 163–66
political career in Australia, 5, 7, 11–17, 23
political interests in England, 46–47
political interests in Scotland, 197
providing gold for Prince of Wales investiture, 194–96
relationship with the press, 58, 61, 65, 66, 69, 76, 88–9, 124, 155, 157
struck heavy gold, 36–42
visiting China, 166–67, 170
visiting Korea, 174
worked as a labourer, 4, 63, 78, 132
Protheroe, Thomas, 87, 182
Pugh, Hugh, 44

Queen Elizabeth II, 202, 207
Queen Elizabeth, the Queen Mother, 202, 206
Queen Victoria, 37, 46, 93, 97, 100–101, 142, 190, 207

Randell, David, 98, 121, 122, 138, 135, 155,
Readwin, Thomas Allison, 31–9, 41, 52–5, 100, 126, 191
Rendel, Stuart, 93, 143, 145
Rhaidr Mawddach, 36, 44, 102
Richard, Henry, 60–63, 67, 72, 91
Rothschilds, 41–2, 97, 108, 137
royalties, 32, 85, 93, 98–109, 111–113, 121, 123–24, 126–130, 136–141, 143, 148, 152–53, 160–161, 174, 189, 205

Smith, W.H., 106
Smith, William, 31
Smyth, Sir Warington, 57, 109, 137, 139–140
Stanley, Henry Morton, 30, 61
Stirling, A.W., 25, 28, 46, 59
suffrage, female, 49, 175
suffrage, male, 7, 65, 88

Thomas, Alfred, 97, 121–23, 145
Thomas, D.A., 67, 75, 80–83, 86–87, 89, 94, 96–97, 112, 117, 119–121, 122–23, 130–133, 135–36, 143, 145, 149–150, 153–160, 165, 175–182, 191, 197
Thomas, Julian, the 'Vagabond', 8, 11, 17, 25, 63, 65

Vaughan, John, 61–2, 65, 68, 90, 94, 96, 120, 130–131, 153, 155–56, 158, 163, 164, 166
Vigra Gold Mine, 32, 52, 53

Welsh Exhibition, 95–6
Welsh gold miners in Australia, 4
Welsh gold wedding rings, 102, 141–42, 162, 163, 175, 201–204, 206, 209
Welsh language, 2, 36, 60, 64, 69, 70, 76, 79, 88, 91–2, 132, 151

Zeta-Jones, Catherine, 204